Declining Sri Lanka

Terrorism and Ethnic Conflict:
the legacy of J R Jayewardene (1906–1996)

Rajiva Wijesinha

Delhi • Bangalore • Mumbai • Kolkata • Chennai • Hyderabad

Published by
Cambridge University Press India Pvt. Ltd
under the Foundation Books imprint
Cambridge House, 4381/4 Ansari Road, Daryaganj, **New Delhi** 110002

Cambridge University Press India Pvt. Ltd

C-22, C-Block, Brigade M.M., K.R. Road, Jayanagar, **Bangalore** 560 070

Plot No. 80, Service Industries, Shirvane, Sector-1, Nerul,
Navi Mumbai 400 706

10 Raja Subodh Mullick Square, 2nd Floor, **Kolkata** 700 013

21/1 (New No. 49), 1st Floor, Model School Road, Thousand Lights,
Chennai 600 006

House No. 3-5-874/6/4, (Near Apollo Hospital), Hyderguda,
Hyderabad 500 029

© Cambridge University Press India Pvt. Ltd
First Published 2007

ISBN 978-81-7596-532-4

All rights reserved. No reproduction of any part may take place without the written permission of Cambridge University Press India Pvt. Ltd, subject to statutory exception and to the provision of relevant collective licensing agreements.

Published by Manas Saikia for Cambridge University Press India Pvt. Ltd and
Printed at ANAND SONS

To
George Cawkwell
for inculcating
Thucydides and Tacitus

Contents

Preface vii

Part I
Kingdom and Colony: The Mythology of Race (Pre-history to 1948)
Chapter 1 Multiple Migrations 3

Part II
Dominion to Republic: The Politics of Language (1948–1977)
Chapter 2 Developing Majorities 17

Part III
The New Monarch: Jayewardene in Control (1977–1983)
Chapter 3 Consolidating the New Regime 37
Chapter 4 The Proliferation of Violence 52
Chapter 5 Tightening the Reins 61

Part IV
The New Dominion: India in the Driving Seat (1983–1987)
Chapter 6 The Bang and the Whimpers 77
Chapter 7 Raising the Stakes 88
Chapter 8 Holding the Centre 99

Part V
Changing the Guard: Premadasa's Emergence (1987–1989)
Chapter 9   The Accord in Action 119
Chapter 10 The Façade Cracks 131
Chapter 11 The Last Hurrah 141

Part VI
Using the Executive Presidency: Premadasa in Action (1989–1993)

Chapter 12 Controlling the Country	159
Chapter 13 Reform and Reaction	176
Chapter 14 Restoring the Balance	187

Part VII
Using the Spoon: Wijetunge as President (1993–1994)

Chapter 15 The New Dispensation	197
Chapter 16 Internal Combustion	208
Chapter 17 The End of a Long Road	218

Part VIII
The Procrastination of a Princess:
Kumaratunga in charge (1994–2001)

Chapter 18 Wasted Years	233
Chapter 19 Hurried Elections	243

Part IX
The Baby without the Bathwater:
Wickremesinghe as Prime Minister (2001–2004)

Chapter 20 Jayewardene's Heir	255
Chapter 21 The Tiger's Tail	264

Part X
Guarding the Change: Rajapakse's Emergence (2004–2006)

Chapter 22 The General Election of 2004	277
Chapter 23 Kumaratunga under Siege	287
Chapter 24 The New Regime	300
Select Bibliography	313
Index	317

Preface

This book is an updated version of two earlier books, *Sri Lanka in Crisis: JR Jayewardene and the erosion of democracy, 1977–1988* and *Civil Strife in Sri Lanka: the United National Party Government, 1989–1994*.

The first of these was an expanded version of *Civil Strife in Sri Lanka*, published in India in 1986 after the ethnic crisis exploded in July 1983. With every year that passes I am more convinced of the accuracy of the analysis in that first book, which put the blame for the crisis foursquare on the President at the time, J R Jayewardene.

Such an analysis was unique at the time, because commentators either engaged in virtual hagiography of Jayewardene, and saw Tamil claims as illegitimate and associated with terrorism, or else they presented the Sri Lankan state as a Sinhala majoritarian monolith that necessarily oppressed Tamils. My own view was that Tamils had been the victims of majoritarian excesses, but these were piecemeal and often due to political rivalry amongst Sinhala majority parties.

Though in the late seventies I shared the general view in Colombo that Jayewardene was an intelligent and forward looking politician, able to lift the country from the trough, economic, social as well as racial, into which it had fallen, it rapidly became clear that all he was interested in was perpetuating his own power. He entrenched himself through a constitutional change that elevated him to becoming an American-style Executive President. However, since he kept elements of the old British Parliamentary system, with a Prime Minister, he should also have ensured that elected representatives from all over the country saw him as their leader.

For that it would have made sense for him to have worked out a compromise with the major Tamil party, but underlying Jayewardene's greed was a narrow vision, which included a chauvinist streak. Though in Colombo the nationalist element in the Sri Lankan state was attributed to SWRD Bandaranaike who introduced the 'Sinhala Only' bill in 1956, making Sinhala the sole official language, the historical records, unfortunately ignored in Sri Lanka, reveal that it was Jayewardene who had first proposed an exclusive status for Sinhala. Despite this, following the excesses of Mrs. Bandaranaike's 1970–1977 government, the Tamils saw Jayewardene as their potential saviour and, while endorsing the Tamil United Liberation Front in majority Tamil areas, they voted for the UNP in 1977 in the rest of the country. Given the massive majority the UNP got, correcting the excesses the Tamils had suffered would not have been difficult. Greater devolution and the entrenchment of fundamental rights in the new constitution Jayewardene introduced would have worked towards equity.

But nothing was done. The story of Jayewardene's useless carrots and monstrous sticks over the next six years was the subject of the original version of the first book incorporated here. It illustrated my theme that violence and internal hostilities were exacerbated by the authoritarian policies of the Jayewardene government.

That book was expanded later, following the Indo-Lankan Accord of 1987, which aggravated problems amongst both Sinhalese and Tamils. It was seen, not as a corrective to Jayewardene's previous erosion of democratic practice, but as capitulation to Indian pressure. Previously his approach, in line with his admiration for the economies and the political structures of South East Asia and what he saw as their adherence to Western capitalism, had involved belittling the role of India in the region. This ironically occurred at a time when India had succeeded in establishing itself as a regional superpower. The Indian reaction to Jayewardene's approach was to make use of Tamil militant groups and strengthen their military capacity until the Sri Lankan government was forced to come to terms.

The Indo-Lankan Accord of 1987, however, in catering to Indian interests, left the largest Tamil militant group dissatisfied. The consequence was that, even with a peacekeeping force of over 50,000 men in the Tamil areas of Sri Lanka, the Indian government was not able to establish

Preface

satisfactory control. In the rest of the country, Sinhalese resentment at what was seen as Jayewardene's sellout to the Indians enabled a militant Marxist group to increase its influence to the point at which its calls for general strikes and stoppages brought the country virtually to a standstill on several occasions. Pressures from this group, together with agitation by all other political parties, forced the government to hold elections, first a Presidential election in December 1988, and then parliamentary elections in February 1989. Jayewardene himself was compelled to step down but his Prime Minister Premadasa won the December election by a small majority.

Meanwhile the Indian offensive against the terrorist Liberation Tigers of Tamil Eelam, who were dissatisfied with the 1987 Accord, brought them to their knees. But political changes in both India and Sri Lanka allowed them to regroup. Emerging then as a more powerful organization they killed Rajiv Gandhi and the Sri Lankan President, both of whom at earlier stages had sought to use their services. That period was the subject of the second book incorporated here.

The last section of this book deals with the new government of Chandrika Kumaratunga, daughter of the two former Prime Ministers, SWRD Bandaranaike (1956–1959) and Mrs Sirimavo Bandaranaike (1960–1964 and 1970–1977). In looking at the history of her Presidency, I concentrate mainly on the failure of her attempts at a settlement, and the re-emergence of the UNP, under Jayewardene's nephew Ranil Wickremesinghe, as the hope of the Tamils. His election as Prime Minister in 2001 led to a period of what should have been peaceful co-existence with her as President, with each respecting the powers of the other in their different spheres of responsibility. In fact his reversion to Jayewardene style authoritarianism led to another election in which her party easily defeated his. One of the reasons for this was the overwhelming perception of the electorate that he was indulging the Tigers to unacceptable extents.

The remaining years in which Kumaratunga exercised power saw little progress in the peace process. The book ends with the election in November 2005 of her last Prime Minister, Mahinda Rajapakse, as President, and the developments during the short period he has been in office.

***

I have edited the first two books heavily, to reduce their content to what is essential for understanding the current situation. My purpose continues to be to chart the erosion of a promising democracy that had peacefully changed governments over the previous thirty years into a banana republic lurching towards self destruction. Jayewardene had a significant role in this process; the power of his personality as an elder statesman led to his party accepting extreme proposals with disastrous consequences. At the same time I have also tried to suggest the tragic repercussions of the system set up by Jayewardene on many politicians. Though internal conflicts in the UNP led to the system being finally opened up under his successor Premadasa, neither he nor his principal opponents, Lalith Athulathmudali and Gamini Dissanayake, lived to function in the new democratic dispensation. They were all killed by assassins, a deadly reminder of the background against which they had functioned. Though they too can be seen as cogs in the wheel, the fact remains that the terrorism which has been more decisive than political activity in Sri Lanka over the last decade springs from the authoritarianism of the previous government. For this all three victims too must accept some responsibility.

However, one of the principal arguments of this book is that, despite the dispensation he inherited, there was a difference in the approach of President Premadasa who succeeded Jayewardene. Elections became free again after he came to power. Premadasa was convinced that the people appreciated what he was doing, and would support him. In this he was unlike Jayewardene, for whom there was no question of allowing the electorate to choose freely, in case it upset things for the government.

I have also tried to do justice to both Athulathmudali and Dissanayake, of whom it could truly be said that nothing became them more than the last few months of their lives. Athulathmudali's energy in building up the possibility of an opposition victory was crucial in a context in which nothing like it had occurred for years. That he did so against the odds, and clearly relished the process, was a salutary reminder that politics was not simply about enjoying the benefits of office. Dissanayake, in the brief period after he took over, was able to rebuild confidence in the importance of opposition, if the new government were not to turn into a carbon copy of the old.

Preface

The second book was written largely in response to Dissanayake's assassination. When the revised edition of the previous book was published he was thoughtful enough, despite the criticisms of him and his colleagues that that book contained, to write to express his appreciation of the work, and to suggest that I apply the same analytical skills to the prevailing dispensation. I felt unable to do so then, because while it was easy to understand and predict the consequences of Jayewardene's actions that were basically transparent in their destructiveness, the complexity of what followed left me uncertain. The ambivalences in the various characters who now dominated the scene were not so easy to explain.

It was only with Dissanayake's death that a pattern emerged that required to be recorded. Though deeply flawed, all three characters with whom the second book dealt were able men who made a considerable contribution to the nation. That was a tribute to what seems to have been the lost generation of the UNP. And if this book has a message, it is that a party, like a country, needs to uphold and encourage pluralism and tolerance to survive.

Unfortunately, this is lacking in the dispensation that took over the UNP after Dissanayake's death, a dispensation that has remained in the opposition for a dozen years now, save for a couple of years in which it squandered its electoral advantage. The years in which President Kumaratunga dominated the country seem to me to have been wasted, despite the enthusiasm with which she was elected. Her failure stems from the authoritarian position in which she found herself, without the capability of developing a collegiate system of government. The heady isolation provided by the Presidential system created by Jayewardene seems to me a recipe for destroying the abilities even of an idealistic successor. I can only hope the current President realizes this and ensures that he continues in touch with other politicians on a basis of equality, rather than relying on the exalted position which the present constitution assigns him.

This is the theme of this book, though I have tried to present it through a fast moving account of events rather than analysis. Footnotes and references have been eschewed. At the same time brevity has occasionally been sacrificed in the interests of thoroughness since the view that the ethnic crisis is inextricably intertwined with the decline of democratic practice in Sri Lanka is one that requires detailed substantiation. For further study of the issues discussed, I have included a bibliography that has been divided into three sections, in terms of the main focus of each of the works listed, though there is necessarily some overlap. The first section consists of books that are primarily concerned with the period before 1977 in exploring the background to the violence that overtook Sri Lanka in the eighties. The period of J R Jayewardene's government, from 1977 to 1988, is covered in the second section.

The last section of this bibliography deals with developments after 1988 and therefore emphasizes the peace process. Also included however are narratives, sometimes of a journalistic nature, that capture the outlook of different protagonists, and therefore suggest why the process has not been successful.

***

I am grateful to Gillian Peele, of Lady Margaret Hall, Oxford, for having initiated this book by arranging a lecture on the subject soon after the riots of July 1983; to the Fellows of University College for granting me membership of the Senior Common Room which allowed me to complete the first version of the book; and to Chanaka Amaratunga, my fellow editor of the Liberal Review, in which later sections of the book first appeared after useful discussions with him. Finally, I should once again express my thanks to George Cawkwell, who developed my understanding of history and historiography thirty years ago. His interpretation of Thucydides and Tacitus and their studies of the decline of societies they cherished, has contributed in no small measure to my reading of events. Human nature has changed little, and the corrosive effects of authoritarianism, on people and countries and in particular on those who perpetrate it, needs constant attention.

Rajiva Wijesinha
January, 2007

Part I

Kingdom and Colony

The Mythology of Race (Pre-history to 1948)

Chapter 1

Multiple Migrations

The early Sinhalese Kingdom

Story has it that the Sinhalese, long the majority race in Sri Lanka, descend from a lion. 'Sinha' refers to the lion who abducted a princess by whom he had two children. The son Sinhabahu, tired of being cooped up in a cave, escaped with his mother and sister to his grandfather's kingdom. The enraged lion began to ravage the area; it was only his son who was able to kill him. Then Sinhabahu married his sister. Their son Vijaya turned out a reprobate and was sent into exile. His boat landed in Sri Lanka whose monarch at the time was Queen Kuveni, who fell in love with Vijaya and made him her consort. Before long he got rid of her and brought reinforcements from his home in India, through whom the race flourished and filled up the island.

Bestiality, parricide, incest, wantonness and betrayal may not seem a promising beginning for a race. These are parts of a legend, and legends are only taken as seriously as required. What is significant here is the assumption that Sinhabahu came from the north of India, which makes him Aryan, of the conquering race that pushed down to the south the original Dravidian inhabitants of the subcontinent. Thus the Sinhalese too become Aryans, and can share in the distinctive heritage of that important race, constructed so lovingly by European ethnologists in the nineteenth century.

There are those who reject the legend. Yet in considering Vijaya as at best a detail, they stress the independent identity of the pre-Dravidian tribes over whom Kuveni ruled. If the influence of northern India is to be minimized, it is not to promote influences from the south. Wherever the emphasis, if the area geographically nearest Sri Lanka, southern India, is kept at bay, the singularity of the Sri Lankan heritage can continue to be asserted.

History perhaps provides a reason for this insistence on independence. Though there are still legends, we have moved to a period of greater certainty in dealing with the arrival of Buddhism to the country. It was sent in the third century BC by Ashoka, the Mauryan emperor of India, who converted at the height of his conquering career and then turned proselytizer. The kings of Sri Lanka at the time embraced the faith wholeheartedly, and helped establish an order of monks who gained immense authority in the country. After the collapse of the Mauryan Empire, Buddhism died out in India; in Sri Lanka however it continued strong, and the island became the repository of the purer Theravada version, as opposed to the Mahayana variety that took root in China. In South East Asia, where Theravada is followed, the preeminence of Sri Lanka is acknowledged. In the island itself the belief is that the Buddha selected it personally as the place to preserve his teaching.

So much for the positive side as far as India is concerned. The reverse is provided by periodic invasions of the country by Tamils from southern India, by now irrevocably restored to Hinduism. The Tamils are the Dravidians who occupy the south-east area of the subcontinent, the present state of Tamil Nadu. There are other Dravidians too, most significantly for Sri Lanka those of Kerala in the south-west. Throughout the first millennium AD however the Tamils were the dominant force in the region, and the Sinhalese in Sri Lanka had to face invasions from various Tamil kingdoms. The best known of these was that of Elara, acknowledged as a just ruler, but nevertheless an alien. Just over two thousand years ago he occupied the old Sinhalese capital of Anuradhapura in the north-central plains. It was many years before he was dislodged by King Dutugemunu, a prince from the southern Ruhunu area, who became the most important of Sri Lankan heroes.

The drift to the South West

As the centuries passed however the pressure of repeated Tamil invasions proved too much. A thousand years after Dutugemunu, King Vijayabahu, having defeated another Tamil king, did not venture back to Anuradhapura

Multiple Migrations 5

but instead fixed his capital at Polonnaruwa, still in the north-central plain, but some distance to the south-east. Though it produced architecture that rivals the remains at Anuradhapura, Polonnaruwa did not last long. From then on the move southward took on the character of a rout: if, that is, only invasions prompted it.

In the fourteenth century the capital was in the central hill country. By the fifteenth it had moved to the west coast, to Kotte, just next to the present Colombo. Meanwhile in the very north the Tamils had settled down, with a distinct Tamil kingdom in the northernmost Jaffna peninsula, often in theory, and sometimes in practice, subject to the sovereignty of the central kingdom. On the east coast too there were Tamil settlements, though without any coherent structure. In between, the great north-central plain where the Sinhalese kingdom once flourished, was virtually deserted. The vast irrigation works that had nourished that dry area had fallen into disrepair, so that the few peasants who remained to confront proliferating sickness and encroaching jungle found it difficult to eke out a living.

Yet the popular impression of unremitting hostility between Sinhalese kingdoms and Tamil invaders from India is countered by some important facts. Even early on there seems to have been synthesis. In the fifth century AD for instance, it was to India that prince Mugalan fled from his parricide brother Kasyapa, and returned with Indian aid to take over the kingdom. Kasyapa's magnificent citadel Sigiriya, may be a renowned monument now, but in the histories of Buddhist monks the hero is Mugalan. Again Polonnaruwa architecture is replete with Hindu influence. Though Vijayabahu, and his great nephew Parakramabahu (under whom the Sinhalese kingdom had its widest range, extending to Pagan in Burma), came from the south, the third memorable king of that era, Nissanka Malla, was originally from India. A convert to Buddhism, zealous about his new faith and about asserting his position within the tradition of his predecessors, he is ample evidence of the communion that was as important as confrontation, even at the highest levels.

Interesting phenomena can be seen also in the fourteenth century hill kingdom. Bhuvenekabahu IV built Hindu temples within the precincts of the two beautiful Buddhist shrines he constructed at Lankatilleke and

Gadaladeniya. The former is architecturally unique in that the two are built back to back; the colossal Buddha statue has a collection of Hindu deities behind it, with separate entrances at opposite ends to the two sections of the building. In this period too began the proliferation of cults of various minor Hindu deities, some of which are now associated with the annual procession of the Tooth, the most sacred of Buddhist relics. By the time the kingdom moved to the western coast there is no doubt that Sinhalese culture, inextricably connected as it was with religion, had been subject to strong influences from the south of India.

And so was the race itself. With the move to the south-west there is evidence of whole groups from the subcontinent being absorbed amongst the Sinhalese. All of them now speak Sinhala, and even those who did not do so until relatively recently, such as the fishermen in the area north of Colombo, would baulk at the suggestion that they had not always been identifiably Sinhalese. Yet some of them can still be distinguished through caste as relatively recent immigrants, while even among the dominant farmer caste (the majority of which go back a couple of millennia) there is documentation of ancestors coming from India around the fifteenth century.

These immigrants came primarily from the south-west of India, the Malabar coast. Its influence is apparent in the distinct similarities in styles of dress and forms of food between the Sinhalese and the people of Kerala. Significant too is the date of these migrations, at a time when the pattern of livelihood of the people of Sri Lanka changed decisively.

The legend is that it was predominantly Tamil invasions that drove the Sinhalese southward. The spread of sickness in the dry zone contributed; the invaders did not occupy the area themselves but left it empty. These were also times when new trade routes were being opened up; this would also have contributed to the shift from an agriculture based economy to one that relied more obviously on commerce. The great traders, first Arabs and then the Europeans led by the Portuguese, had come to stay. This made the trend of migration to the south-west irreversible. It was there that the trade routes led, and the commodities in demand grew better in those parts. Cinnamon, in particular, gave its name to one of the more prominent caste groups in the area, many of which originated in the

Malabar coast. As the occupation flourished a proportion of the indigenous population might well have been absorbed into the caste.

By the time the Portuguese took over in the sixteenth century, the racial purity of the Lion race had definitely been diluted. Religious practices had been adapted in various ways under new influences, along with other aspects of culture. At the same time the distinctive nature of the dominant race and culture should not be underestimated. The appeal of Buddhism, preserved against many vicissitudes, continued undiminished. Despite the trading power of Muslims, and then Christians, sometimes accompanied by enforced conversions, the majority of the Sinhalese, including all those they absorbed, remained Buddhist. Through this, and also through the acceptance of the language by all who had been added later to the original stock, the identity of the race remained unshaken. This understandably was a reason for pride. What was less clear was that the resilience of that identity, in a small country subject to so many outside influences, was based on its capacity to absorb so much and so many without insisting on distinctions.

Colonial Rule

The first colonial power to possess territory in Sri Lanka was Portugal. The Portuguese came originally to trade, not to conquer, but internal rivalries in the royal family led to what was a unique achievement for a colonial power in Asia: the king of Portugal became successor to the last king of Colombo. The Portuguese defeated the other contenders for the throne, established their sovereignty in the coastal areas, and won Jaffna too. Only in the central hills did another Kandyan Sinhalese kingdom maintain its independence, established by an agent of the Portuguese whom they had sent with an army to overcome resistance there. The dynasty that he set up lasted in various forms for three hundred years, resisting several attempts by the Portuguese and then by the Dutch (who supplanted them with Kandyan help but then fell out with their allies) to complete their conquest of the island. The British who replaced the Dutch were also defeated in an assault on Kandy in 1803. Finally in 1815, following the betrayal of the last king of Kandy by his chieftains, a convention between them and the British erased the last traces of sovereignty.

The rebellion of the chieftains was prompted by the personal unpopularity of the king. He was foreign, but this was not surprising nor should it have been a cause of unpopularity, for the dynasty had long ceased to be Sinhalese. The original line died out in the early eighteenth century, and the throne had passed to the previous king's brother-in-law, who had accompanied his sister from south India. The new king became a Buddhist, as did his brother-in-law who succeeded him, having also arrived from India; they were certainly more careful than earlier Kandyan kings about limiting the admixture of Hinduism in the temples they constructed; but, perhaps because the territory over which they reigned was so small and regal requirements necessitated continuing marital alliances with India, they were never fully assimilated. So, when they became unpopular, it could be argued, as was done by the chieftains who rebelled in 1815, that they were aliens. Correspondingly the British agreed in the convention that they would maintain Buddhism as the state religion. It could therefore be claimed that nothing had changed fundamentally. One foreign sovereign had simply been exchanged for another, and the essentially Sinhalese character of the state would continue.

Yet things were different now. When the Kandyan aristocracy found British rule oppressive and rebelled barely three years later, they were put down firmly and the convention was abrogated. Though there was no doubt who was in charge, cultural domination came more slowly. Perhaps because the concept behind the convention was still respected, perhaps because British policy in the area was still unaffected by the Anglicizing reforms that Macaulay spearheaded a couple of decades later in India, Buddhism continued to have a prominent position. Crucially, education was still largely left to the temples. It was only in the 1830s that a government school was started in Colombo on a British model, and only in the 1850s did the Anglican Church begin its educational activities. Thus it was long after the British had taken over the country that English became a medium of instruction in the Sinhalese areas, to produce a generation capable of functioning in English and taking up posts within the colonial administration. Until that time the British had to draw their functionaries from elsewhere.

Though a few of these were Sinhalese who had taken the initiative themselves, the majority were Burghers, descendants (often of mixed blood) of the Dutch and the Portuguese, who were happy to learn the language of the latest of the Europeans and be absorbed within the system; significantly, there were also a number of Tamils, since in Jaffna an English educational system developed long before it was started in the rest of the country. This was due to the American missionaries who were allowed a free hand in the Jaffna peninsula when the colonial power still trod warily in the rest of the country. Thus, perhaps because of a historical accident arising from British delicacy and the Kandyan convention, perhaps because of a policy of divide and rule whereby the majority was comparatively disadvantaged, a disproportionate number of places in the administration came to be held by Tamils. This remained the case until independence and for some time after.

Another contributory factor may have been the relative barrenness of the Jaffna peninsula. Education therefore was doubly significant, and the white collar jobs it guaranteed played a larger part in expectations than elsewhere in the country where other occupations were available. Whatever the cause, the result was a fact, and associated with it was the relative command of English possessed by the average Tamil as compared with the Sinhalese.

Another more obvious complication was introduced by the British when they opened up the centre of the country to large scale plantations. This began with coffee, replaced after blight by tea. The Kandyan peasant rebellion of 1848 happened largely because of the extensive alienation for this purpose of land which had been used in common for generations. The plantations were bitterly resented and the average villager, though deprived of some of his previous livelihood, preferred to eke out an existence some other way rather than provide labour for them. This was not a problem for the British, who imported labour from south India to work the estates. The labour was predominantly Tamil; between them and the people of Jaffna lay a wide gulf which was not bridged during the century and more that followed. No educational facilities were provided for the Indian Tamils, as they were called; they were lodged on the estates on which they worked in primitive accommodation known appropriately as 'Lines'; it was generally assumed, however old they grew at their labours, that they would return to India once they had earned enough. They were thought to have no stake in the country, and were treated as undesirable, if necessary, aliens.

Moves towards self-government

In accordance with this attitude the Indian Tamils were not represented for many years in the Legislative Council that was set up as early as the 1830s. Originally the Legislative Council had a membership of 15, nine Officials of the government and six Unofficials as they were called, three English and one each to represent the Sinhalese, Tamil and Burgher communities. Fifty years later a Muslim was added, and also an Upcountry Sinhalese, to register the distinction between the old maritime province and the Kandyan kingdom. In the first quarter of the twentieth century the government gradually gave up its control of the Council, various reforms leading first to a majority of Unofficial members over Officials and then to a majority of elected members over members nominated by the Governor, Official or English or Sri Lankan. It was late in the course of these manoeuvres that the Indian Tamils received representation but, as with the Muslims, it was through nomination by the Governor.

In 1931 however, along with a State Council with some executive power, Sri Lanka received universal franchise, some years before India and just five years after it had been extended to women in Britain. For the Indian Tamils this was a tremendous advance - in one respect at least they were now on a level with the rest of the population. For the other Tamils however the new system came as a disappointment. At first glance this seems odd, for during the previous two decades they had been closely associated with the Sinhalese in the agitation for self-government. Indeed at the very first election permitted to Sri Lankans for a single seat on the Legislative Council (the seat for an 'Educated Ceylonese Member' as it was happily called in 1912), a Tamil was elected despite the majority of the voters being Sinhalese. Communal tensions that arose in the years that followed out of clashes over business interests were between Sinhalese and Muslims; after the 1915 riots the 'Educated Ceylonese Member' of the Council proved a forceful champion of the Sinhalese who had been victimized by the British administration.

In 1931 however, the Tamils opposed the new reform. Under universal franchise and a system of single member constituencies which would go to whoever obtained a majority of votes in each, they would have fewer members proportionately, and also would be deprived of representation from Colombo. It was not a very grave objection, and they soon abandoned their boycott and contested seats in the northern and eastern areas that had been deemed their rightful field; but their response was symptomatic of the dilemma that would increasingly confront the Tamils, many of whom had established themselves securely in Colombo under the British. They were in a minority there, but felt that their importance in the capital, springing from their numbers within the public service, warranted representation there too instead of their being treated as a regional group.

What occurred after the elections of 1936 seemed to justify their fears. Under the 1931 reforms members of the State Council were divided into seven committees which looked after different departments of government. Heads for these were elected, to constitute a Board of Ministers together with three key officials of the colonial administration. The Board functioned under the control of the Governor who continued to be answerable to the Colonial Secretary in Britain rather than to the State Council or its Board. It was however understood that the setting up of this sort of cabinet was a test and indeed a preparation for the conferment of further powers on Sri Lankans in time. It was therefore a bitter blow to the Tamils when, after contesting the elections of 1936 in full harmony with the system, they found that the hierarchy of the Ceylon National Congress arranged the elections so as to ensure that all seven ministers were Sinhalese.

The Tamils felt left out. It was that very Board of Ministers that finalized the negotiations that led up to independence in 1948. In such a context G G Ponnambalam the leader of the Tamil Congress put forward a demand of 'fifty-fifty', namely that all the minorities together, Tamils and Muslims and Christians, should have equal representation with the Sinhalese Buddhists if independence were granted. This concept had not been enunciated previously and was ignored. In the light of concessions to minority interests in India, extending to partition, surprisingly the majority in Sri Lanka was left in almost absolute control of the political process; surprising that is, unless one considers the relative roles of the Indian Congress and the Muslim League during the war; in Sri Lanka it was the National Congress that gave support to the British as the Muslim League did in India.

The leaders of the Tamil Congress bowed to the inevitable, and accepted office in the first government after independence. Of the Tamil ministers in that cabinet (which seemed by its multiracial character to justify the optimism of the British in rejecting the arguments of the Tamils), two had been leaders of the agitation for parity of status. But there had been a split in the Tamil Congress; and, though this was not to prove significant again in mainstream Tamil politics, it had been fuelled by what had happened to the Indian Tamils.

Unlike their counterparts in Jaffna and Colombo, Indian Tamils were satisfied with the 1931 constitution, since under it they were equals, for the first time, in the political process. As it happened, given the boycott by the Ceylonese Tamils, an Indian Tamil representative even became a Minister. Unfortunately, not for communal but for ideological reasons, the participation of Indian Tamils in the elections, in 1931 and then in 1936, and again in 1947, did not satisfy the Ceylon National Congress; they were heavily unionized and voted accordingly, and it was primarily because of their votes that the left did comparatively well. The result was that the Indians were disenfranchised in 1947 in accordance with a hurriedly passed citizenship act, which reinforced their status as migrant labour with no automatic right of citizenship. The Tamil members of the Cabinet acquiesced to this monstrous piece of legislation. Doubtless they too believed that keeping Socialists out of parliament was more important than ensuring representation and rights for people who seemed fundamentally different from themselves.

Jawaharlal Nehru, visiting Sri Lanka a decade earlier, had drawn attention to the plight of Indian Tamils and suggested that the Ceylon Tamils look on them with greater sympathy by virtue of consanguinity. Given too the disappointments they had suffered with regard to the constitutions of 1931 and at independence, his advice seemed to have been heeded by those Tamil politicians who set up their own party in opposition to their leaders who joined the government. Yet the average Ceylon Tamil voter was not especially taken by their arguments. The Tamil Congress did better at the polls; it took other issues closer to home to enable the Federal Party (FP as the breakaway Tamil group was called, rather boldly at the time) to come into its own.

Racial distinctions at independence

To recapitulate then, when Ceylon became independent in 1948 as a Dominion on the lines of Australia or Canada, there were a number of racial groups with various subdivisions. The Sinhalese were still classified in census returns as Low-country or Up-country, though before long the distinction was forgotten. Amongst Tamils however divisions ran deeper. First, there were the Tamils of the north, concentrated largely in the Jaffna peninsula. Springing from invasions that had commenced two thousand years previously, they regarded the lifestyle they had developed as distinctively their own, just as the Sinhalese did theirs. Largely from amongst them came the Tamils who had settled in Colombo and other predominantly Sinhalese areas in the south. Though still with roots in the Jaffna peninsula, they were more cosmopolitan than their relations who had stayed back. Right up to independence and beyond their numbers increased, for they were still being recruited into the administrative service and other government departments in large numbers, and such employment continued to be amongst the most prestigious for the youth from Jaffna.

Further down the social scale were the Tamils of the east coast. Culturally they did not possess as strong a sense of identity as the Tamils of the north, for their settlements had been more precarious and they lived amongst people of other races. There were a number of Muslims in the east, and though they spoke Tamil they were very conscious of their separate identity. This last applied too to the Sinhalese, especially the migrant fishermen who, in going back to the west coast for the fishing season there, looked on it as their true home. Whether it was because the pure strain was thus seen as diluted, or whether the explanation lay in the clannishness the geography of Jaffna encouraged, or in economic or occupational disparities (educational facilities in the east being comparatively poor), there was little social intercourse between Tamils of the north and those of the east.

Yet both these groups were classified as Ceylon Tamils. Lower down in the pecking order in their eyes, and those of everyone else, were the Indian Tamils who had just been disenfranchised and in effect debarred from citizenship. Stranded as they were within their estates, they derived no benefit from the educational and other welfare schemes available to others. They had no political representation now except for individuals who might or might not be appointed at the pleasure of the government. Six seats had been allotted in the constitution for those who would not otherwise be represented, to include both the British business houses which had every other advantage, and the plantation workers who had none. Meanwhile the conditions under which they lived and worked for their British masters, who continued for a quarter of a century to own the estates, were deplorable.

Apart from these there were the Muslims. In the east their first language was Tamil. This was also true of many of those who lived inland and on the west coast, but almost all of them knew enough Sinhalese to be more or less assimilated. Since the riots of 1915 they had had no problems. Though in the census returns they were distinguished as a race, what was significant to them and others was the difference in religion. Thus they were not much different from the Christians, who were only distinguished by religion in the census returns. The aggressive attitude of the Portuguese had led to there being many more Catholics than Protestants. Though the Anglicans were socially dominant at this time, owing to continuing British influence, because of their small numbers they presented no threat whatsoever.

Finally, in terms of race, there were the Burghers. Their percentage was miniscule but, even more disproportionately than the Tamils, they exercised administrative and professional influence due to their command of the language of administration. Their small numbers made it unlikely that this would ever be a problem. Nevertheless, it is with regard to this sort of disproportionate influence and its source that one finds problems springing up after the first few years of contentment, years in which the leaders of the newly independent nation congratulated themselves on having achieved their goals in such a civilized manner, without the communal bloodbath that had torn India apart.

Part II

Dominion to Republic

The Politics of Language (1948–1977)

Chapter 2

Developing Majorities

The first UNP years

When the problem of the Indian Tamils was discussed at the time of independence, it was suggested that they be granted citizenship and educated in Sinhalese. A Sinhalese Civil Servant of the period rejected this on the grounds that the Indian Tamils were so industrious that they would soon dominate the Sinhalese from within. The legend had been swallowed wholesale, and the man clearly had no idea of the kind of assimilation that had been going on for a millennium and more. Perhaps he would not have been capable of appreciating that new groups, which exercised influence amongst their peers after they had learned Sinhalese, would do so virtually as Sinhalese themselves. It was in that way that, far from being dominated by immigrant groups with different identities, the Sinhalese had over the centuries absorbed new blood that enabled them to develop, and to preserve traditions that were constantly being renewed and rejuvenated.

But at the time of independence the Sinhalese language was a sort of relic, to be carefully conserved but scarcely ever used. The bureaucrat belonged to the old aristocracy that functioned best in English and never questioned the fact. Interestingly enough it was someone from the same sort of background who initiated the revolution. But, as is usual in such instances, charismatic as the individual was, his influence was immense precisely because he responded to real public need.

The United National Party (UNP), under which title the National Congress governed after independence, faithfully followed the West. It was content to rely largely on the plantation economy left behind, or rather still owned and managed, by the British; despite changing circumstances the country seemed able, partly because of the boom in rubber prices caused by the Korean War, to survive and indeed thrive on its traditional exports. The socialist forward planning based on industrialization that was happening in India was unknown in Sri Lanka. Though there were some attempts to develop new industries, these were on a small scale, and it is significant that the Tamil Minister of Industries at the time was able to site many of the new factories, for cement and for paper for instance, in Tamil areas. The complacent Sinhalese in the Cabinet could not have conceived that therein lay the future.

It is often claimed that the 1951 split in the UNP was prompted by ambition. But long before independence there had already existed a separate political grouping known as the Sinhala Maha Sabha, led by an Oxford graduate from a prominent Sinhalese family, albeit one documented as having hailed from India round about the fifteenth century. In a Board of Ministers composed largely of Congress stalwarts S W R D Bandaranaike had functioned quite satisfactorily, so it is not surprising that he joined the UNP and served in the first Cabinet after independence under its leader, D S Senanayake. There is no doubt that he wished to be designated as Senanayake's successor, and it is held that he broke away only when this was in doubt.

But Bandaranaike's speeches reveal from the very start a vision that was not shared by his colleagues within the UNP. He saw himself as representing the ordinary Sinhalese, not as opposed to the Tamils but rather to the English oriented upper classes who ran an administration that did not cater to the needs of the average citizen. It was precisely that upper class that constituted the core of UNP support.

In the elections of 1952 the Sri Lanka Freedom Party (SLFP) that Bandaranaike had set up had only a limited impact. Dudley Senanayake, having succeeded his father on his sudden death, led the UNP to a convincing victory and formed a government. A year later he resigned when a worker was killed by security forces during a demonstration. Senanayake was a sensitive man; he accepted responsibility for the incident and gave up office. He was succeeded by Bandaranaike's erstwhile rival, John Kotelawala, who had stomached his disappointment after the elder Senanayake died but could not be overlooked again. His lifestyle as well as his whole approach to politics was strikingly western. As the years passed it became clear that Bandaranaike would be a threat at the next election, and the UNP accordingly took stock of its position.

Bandaranaike's language policies

The main plank of Bandaranaike's platform was a commitment to make Sinhalese the language of administration in the country. This was primarily in opposition to English, which was beyond the reach of the average citizen. Indeed there were elements in the UNP that had not been blind to this. J R Jayewardene, considered their chief strategist, had moved in the State Council in the early forties that the compulsory medium of instruction in all schools be Sinhalese (and Tamil, which he agreed to add when reminded of the Tamils). At that stage the final decision had been to restrict this to primary schools, but in the early fifties it was extended to the entire school system.

So it was not entirely surprising that, under pressure from its populist wing, the UNP adopted a Sinhala Only policy at sessions held in Jayewardene's Kelaniya electorate early in 1956, and chose to call an early election to seek a mandate to implement it. This however could not be perceived as being in opposition to English: the UNP was seen as the party of the ruling elite who were entirely at home in English. Rather the determination to make Sinhala the official language of the nation was seen as a method of denigrating Tamil. Kotelawala himself had previously pledged parity of status for the two languages, a pronouncement to which the Kelaniya sessions were seen as a corrective.

Tamil members of the UNP abandoned it. In what became a race for popular favour on the part of the two main parties, far from attempting to correct the impression of racism, chauvinistic elements were permitted a free hand. Conversely Tamil politicians, spearheaded by the FP which at last had concrete evidence of the racist duplicity it had all along attributed to the UNP, reacted vigorously.

Bandaranaike swept into power in the Sinhala areas; the rout of the UNP suggested that, far from chauvinism, it was the social issue of greater egalitarianism that had proved crucial. More significant for the future was the fact that the UNP and its former allies of the Tamil Congress

(TC) were heavily defeated in the Tamil areas. The FP swept to the fore. No matter that its leader SJV Chelvanayakam, who had first split with the Tamil establishment over the disenfranchisement of Indian Tamils, functioned from Colombo and was more at home in English rather than Tamil: the lines of opposition had been drawn.

There was however a period of respite. Bandaranaike's own priorities were not anti-Tamil, whatever the inclinations of some of the motley crew that formed his unexpectedly large parliamentary majority. He was prepared to negotiate with the FP, and worked out a series of measures known as the Bandaranaike-Chelvanayakam pact.

The question of language policy was read in simplistic terms. Bandaranaike had perhaps assumed that, since English had been readily accepted by Tamils as the language of administration, so would Sinhalese be. When he found that this was not the case, he accepted the consequences of the resentment too easily. Sinhalese had hitherto been available as a subject in Tamil schools but, since Tamil politicians now opposed this, Bandaranaike expedited the changes the previous government had initiated. He allowed the establishment of two parallel educational systems, divided racially by two different mediums of instruction.

Again, he was quite happy to permit the language of administration in the northern and eastern provinces to be Tamil, and also to permit to citizens there the right to communicate in Tamil with the central government. The impracticality of producing translations from Tamil to Sinhalese and vice versa, in a context in which individuals received their education in one language and did not study the other, appears to have escaped him completely. But then, English was to continue in theory as a second language for all, and even as a medium of instruction for a lucky few – Burghers and those of mixed blood and also Muslims (the Minister of Education at the time happened to be one, which may have influenced the conferral of what proved a distinct advantage). Bandaranaike and Chelvanayakam, having conducted their own negotiations in English, doubtless assumed that bridges would always be available.

In accordance with the mandate the FP seemed to have received, but also in terms of his own reflections enunciated twenty years before about

Developing Majorities

the unsatisfactory nature of highly centralized government, Bandaranaike was prepared to allow the devolution of power through regional councils. Ironically this particular measure roused fierce opposition. The incoherence of an Official Language policy, while there was another language that could also be used officially even though it was not compulsory that both languages be studied by all, occurred neither to Bandaranaike, nor to more communal minded politicians on either side. To regional councils however a variety of Sinhalese politicians advanced violent objections, asserting that what amounted to autonomy for the Tamils could lead to the eventual dismemberment of the country.

J R Jayewardene and the UNP

The UNP at this time was dominated by Jayewardene. He had not been a member of the pre-independence Board of Ministers, having entered the State Council only in 1942 through a controversial by-election. The Congress did not field a candidate, but allowed its members to support either a veteran politician named E W Perera or the relatively young lawyer who also put forward his claim. Jayewardene's victory was tainted by his taking advantage of his opponent being a practising Christian. His own father was Christian but, having reverted now to his mother's faith, Jayewardene roused chauvinistic feeling by presenting himself as the only Sinhala Buddhist candidate.

The feelings generated by the campaign amongst the senior members of the party soon died down, for Jayewardene was rapidly recognized as being a reliable party man. At independence he became the first Sri Lankan Minister of Finance, the post had previously been reserved for a British Civil Servant. Though this did not give him a high profile nationally, his authority within the party grew in this office, and when D S Senanayake died his was the deciding voice in Kotelawala being passed over and Dudley Senanayake forming the government. Despite this, his own hopes of succeeding were disappointed when Senanayake advised the Governor-General on his own resignation to send for Kotelawala. Kotelawala would have presented a danger if thwarted a second time, but Senanayake may also have felt that Jayewardene did not command popular support. A popular satirical column of the time called him the Cold-blooded Tiger, as opposed to the more lively sobriquets of Rogue Elephant, Tired Tortoise and Electric Eel that had been bestowed on Kotelawala, Senanayake and Bandaranaike respectively. Though his abilities were respected, especially in urban society, he was never thought of as a charismatic figure.

Kotelawala remained in parliament as party leader, but after the UNP's defeat in 1956 he lost interest in politics and soon left the country to settle down in Britain. It was Jayewardene who, though he had lost his own seat and remained outside parliament, assiduously built up the party again, with the assistance of loyalists such as the party General Secretary Cyril Mathew. By the time of the next election Dudley Senanayake had been recalled from retirement, and Jayewardene, recognising his electoral appeal, was willing to serve as his deputy over the next decade. He was seen as the architect of party strategy, and in the crucial couple of years following Bandaranaike's victory he was its single major public figure.

During the agitation against the Bandaranaike-Chelvanayakam pact, he both formulated party policy and played a leading part in its implementation. His chief move was a protest march to Kandy, recognized as the repository of Sinhala Buddhist culture. The march was disrupted but its propaganda value is not to be underestimated, in particular to those in Bandaranaike's own party who were keen on a communal line. Under these pressures Bandaranaike abandoned the pact. Unfortunately new administrative institutions that might have helped in implementing the new language policy were not put in place; the language policy itself, the fatal acceptance of two separate languages in the educational system, went unquestioned.

The tensions to which all this political manoeuvering gave rise burst out in communal violence in 1958. Bandaranaike could not act with sufficient ruthlessness to stem the tide, but he permitted absolute authority to the titular head of state, Sir Oliver Goonetilleke, a former minister appointed as Governor-General when the last British occupant retired. Using to maximum effect the armed forces, staffed at the higher levels mainly by Sinhalese or Tamil Christians, Sir Oliver soon brought the situation under control. For twenty years after that there was scarcely any communal violence in the country. It was only in 1977, after the massive electoral victory of the UNP under Jayewardene, that attacks by Sinhalese on Tamils began again, to be repeated both in 1981 and 1983. On the last two occasions, unlike before, even if the government officially opposed the violence, some leaders of the ruling party sanctioned the active involvement of unruly elements. It may not have been a coincidence that both these attacks took place shortly after the UNP had won handsome electoral victories all over the country except in Tamil areas.

Social change under Mrs Bandaranaike

In 1959 Bandaranaike was assassinated by a Buddhist monk, the tool of forces that thought that he had conceded too much to the Tamils and had also been too left-wing. In the election of March 1960 that followed no party won a majority, but the UNP was the largest single party and Dudley Senanayake formed a minority government. His reason for accepting the post was to prevent the SLFP from forming a coalition with the FP after conceding several of their demands. Though Senanayake lost a vote of confidence as soon as parliament met, as Prime Minister he advised the Governor-General to dissolve parliament and hold fresh elections.

At this point however the SLFP invited Bandaranaike's widow to lead the party; in July 1960 she won a substantial victory which enabled her to continue his work. Bandaranaike had introduced measures such as a Paddy Lands Act which liberated tenant cultivators from the previous almost feudal system and gave them a right to a share of their labours. Pressures from the right of the SLFP had led early in 1958 to the resignation of Philip Gunawardena, the Minister who had pushed through the Act, but its impact continued. Bandaranaike had also embarked on a limited programme of nationalisation, of transport services for instance. Mrs. Bandaranaike went much further, to the extent of nationalizing even foreign oil distribution networks, which led to a stoppage of American aid. Correspondingly she began, with increased Russian aid, to industrialize to a greater extent than before.

Though without any formal ideological position herself, she displayed a remarkable capacity to reflect what could be thought of as international trends. For the first time Sri Lanka began to fit prominently into the mainstream of Third World governments. In terms of international relations its stature in the emerging non-aligned movement grew considerably. It made a concerted attempt to diversify its economy and emerge from the control which the First World had exercised over it.

Although early in Mrs. Bandaranaike's tenure there were some political conflicts with the FP, implementation of the language policies with regard to administration that had been enunciated in the Bandaranaike-Chelvanayakam pact led to a period of equanimity. For the moment the problem seemed to have diminished. Much more controversy was generated by the campaign against what was termed Catholic Action, the opposition of some prominent Catholic institutions and individuals to the socialist and nationalist policies advocated by the Bandaranaike governments.

Unfortunately the Catholic Church in Sri Lanka was still in a traditionalist phase, which contributed to the assumption that the opposition the government encountered was formal and organized. To deal with this at its roots perhaps, the government took over most Catholic schools, which seemed to Catholics an attack on a crucial element of their identity.

This may well have contributed to the attempted coup of 1962, in which the first accused was Douglas Liyanage, a leading Catholic Civil Servant, while a number of the military officers involved were also Catholics. This, and the fact that most of the leading conspirators were Christians, from prestigious schools and cosmopolitan backgrounds, had a serious long-term effect. The coup itself was easily forestalled, but in subsequent recruitment to the army a Sinhala Buddhist background was stressed. The consequence was that twenty years later there were far fewer Tamils amongst the middle-rank officers in the field, many of whom (given too the divisive educational system that had been in operation) had a relatively restricted outlook. This proved unfortunate when the communal issue blew up.

Much more important in the public eye than dealings with the FP was Mrs. Bandaranaike's success in negotiating a pact in 1964 with the Indian Prime Minister Shastri concerning the repatriation of the Indian Tamils who were without Sri Lankan citizenship. These had not figured in the agitation of the FP over the previous decade about the language issue and devolution, and they had not suffered noticeably in the disturbances of 1958, but their status remained a problem. The compromise arrived at involved granting Sri Lankan citizenship to some, repatriation of more, with the fate of another 100,000 to be decided later. Mrs. Bandaranaike's government fell soon after the agreement was reached, so that it was left to subsequent governments to oversee the implementation of the scheme.

Among those whose abstentions caused the government's defeat in the crucial vote was S Thondaman, the leader of the Ceylon Worker's Congress (CWC), the Indian Tamils' main trade union. He had been nominated by the government to represent his people in parliament, so that his defection suggests he disapproved of the pact. The government view was that something definite had been decided about a people whose status was otherwise uncertain, and this had been possible because of Mrs. Bandaranaike's good relations with India, a factor that was to be significant throughout her political career. From Thondaman's point of view, however, this could lead only to a diminution of his own influence in Sri Lanka.

Certainly the claim that he was concerned about press freedom, the crucial vote having arisen over a proposal to nationalize the Associated Newspapers of Ceylon (the major newspaper group known also as Lake House that had forcefully opposed both Bandaranaike governments), rings hollow in the light of his subsequent adherence to a government that exercised careful control over the press. In his case though, financial incentives were never alleged, as they were for many of her own party who voted against her on this occasion.

It was generally accepted that Jayewardene, whose mother had been the sister of the founder of Lake House, was the brains behind the government's defeat. He was closely supported by his cousin-in-law Esmond Wickremesinghe, the Managing Director of the group who had looked after the financial aspects of the operation. But, Mrs Bandaranaike's coalition earlier in the year with a couple of Marxist parties, that had provided the impetus for the nationalization of the newspapers, had also raised sincere worries in some of them about a drift towards totalitarianism. Having crossed over just before the crucial vote they set up their own party which contested the ensuing elections in association with the UNP. Also attached to this grouping was Philip Gunawardena's United People's Party (MEP, in accordance with its Sinhalese name), which had earlier formed a United Left Front with the Communist Party (CP) and the Trotskyist Lanka Socialist Party (LSSP), but had disdainfully stayed out when the other two went into coalition with the SLFP.

Dudley Senanayake led the coalition for the election, and was its candidate for Prime Minister, but they were just short of a majority. He then entered into an agreement with the FP, to establish a majority, which allowed him to nominate six more members (including Thondaman). His position was thus secure even without the FP, but he made a genuine attempt to push through the bill which had been the condition of their support. This was a District Councils Bill, which gave Tamil areas less autonomy that the Regional Councils envisaged by the Bandaranaike-Chelvanayakam Pact. Now even Provinces seemed too large as units and local administrative responsibilities and powers were contemplated only for the Districts into which the Provinces were divided.

Even this limited measure did not prove practicable. There were protests throughout the country by opposition political parties and various interest groups that had supported the UNP at the elections, and rumblings of discontent within the party too. These were expressed most prominently by Cyril Mathew, who was removed from his party post as a consequence, but the pressures proved too strong in the end and Senanayake dropped the offending bill. Given that around this period he had both Jayewardene and Wickremesinghe tailed by the CID, it is possible that he also feared Jayewardene would pull the rug from under his feet.

Unlike Bandaranaike, who had unilaterally abrogated his pact, Senanayake withdrew the District Councils Bill after discussions with the FP which apparently accepted the position, and persuaded him not to resign. Soon after however, its sole representative in the Cabinet, Senator Tiruchelvam (not an elected member but one who had been appointed to the Second Chamber that then existed), resigned from the Cabinet, ostensibly over another issue. The FP nevertheless continued to support the government right through to the elections of 1970. Incidentally the

TC too remained a member of the governing coalition throughout its lifetime, though at no stage did it hold a Cabinet portfolio.

Mrs. Bandaranaike was returned to power in 1970 with a massive majority. In her Cabinet, in vital portfolios such as Finance, Plantations and Constitutional Affairs, were representatives of the Marxist parties she had allied with. As a consequence socialism was pushed with far more determination and thoroughness than had been the case during the two previous Bandaranaike regimes.

The government began with the introduction of a new republican constitution, as had been pledged in its manifesto, and which the two-thirds majority it had achieved made legally possible. To many young people who had campaigned for the government at the election the deliberations of the Constitutional Assembly, which parliament had set itself up as, seemed intolerably slow. Agitation led to government reaction, and perhaps to pre-empt further measures an armed insurrection was launched, in April 1971, less than a year after the election. The moving spirit behind all this was a new neo-Marxist political grouping, the People's Liberation Front (JVP), led by Rohana Wijeweera, a former student of Lumumba University who had been found *persona non grata* by the Russians for excessive revolutionary fervour.

Apart from the tightly organized JVP itself, participants in the insurrection included several youngsters still at university or even school, who had been carried away by idealistic enthusiasm and expected swift success. Confined though it was to Sinhala areas only, the widespread and intense nature of the uprising at first took the government aback. It was quelled before long, but not without much bloodshed. The government was offered and accepted assistance from a whole range of foreign governments, eastern and western. It was also strongly supported by the UNP in parliament, led now by Jayewardene. Senanayake had declined the post of leader of the opposition after his defeat at the polls, although he still continued to sit in parliament and lead the party.

Perhaps spurred by the insurrection, the government now moved fast. Amongst its most important measures was a ceiling of fifty acres for land in private ownership, which meant the break up of the large estates that had hitherto provided the landed aristocracy with so much influence as well as wealth. This was followed by the nationalization of foreign-owned plantations. Significantly it was only when this process had been put in train that the British press began to draw attention to the sorry plight of the Indian labour on the estates; in fact there were some attempts to improve their condition after they came under state management. Despite the sincere critiques of individual reporters, the whole exercise indicates the skill with which the foreign proprietors of the estates avoided investigation of much worse conditions that had obtained in their time. The result was the beginnings of international interest in what appeared as the racist policies of the Sri Lankan government: and some confusion with regard to the claims of the Tamil Separatist movement that began.

The beginning of Separatism

That movement arose primarily in the Jaffna peninsula, and there were specific reasons for the bitterness which generated it. One sudden change in particular struck very deep. Education had long been one of the prime concerns of the area; of the relatively large number of Tamils who gained admission to the various Sri Lankan universities, a high proportion came from Jaffna. Since hardly any Indian Tamils gained entrance, and relatively few from the Eastern Province, the proportion of students from Jaffna now prompted a critical reaction.

The context was one in which university education had scarcely been expanded over the previous decade while numbers in schools had increased dramatically. The proportion of students gaining admission to university in any particular year, therefore, was miniscule. Those hardest hit were students from rural areas where schools were comparatively poor. The government with its egalitarian outlook felt this was not the fault of these students who had to compete against others who enjoyed much better facilities. There was no system of interviews nor did the different universities have individual intakes; the system of admission for the whole country was through a consolidated merit list based purely on marks at the final school public examination. This was considered unfair to the rural student. In addition, while different standards were adopted in the marking of different subjects, the high rate of success amongst some Tamils suggested that the same applied with regard to the different languages in which scripts were submitted. It was decided accordingly to standardize marks, with regard to different districts and subjects and the various mediums of instruction. The goal was to make admissions to university reflect proportionately the actual numbers in the various categories that had sought admission through the examination.

The theory was in accord with the egalitarian principles that the government was determined to promulgate. The scheme however was complicated, and the main reaction was the cynical and often bitter one that all the government wanted was a result that pleased its principal base of support, the rural Sinhala areas. This certainly did occur and, though areas such as the Eastern Province also benefited, the proportion of Tamils gaining admission to university came down drastically. Had the scheme been perfect and readily understandable, Jaffna would still have suffered, given the absence of private sector tertiary education and other suitable substitutes for able youngsters. As it was, the whole scheme was handled with arrogance and insensitivity, so that to the disappointment was added the conviction that the motivation behind the scheme was entirely racist. The result was a rapid increase in militant feeling amongst Tamil youth.

Connected with this was the problem caused by the fruition of the educational policies put into operation in the fifties. Tamil children now growing up had no knowledge whatsoever of Sinhalese, the language in which much of the administration of the country was conducted. Their second language in school was English but, apart from being badly taught, it was now of little use to those seeking official employment. The argument might have been that Tamils could serve in the Northern and Eastern Provinces, but in a highly centralized system of government the jobs available in those areas were disproportionately few and not especially promising. Thus, given their lack of fluency in the main language in which the business of government was carried on, the Tamils found themselves shut out of many government jobs, the occupation they had fitted into so easily over the past several years.

The sense of frustration thus roused led to a drastic change in outlook, while the general attitude of the government did nothing to help. In preparing the new constitution it rode roughshod over the objections of the opposition, and in particular introduced a clause giving Buddhism a special position. This violated clause 29 (d) of the constitution that the British had left behind, which guaranteed that no race or religion could be discriminated against or given any special privileges. That clause was supposed to have been entrenched, but could be changed with a 2/3 majority, which the government had. There was no further legal remedy, since the government had stopped appeals to the Privy Council in London, which had in any case not responded actively to a previous appeal on the provision. The Constitutional Assembly saw itself as composed of sovereign representatives of the people, given the mandate it had received, and in British practice that meant a majority could do whatever it wished. In addition, the government claimed that it was simply restoring the position that prevailed at the time of the Kandyan Convention, which the British had unfairly abrogated. The fact that Convention had not applied to Jaffna was totally ignored.

The Trotskyist architect of the constitution argued that sufficient safeguards against discrimination had been retained. The Tamils felt imposed upon, and no attempts were made to hold discussions with them that might have produced a compromise. Rather, the government continued to assert an authority it felt was absolute, to the extent even of postponing for three years, under Emergency Regulations introduced for a very different reason, the by-election necessitated by Chelvanayakam's resignation from his parliamentary seat. His aim had been to show the continuing, indeed increasing, support he commanded in the Tamil areas. When the government did finally hold the election it was clear that the long postponement had only served to vindicate his stand.

Apart from these factors the incident that is widely held to have seen the birth of militancy occurred at a Tamil Cultural Festival held in Jaffna, over which, perhaps because of South Indian participation, the Government grew extremely alarmed. A shot fired by a policeman hit a high tension wire with fatal consequences. The official investigation, conducted by a Burgher judge of the Supreme Court, found that the deaths had been caused accidentally, but the government was thought to have instigated the incident. Soon after there occurred the murder of the mayor of Jaffna, a member of the SLFP, who had been condemned as a traitor. The group responsible for the assassination, at that time very small, called itself the Liberation Tigers of Tamil Eelam, meaning independence. Amongst those involved was Velupillai Prabhakaran who, whilst various splinter groups split off and others were formed, rapidly emerged as the most prominent figure in the ensuing terrorist campaign.

At that stage however the campaign was still predominantly peaceful. In 1976 the Tamil United Liberation Front was established to campaign for a separate Tamil state at the general election due the following year. The FP was its chief component, but the TC was also involved, along with Thondaman's CWC. Though a separate state that encompassed the central hill region too would have been a geographical anomaly, Thondaman had very good reason to oppose the government. He was not in parliament since the appointment on behalf of the Indian Tamils had gone to the leader of a rival grouping called the Democratic Workers Congress that commanded little public support. Besides this, repatriations in terms of the pact with Shastri were proceeding apace during this period. The Senanayake government with Thondaman supporting it had no reason to implement the pact assiduously but, apart from the present government wanting to anyway, its task was facilitated by the the economic position of the country which made vast numbers anxious to leave.

To be quite fair this was not entirely the fault of the government. The massive increase in oil prices during its tenure had thrown all calculations out of gear. Besides this, tea was one of the very few commodities the price of which did not increase substantially during the early seventies; and the fact that the markets were still largely controlled by the major British companies whose estates in Sri Lanka had just been nationalized did not help. But the government had also alienated a number of professionals who emigrated, while the business community in general had little confidence in it. The calibre of most politicians in office or power left much to be desired; many able and influential policy makers were Marxists who were not trusted by the bulk of the SLFP.

In 1975 indeed the LSSP was got rid of from the government, though the CP continued part of the ruling coalition until just before the election, when it went away taking with it a section of the left wing of the SLFP. The net result, particularly in the last two years, was general incoherence as politicians with a fundamentally right wing outlook attempted to run a highly socialist economy, while the human and material resources dwindled.

Mrs. Bandaranaike herself was more interested in foreign policy, and in this field Sri Lanka achieved prominence as Chairman of the Non-Aligned Movement. She also succeeded in maintaining close relations with both India and Pakistan in spite of their own hostilities. Though Pakistan was permitted aerial facilities during the 1971 war, India continued amicable, and indeed gave up its claims to an island in the strait between India and Sri Lanka. Again the pact regarding the Indian Tamils was finalized with Mrs. Gandhi, with both countries agreeing to divide equally those whose fate had been left undecided. As far as Sri Lanka itself was concerned however none of this helped a population that saw a drastic decline in its standard of living, while the programme of nationalization failed to provide any appreciable assistance to the landless or the deprived.

The return of the UNP

The result was that the UNP was swept back into power in 1977 with over three quarters of the seats in parliament. When the new constitution had been introduced the next election was postponed a couple of years beyond the date it was due. The government claimed that this was in accordance with its manifesto that had argued for an extension of the parliamentary term, but the delay only served to strengthen the appeal of the opposition.

During his first few years as leader of the opposition Jayewardene had a great deal of trouble within the UNP. His relationship with Senanayake had deteriorated during the latter part of the UNP regime. Senanayake voluntarily gave up the leadership of the party in parliament, but he remained wary of his successor. Many former Cabinet Ministers were worried by what they saw as Jayewardene's overtures to the government at the time of the 1971 insurrection and after that, and they moved to expel him from the party. As it happened a number of his senior opponents died, while efforts at conciliation produced an uneasy truce between him and Senanayake; but what finally settled things was that the latter, younger by five years, died unexpectedly in 1973. The massive crowd that attended his funeral convinced Jayewardene that he did not now need an understanding with the SLFP, and that the UNP could, despite its shattering defeat, return to power by itself.

Having consolidated his hold over the party, once again as after 1956, he set about the task of rebuilding it. By 1977, though by then seventy, he was in a position to run a very effective campaign. Apart from the shortage of necessities and economic mismanagement, there were two other sources of bitterness on which he capitalized. One was the sense of betrayal amongst young people, and even the old, in particular in the rural areas which had been hardest hit, about those killed during the 1971 uprising. After the first shock and consequent brutal repression the government had altered its approach, and even disciplined some military personnel involved in the excesses. Many of those captured were released without trial, while the tribunal that tried the rest was acknowledged by them to have been very fair and even indulgent. Few were punished, and their sentences too were not heavy. The memory of the numbers slaughtered in 1971 however died hard. Though Jayewardene had at the time pledged support to the government at what he acknowledged was a national emergency, he now deplored its excesses and helped to build up a myth that multiplied several times over the number of those who had died. Having promised an amnesty to those found guilty, a promise he fulfilled as soon as he took office, in the first few years of his government he found in the JVP, and its leader Wijeweera, extremely useful allies against Mrs. Bandaranaike.

Not less significant in terms of votes, and more so in terms of financial support and bloc votes in particular constituencies, was the backing he received from Tamils living in Sinhalese areas as well as from some from the east. In his manifesto he promised to alleviate what was described as the 'just grievances of the Tamils', after holding an all-party conference to discuss the relevant issues. Apart from their resentment of Mrs. Bandaranaike's economic dispensation, the majoritarian arrogance of the government led Tamils, in electorates where the TULF did not stand, to rally behind the UNP. Thondaman, it is true, did field some candidates. With a multi-member constituency having been created at the highest point in the hill country to ensure the return of an Indian Tamil representative, he himself was elected to parliament. But in general those of his people who had the vote used it on behalf of the UNP.

Apart from the general commitment of the UNP to redress their grievances, and the particular commitment to repeal the standardization procedure for admission to university, there was further reason for rejoicing amongst Tamils at the magnitude of the UNP victory. The SLFP was routed at the polls and reduced to a rump of eight seats, which included Mrs. Bandaranaike and her son Anura, who had just entered politics but was returned from the same multi-member constituency as Thondaman. The TULF which had swept the north and done well in the east had the second highest number of seats in the new parliament, albeit only a fraction of those held by the UNP. It was thus entitled to the office of leader of the opposition, the first time in Sri Lanka that even that post had gone to a Tamil. Thondaman might well have claimed the office, being the only surviving Joint President of the original three, both Chelvanayakam and Ponnambalam having died shortly before the election. He yielded however, since that represented a larger and more senior grouping of Tamils than the CWC, to Appapillai Amirthalingam the new leader of the FP.

Part III

The New Monarch

Jayewardene in Control (1977–1983)

Chapter 3
Consolidating the New Regime

The new order and its President

The period immediately following the election of 1977 was one of great hope. In the economic sphere certainly this seemed justified. Massive devaluation and a vigorously pursued open economic policy that contrasted sharply with the restrictions of the last seventeen years prompted much aid from the First World and its agencies, and a renewed interest in investment, local as well as foreign. Some of this was in a Free Trade Zone set up just north of Colombo, in emulation of Singapore and other success stories of the seventies. There was however general interest in the country as a whole, and a period of stagnation was succeeded by one of intense activity.

Tea prices too finally took off, while another large source of income developed through remittances from Sri Lankans working in the Middle East. The increase in oil revenues there had contributed to a proliferation of jobs for foreign workers, unskilled as well as skilled. The dearth of satisfactory employment in Sri Lanka in the preceding years had propelled many in that direction. Both these avenues opened up shortly before the elections, but their full impact was felt only afterwards, contributing to the feeling that the millennium had at last arrived.

There was a greater sense of purpose in the air, and several large projects were devised for concentrated action. Most important of these was the Mahaweli Scheme, planned some years earlier, but implemented very slowly, to harness the waters of the largest river in the country for hydroelectric power and irrigation of the Dry Zone. Unlike previously, funds now flowed in for the project. A separate Ministry was established to accelerate the project, headed by Gamini Dissanayake, one of the rising stars of the party thought to have Jayewardene's confidence.

Jayewardene had his own pet project too, the creation of a new capital through the building of a new parliament, so that the administration could shift from congested Colombo. The new capital was situated only a few miles from Colombo, in the already relatively crowned suburb of Kotte, known in the past as Sri Jayewardenepura.

The third major project, a Housing Development Scheme, was the brainchild of Ranasinghe Premadasa, who had been elected Deputy Leader of the party by the parliamentary group, defeating Dissanayake who had come a close second despite his youth. Premadasa had earlier been close to Dudley Senanayake but, hailing from a different caste and a less prosperous background than his peers in the UNP, his influence as a new man, closer to the people, could not be ignored.

Hopes for economic and social development then may have seemed justified; politically, however, indications were depressing from the start. With hindsight it is clear that Jayewardene intended from the beginning to establish an authoritarian one party state. Having a two-thirds majority in parliament, which according to the prevailing constitution meant that any change was possible, he set about using it with clinical determination to consolidate firstly his own power, secondly that of his party.

Unlike the first Republican Constitution of 1972 which came into operation through a Constitutional Assembly as proposed in the government manifesto, the Constitution of 1978 was introduced simply as an amendment to its predecessor. At the same time no bones were made about the fact that it involved a complete overhaul of the previous system, with two fundamental changes that struck at the roots of Westminster style parliamentary democracy.

The first change, culminating in the claim that he was the first elected Head of State in a line stretching back over two thousand years (the 193rd to be precise, including British sovereigns such as George III, as he used to stress), was the institution of an Executive Presidency to which Jayewardene elevated himself. He had previously suggested the desirability, on the American model, of freedom from the trammels of legislative duties for the executive authority. Assuming the post of ceremonial President under the 1972 constitution, appointed by himself as Prime

Minister, he amended the constitution on lines that turned out to be closer to the Gaullist constitution of the Fifth French republic rather than the American one. It was in accordance with this that, though the President presided over the Cabinet, the title of Prime Minister was retained. This he bestowed on Premadasa.

At the same time there was a fundamental difference from the Gaullist model with its separation of powers and functions. Jayewardene ensured that parliament continued under the domination of the executive, as in the Westminster model, since the new constitution also laid down that, apart from the President, all ministers should be members of parliament. This anomaly did not attract much critical attention, even though it contradicted Jayewardene's original published reflections which advanced as one of the main reasons for change the need for the entire executive to be free of legislative and other duties associated with parliament. In the welter of change the precise significance of the wide responsibilities that remained or accrued to parliament (except insofar as the executive President himself was concerned) were not examined. This was unfortunate in that the second major change he instituted made absolute the control over parliament not just of the UNP but of its controlling hierarchy, at the pinnacle of which stood himself.

The basic feature of this second change might not in itself have seemed sinister. The new constitution introduced a system of proportional representation at all elections. The arguments in favour of this were sound. Two elections, of 1970 and 1977, had given massive majorities to one or other of the two major parties, even though the proportion of votes that each had obtained in either election did not differ dramatically. The lopsided result was the consequence of the vast majority of constituencies into which the country was divided being marginals, with basic support for either party being more or less evenly divided; a small swing nationwide to one party therefore resulted, a majority of votes being enough to win the constituency, in its gaining a disproportionate number of seats. It therefore made sense to introduce a system of proportional representation, with parties drawing up lists for the different districts which would constitute the electoral units. Individuals would therefore be declared elected from each party list according to the proportion of votes it polled in each district.

Understandable in terms of this new system was the abolition of by-elections to fill any vacancy that should occur, through death or resignation, since new elections for individual positions might disproportionately alter the membership of parliament as far as the whole district was concerned. Rather, since members of parliament were elected by virtue of their membership of a party, a vacancy could be filled by another member of the original party list.

The argument became less acceptable after that. The example of the previous government which had been plagued by defections from its ranks was adduced to justify the provision that, should any member abandon the party through which he had been elected, he would forfeit his seat in parliament and be replaced by a substitute from the list. This was presented as an effective way of discouraging crossovers; the constitution however went further and laid down that a member of parliament expelled from his party would also lose his seat, and be replaced by nomination. Finally, the same system was to apply to the existing parliament, according to the transitional provisions of the new constitution. There had not, of course, been any party lists at the previous elections, and members had been elected as individuals from separate constituencies; they too were now subject to replacement for any of the above reasons by individuals nominated at will by their parties.

This meant the absolute stranglehold of the party over members of parliament. None was likely to risk disobeying the party since this entailed risk of expulsion and forfeiture of a seat in parliament. Certainly, as the UNP might well have deduced, having benefited considerably from crossovers from the SLFP in 1964 as well as throughout the lifetime of the 1970 parliament, it was the hope of gain, pecuniary or otherwise, that motivated crossovers more often than conscience. Yet there had also been instances of conscience playing its part, not only in terms of crossovers but also in the case of forceful backbench criticism of government excesses. All that was now bound to be limited, if not altogether stopped. Even worse, the increased power of the party made it more likely that those in office would act arbitrarily, aware that there could be no party revolt.

Consolidating the New Regime

The principal achievement and primary aim of this legislation, that had been so subtly introduced, was to render the authority of the party hierarchy absolute. The subsequent demand in 1982 for undated letters of resignation from all UNP members of parliament, letters which the President held so that he could date and action them at will, was thus simply the frosting on a cake prepared much earlier.

The cynicism of the architect of these provisions became even clearer when he introduced an amendment to the transitional provisions. This was the second of sixteen the new constitution had to endure over the eleven years through which its first parliament persisted. Before it was introduced it could have been argued that Jayewardene's constitutional changes were based on principle and that his purpose was to ensure strong government. The first amendment had already raised grave doubts, and the second made it clear that no principles were of any consequence in comparison with the determination of the government to extend and consolidate its authority.

What it did was allow a member of the existing parliament, who had crossed over or been expelled from his party, to keep his seat, unless a majority of parliament voted to expel him. This meant that members of the opposition were free to join the government if they chose, but not the other way around. One member of the SLFP did in time join the UNP and before that, more significantly, two from the TULF who represented constituencies in the east. The first, on whose behalf the amendment was introduced, was promptly appointed a Cabinet Minister and continued as such until 1988. The other was shot, though not fatally, by Tamil militants. Not long afterwards he died, and the UNP as the party to which he now belonged appointed his sister as his successor. Neither she nor the Minister who had crossed over was able in the years that followed to visit the Eastern Province with any frequency. In 1989, when an election was at last held again, neither could be even nominated for the districts they had represented for so long.

Dealings with the Tamils

The treatment of the Tamil problem as a whole during these early years also indicates Jayewardene's determination to dominate on his own terms.

The promised all-party conference was not summoned. Given the absolute power he possessed, he felt able to handle the matter himself, using his characteristic technique: he would draw all the strands of the decision-making process, all he thought relevant or desirable, under his own broad umbrella, and then from under that he would pull out a triumphant solution.

From his own point of view he had scored a notable success as far as the Tamils of the east were concerned. The UNP had won some seats in the east and now, with two defectors from the TULF, he could claim that a majority of the Tamil elected members of parliament from the Eastern Province supported his government. More satisfying still was his achievement in winning Thondaman over. This was not surprising, for Thondaman made no bones about the fact that his commitment was primarily to the Indian Tamils, and he would do anything in pursuit of their welfare. Though he had joined other Tamil politicians before the election in a party that called for a separate state, this was clearly an absurd position for Indian Tamils, a minority in the areas in which they lived, surrounded on all sides by totally Sinhalese areas. Thondaman had accordingly been an assiduous member of the Parliamentary Select Committee that revised the constitution and had managed to enshrine in it recommendations that favourably affected persons of Indian origin. A few weeks after the constitution was put into operation Thondaman joined the Cabinet, and continued in it right through to the next parliament, with increasing prestige and authority,

His most important recommendation was the withdrawal of the distinction between citizens by descent and citizens by registration that had been introduced in the bill that disenfranchised Indian Tamils. This did not mean that the stateless received citizenship immediately. They were, however, granted the benefit of all the fundamental rights that the constitution recognized for a period of ten years, by which time it was envisaged that the problem would be settled, by grant of citizenship to all those who had not gone to India.

Another important change was that the provisions governing the use of Tamil in official transactions were extended now to the whole island. Earlier, citizens in the Northern and Eastern Provinces were entitled to deal with government there or elsewhere in Tamil, and to receive replies in the same language. This entitlement was now extended to everyone in the country, which was a means of acknowledging that Tamils elsewhere too had basic language rights. Inasmuch as this amounted to recognition of the distinct identity of all Tamils, the largest single group of which outside the north and east was the Indian Tamil plantation labour, it is understandable that Thondaman saw this as a great step forward which warranted his joining the Cabinet. The rest could follow, and indeed much did in the decade that followed.

Jayewardene could be happy then about his achievements in these areas: he could claim to command the confidence of the large sections of the Tamil population who lived in the centre or the east as their elected representatives formed part of his government. What he had to offer them, however, was insufficient for the rest, especially the politicians of the north, where there was greater concern with the specific Tamil cause and its crusade for constitutional rights. In addition, any attempt to break ranks in the north would have led to brutal punishment by the more militant adherents of the cause who were already influential there. It was highly unlikely, therefore, that Jayewardene would find support or even sympathy amongst members of parliament from the Northern Province for solutions on his own terms.

Jayewardene therefore adopted the technique of dealing with Tamils from Colombo who, being detached from Jaffna and more cosmopolitan, seemed to him more in sympathy with his own approach. Of course he could not choose just anyone: what he did was to deal with the descendants of Tamil politicians of his own generation. Though they had no formal authority, the respect inherent in Sri Lankan society for family structures and hence for the children of the revered (Dudley Senanayake succeeded his father and Anura Bandaranaike rose rapidly to be leader of the Opposition) ensured that they carried authority. At the same time Jayewardene could hope that their respect for him as a guru of the earlier generation would make them more malleable than socially less familiar figures from the north.

Amirthalingam, the current leader of the TULF, and indeed of the opposition in parliament, had his roots emphatically in Jaffna and brought his family up there. This was in marked contrast to his predecessor Chelvanayakam who had been a Colombo lawyer. No one however had doubted Chelvanayakam's commitment to his cause, and the only one of his sons actively involved in politics, S Chandrahasan, though also educated and resident in Colombo, was in the radical wing of the party. More to Jayewardene's taste was Chelvanayakam's son-in-law, A J Wilson, a political scientist who had migrated to Canada during the previous regime. He became Jayewardene's link to the Tamils, and the chief negotiator on their behalf, while commuting from Canada. His principal associate in this exercise was Neelan Tiruchelvam, the son of the FP representative in Senanayake's last cabinet. The younger Tiruchelvam had received much of his education abroad and now resided in Colombo. Officially both he and Wilson were attached to the TULF, but it was typical of Jayewardene's style that these two should have represented the Tamils in dialogue with him, while those elected to parliament from the north, where pressures were heaviest, were left out in the cold.

There was no doubt now that the situation was more serious. Firstly, there was an orgy of post-election violence in 1977, much of it directed against Tamils, in particular those on the estates. The commission of inquiry that was subsequently held could not detect coherent patterns or explain the sudden escalation into a situation that recalled 1958. The general impression was that supporters of the new government were responsible and, even if their original intention had been only to avenge themselves on those dominant during the previous regime, it had been easy for interested parties, including some of their own functionaries, to give a racist twist to the exercise. Colombo itself remained relatively unscathed and the makers of opinion there continued optimistic about the new government, but in areas where the damage had been severe Tamils began to feel insecure except amongst their own.

Partly because of suspicions roused by these incidents and the failure to summon the promised conference, in part too because of what were seen as the repressive and provocative actions of some branches of the government while Jayewardene was negotiating with Wilson and Tiruchelvam, younger Tamils in the north, who had supported the TULF at the election, began to turn more forcefully to militant action. At first it

Consolidating the New Regime

was primarily a question of dealing with traitors, as the member of parliament from the east who defected was termed. As time passed, however, confrontation with the armed forces began to escalate.

The Election to District Development Councils

It was probably still not too late when, two years after the election, the Commission on Devolution, on which the Tamil representatives were Wilson and Tiruchelvam, produced its report, and recommended the establishment of District Development Councils. Wilson and Tiruchelvam also submitted a minority report, and some of their additional recommendations were incorporated in the bill brought before parliament in 1980. Even so the Councils were not given much real authority. Making a mockery of the whole principle of decentralization, members of parliament from a particular district were to serve on the District Council together with those who were to be elected specifically for the purpose. In the east, given the crossovers that had been permitted, this made the composition of the various councils lopsided in relation to the popular will. This was particularly significant as, in putting forward the demand for a separate state, the Tamils were especially concerned about the east being accepted as part of a traditional Tamil homeland.

Apart from this, District Ministers too were to serve on the District Councils, and indeed to function as chairmen. The office had been created a couple of years earlier in an attempt to satisfy the demand for devolution. It did nothing of the sort, for District Ministers were appointed entirely at the whim of the President so that he could choose members of parliament from wholly different areas. Such was the case of the District Minister for Jaffna who hailed from the Northwest Province. This was bound to create conflicts with those who had been locally elected. The Tamils had hoped that the office would be abolished with the introduction of District Councils, which they saw as a means of genuinely devolving power from the centre and centrally appointed officials to the periphery.

The result of all this was that from the start the TULF looked on the District Development Councils simply as stepping stones to something more. On the other hand within the government itself there were those such as Cyril Mathew (expelled from the party by Dudley Senanayake in

1968 but now Minister of Industries as well as President of the large and powerful government trade union, the National Workers' Congress (JSS)), who were of the view that the present bill was already extreme and nothing more should be conceded.

The Sinhalese opposition, except for the JVP which had now emerged as a respectable political party, boycotted the elections that were finally held in May 1981, alleging that the Councils were unnecessary. This made things even more embarrassing for the TULF, since it helped to create the impression that the whole exercise had been designed merely to mollify them, whereas from their point of view it was thoroughly inadequate. They entered the fray with remarkable goodwill, resisting those in their own ranks as well as militants outside who had urged a boycott on their part. Some militants at this stage turned to disruption, and in early May they shot dead two policemen, one Sinhalese and the other Tamil, at a UNP rally. Despite the tension generated, it seemed that all political parties involved (though Ponnambalam's former deputy was now the President of the TULF, his son had resurrected the TC and also put up candidates) were determined to continue their campaigns.

At this stage Mathew was sent to Jaffna to spearhead the last stages of the government campaign. He went with Jayewardene's blessing and took in his entourage Gamini Dissanayake. Soon after they arrived in Jaffna it was reported that security forces had run amok, that the Jaffna Public Library had been burnt along with the Central Market, and that the house of the member of Parliament for Jaffna, one of the most radical Tamils in parliament, had been attacked and gutted while he himself had only just managed to get away by scrambling over the back wall.

Despite all this the election was held a couple of days later as scheduled, under conditions previously unknown in the history of Sri Lanka. The government officials who had been detailed to supervise the election were replaced by men handpicked by Mathew; a number of ballot boxes disappeared, twelve were never found; others produced more ballot papers inside than there were eligible voters in the area. Even so the UNP failed to achieve twelve and a half per cent of the vote in the district as a whole. This meant that it did not win any representation since that was

Consolidating the New Regime

the minimum that had to be achieved by a party to warrant representation. As it happened the TULF was the only party to cross the cutoff point in the Jaffna District, so that only its candidates were declared elected. The TC alleged its attempts to prevent the declaration of the results on the grounds of malpractices were forestalled, and that the TULF had joined with the UNP to prevent any judicial investigation.

Unfortunately outrage at what occurred was not expressed widely, and a thorough investigation was not carried out. The government had been keen to ensure that, under the system of proportional representation, used for the first time in the country, it obtained at least one seat in the north, to claim to have some sort of support there. It had failed in this attempt as this was the first election in which it had used such tactics. Clearly this sort of practice would continue on a larger scale if unchecked at the start. At the same time it is difficult to blame the opposition, Sinhalese or Tamil, for its failure to respond forcefully enough. As far as the Tamils were concerned much worse was in store, which effectively put them on the defensive. Before going into that however, or indeed looking more closely at the condition of the Tamils so as to better understand the violence that followed, we should glance briefly at the increase in authoritarianism in the rest of the country, since that may explain the relative quiescence of the rest of the opposition while the whole face of Sri Lankan politics was being radically altered.

Removing the gloves

By 1980 the first traces of doubt about the government's economic miracle had begun to appear. The increase in oil prices which hit the world in 1979 could not have been anticipated, but there were also aspects of government policy and practice that contributed to massive inflation during this period. The mass of people who were still on incomes that reflected the pre-1977 economic order were adversely affected. Even the World Bank began to demand restraint from the government with regard to its more grandiose schemes. Such criticism could not however be aired publicly. The government kept tight control over the media, with monopolies on radio and television, direct control of two newspaper groups, and heavy influence over the third.

Significantly it was only Premadasa's Housing Development Scheme that was questioned in the media, which led to what had been intended as cheap housing being sold at very high prices in the open market to meet costs. Even such mild modifications were not imposed on the other major schemes. It would not have made sense to pull back on the Mahaweli once the whole package had been put in train but, though expenditure regularly exceeded estimates and construction was not satisfactory, there was no careful monitoring or financial accountability. Even more unfortunate was the continuation of Jayewardene's own pet scheme of shifting the capital, involving the draining of a marshy area to build a grand new parliament complex. Though much was made of the fact that this was being built by the Japanese, no grant aid was received for it. Finally, the towering structure that emerged on an island in the middle of a lake cost the country billions of rupees. In the decade that followed no major administrative or commercial undertaking, except the Ministry of Education, under Jayewardene's youthful kinsman Ranil Wickremesinghe, Esmond's son, moved to Sri Jayewardenepura. Colombo continued very much as the capital of the country despite Jayewardene's exaltation of the area that carried his name.

While capital expenditure thus increased and the cost of living escalated, longstanding welfare schemes were subjected to rigid means tests early on in the government's tenure. It became generally known that the government's creditors were insisting on further cuts. They were in a strong position to do so, for the government had borrowed so much in its early years for its programmes that servicing the debts was proving more and more difficult. But the government continued on the course it had embarked upon in 1977, quite content to reach a point when the actual deficit in the annual budget exceeded its income. A natural corollary of this was increased borrowing and reliance on donors. Unfortunately this was the period when the most influential donors, the World Bank and the International Monetary Fund, as well as the more significant countries they represented, were doctrinaire about cutting spending on welfare measures. Thus, while real incomes in Sri Lanka declined, fears grew that the quality of life Sri Lankans enjoyed in health-care, education and

Consolidating the New Regime

basic nutrition would soon decline owing to restrictions on government spending.

Hardest hit were the public servants, still a large part of the work force because the private sector was small and the state dominated practically every sphere of activity. So in July 1980 a general strike was called which appeared to have substantial support.

Jayewardene however was determined. The strike was brutally suppressed, an emergency declared and troops called out. The government's own shock troops, drawn largely if not exclusively from the JSS, were more effective in dealing with pickets and keeping essential services going. Under all this pressure the strike soon collapsed. The government had however decreed that strikers would be deemed to have vacated their posts and a number of people lost their jobs. Some were taken back but ministries such as Education remained adamant, and even a decade later one of the slogans the opposition kept reiterating was the reinstatement of the July 1980 strikers.

After that success Jayewardene moved quickly. Earlier than anyone else he recognized that he could not afford any risks. In October 1980, he consolidated his power by ensuring that he had no opponent capable of confronting him or providing a realistic alternative.

The ground had been prepared earlier by incorporating a provision in the constitution for imposing civic disabilities on individuals found guilty by a Special Presidential Commission of particular charges. Such a Commission, consisting of three judges handpicked by Jayewardene including one who was not on the Supreme Court, had been set up, and charges against Mrs. Bandaranaike of misuse and abuse of power were brought before it. When the Court of Appeal allowed a writ against the proceedings (in accordance with the fundamental rights section of the constitution precluding anyone being charged with actions that were not crimes at the time they were committed), parliament promptly rushed through its first amendment to set aside the Court's judgment. Thus the section on inviolable fundamental rights was unashamedly traduced.

Mrs. Bandaranaike, understandably, refused to appear before a Commission that held office at the pleasure of the President, to hear charges formulated by him in terms of concepts, namely misuse and abuse of power, nowhere clearly defined. The Commission listened to the prosecution and then, in a sometimes self-contradictory judgment, found her guilty of four of the fourteen charges. The most serious of these was that her government had extended a State of Emergency for a period that the Commissioners deemed unnecessary, a view that was in contradiction to the opinion of the Cabinet of the time whose decision it had been. The Commissioners recommended the heaviest penalty available, namely the removal of her civic rights for seven years, which meant that she could not sit in parliament or contest elections during that period.

The punishment had to be imposed by parliament, which it promptly did, before the Supreme Court could deliver judgment on the appeal she had made to it. This was the more serious in that, according to the constitution, once civic disabilities had been imposed by parliament no court had any further jurisdiction. Amirthalingam brought up the point that the matter was *sub judice*; the Minister of State remarked that if the court found in her favour parliament could withdraw the disability; Premadasa however contradicted him and declared that the appeal, a pernicious attempt to circumvent parliament, would not be tolerated. A three line whip was issued for the occasion, and members who were abroad were required to fly back to vote, so that no one could disclaim responsibility afterwards. The motion was carried and, the very next day, in a blatant confession of the real motive behind the whole exercise, the legislation concerning the removal of civil rights was amended: for the future anyone without civic rights was debarred from canvassing on behalf of others standing for elections, or in any other way taking part in the electoral process.

As intended, the SLFP promptly began to fall apart. Conflicting personal ambitions as well as ideological positions led to rivalries and confusion. While Mrs. Bandaranaike was unwilling under the circumstances to stand down as party president, it was alleged in some quarters that this might lead to the disqualification of anyone nominated by the SLFP for any election. This, in conjunction with the splits, reunions and further splits, that began now and continued over the next few years, contributed to the decision to boycott the District Development Council Elections, as much as the disapproval in principle of the proposed councils.

All other opposition parties in the south came to the same decision, except for the JVP which had been the only political party outside the government to welcome the penalty imposed on Mrs. Bandaranaike. That despite its relatively recent entry into electoral politics it did quite well suggests that more established parties might well have defeated the government in several areas. The government's manoeuvres had succeeded admirably. The manner in which it had conducted discussions on devolution, very much as private dialogues with selected Tamils, meant that other parties had little active interest in the process. The sudden emasculation of the SLFP then had meant that the opposition found it difficult to formulate a coherent response either to the establishment of the District Councils or to the manner in which the elections to them were conducted. The TULF meanwhile, though it defended Mrs. Bandaranaike vigorously in parliament, pursued its dream of some form of devolution over the six months that followed, and was therefore unwilling to be involved with the rest of the opposition on matters other than those relevant to its own primarily Tamil goals. In effect the government had a thoroughly fragmented opposition to deal with. In the months that followed it proceeded to flex its muscles still further.

Chapter 4

The Proliferation of Violence

Treatment of Tamil grievances

Before looking at the race riots that errupted in August 1981 after the District Council elections, we should look at some factors that had exacerbated tensions over the preceding four years. In its manifesto, the UNP identified four main grievances of the Tamils. First was education. The incoming government therefore abandoned the system of standardization that increased the number of Sinhalese gaining admission to university, while reducing the number of Tamils. There was some agitation about this change, but it was ignored as having been instigated by loyalists of the previous government. For two years then the admissions to university were purely on marks, which were equated with merit.

The number of Tamils gaining admission to university shot up dramatically in some especially sought after subjects. Complaints from the Sinhalese became more intense, culminating in an allegation by Cyril Mathew in parliament that he had evidence of cheating by some Tamil examiners. Instead of inquiring into Mathew's allegations, the government seemed to accept them in that it reintroduced the effects of standardization through a system of district quotas. Though this benefited deprived districts, some of them Tamil, the net result was that Tamil areas, where education was very much an industry, were the hardest hit. In particular this meant Jaffna. This time the response was more bitter. Expectations roused by the 1977 reforms were dashed; whereas in 1970, the ostensible grounds for change had been egalitarian principles, now it was in direct response to an allegation of cheating, and was deeply resented by the majority of Tamils. The resulting sense of betrayal had much to do with the increase in militancy amongst the younger generation in the north.

The Proliferation of Violence

In the field of education then, far from grievances being remedied, by 1981 resentment had increased. Two other points mentioned in the UNP manifesto may be considered next, namely language rights and employment in the public sector. The remedy advanced with regard to language rights was the constitutional right to deal officially in Tamil all over the country. This proved largely theoretical, for most officials functioned normally in Sinhalese and translation was neither quick nor reliable. Again, the concession did not help with public employment, since most people except in the north and east functioned in Sinhalese, and it was therefore impractical to recruit large numbers of Tamils to official positions elsewhere. This is where decentralization might have helped; but nothing was done for over three years and, when the District Councils were finally set up, they were so limited in their scope that they were not likely to provide much employment. The government did not consider a quota system for state employment to help the Tamils, even though it did so with regard to university admission to help the Sinhalese. Thus in these two areas too, no practical alleviation was offered for identified grievances.

The issue of Colonization

The final grievance identified in the manifesto, colonization, requires extended clarification. The Tamil claim was that their traditional homeland, as they termed the Northern and Eastern Provinces, was being occupied by the Sinhalese as a deliberate act of government policy. The claim that the north was inherently Tamil went largely unquestioned. The overwhelming majority of the population there was Tamil and had been for generations – though Mathew was busy unearthing evidence of Sinhala Buddhist structures in the region that, he claimed, had been recently destroyed by the Tamils.

With regard to the east however, as the census records for 1921 indicate, only a bare majority of inhabitants that far back had been Tamil. Of course the Muslims, who made up forty per cent of the population then, spoke Tamil, while Sinhalese accounted for a very small proportion. Over the next half century however, before and after independence, the picture changed considerably.

In the Trincomalee District, the northernmost in the Eastern Province, the proportion of Sinhalese in the population rose from three per cent in 1921 to twenty in 1946 and thirty by 1971. This led to the creation before the 1977 election of a Sinhalese constituency in the District. Meanwhile the proportion of Tamils had fallen to less than forty per cent. The change was even greater in the Batticaloa District in the south, which was divided in 1963 to accommodate the predominantly Sinhalese Amparai District. Despite this hiving off, the proportion of Tamils in Batticaloa dropped to less than half. These last changes may be attributed to the effects of government sponsored schemes of colonization, though higher Muslim birthrates also contributed.

The increase up to 1946 suggests that, even before there were large government resettlement schemes in the Province, more Sinhalese elsewhere than Tamils were landless and in search of fresh pastures. Certainly there were never claims that Tamils or Muslims had been displaced to make way for Sinhalese. Such explanations did not affect the Tamil response to what had actually happened. Even if the central government could not be accused of a deliberate policy, the concept of a Tamil homeland meant nothing to it. As far back as the fifties, the Tamil Civil Servant in charge of the Galoya irrigation and colonization scheme in Amparai was accused by Tamil politicians of abetting Sinhalese attempts to take over Tamil areas. Further north, some of the more violent incidents in the race riots of 1958 had taken place in areas where other colonization schemes were in train. The issue then, had long been a source of irritation to the Tamils.

By 1981 the situation was further confused by two new factors. The first was the accelerated Mahaweli scheme to bring vast tracts of previously uninhabited land under cultivation. Much of this was in the Eastern Province or in Vavuniya, the southernmost district of the Northern province. The cry for land had previously been strongest amongst the Sinhalese, and the government had assumed from the start that most of the new colonists in these areas would be Sinhalese. Given existing suspicions about demographic alterations, this was contentious enough; but on top of that there was a second complicating factor: the Tamils too were now in the market for land.

There were two reasons for this development, relating to different groups geographically. For the Tamils in Jaffna and its adjoining areas previously pursued occupations were diminishing. The protectionist agricultural policies of the SLFP government had created a very healthy economic situation for the farmers of Jaffna. Thus the attractions of agriculture and land appeared in a new light in comparison with when the height of ambition had been white collar jobs based on educational qualifications. Secondly, after the race riots of 1977, Tamils in the rest of the country wanted to move to more secure places. For Ceylon Tamils who had been settled in the south this meant migration if possible, but that was not always easy. For some of them, and for almost all Indian Tamils who wished to move away from the centre, the lands in the north and perhaps the east too, previously empty but contiguous to established Tamil populations, seemed most suitable.

So the issue of colonization became the subject of intense debate and anxiety. In addition to official schemes, relatively slow to get off the ground, several sponsored settlement schemes, usually exclusive to Sinhalese or to Tamils, sprang up. Inevitably suspicions arose on either side that these were aimed at establishing claims on land with a view to strengthening or demolishing the case for a separate state, or to expanding or contracting its boundaries. Two examples which were later of significance are worth mentioning. A Buddhist priest from the Dimbulagala temple on the borders of the Eastern Province actively encouraged Sinhala settlements in the area with the blessings of Dissanayake and of N G P Panditharatne, President of the UNP as well as Chairman of the Mahaweli Board. Conversely, in the north an organization entitled the Gandhiyam Movement was busily settling a great number of Indian Tamils in the Vavuniya District. It had no formal political allegiance, but was held to have close links with younger militant elements amongst the Tamils whose activities were increasingly being characterized, and with reason, as terrorist. An originally pure humanitarian movement to assist Tamils rendered homeless in 1977 took on a different character because of the aggressive reactions its initial anodyne activities had provoked.

Oppression and alienation in the North

Certainly the handling of the situation in the north by the government left much to be desired. This cannot be attributed simply to misfortune. For instance, the government decided to make a political appointment in Jaffna immediately after the 1977 election to the post of Government Agent, the officer in charge of the day to day running of the local administration. Lionel Fernando, the previous incumbent, a senior Civil Servant, though Sinhalese, had established excellent relations with the people of the area. Despite this, since he was thought to favour the SLFP he was replaced by a Tamil who was a defeated electoral candidate in the area. Naturally his appointment was resisted and, despite his personal efforts, he was seen throughout as the tool of an unsympathetic central government.

Even more serious was the transfer of the army regiment that had been stationed peaceably in the area for some time. There had been some violence there previously, for instance the murder of the mayor of Jaffna, but tensions had subsided before the 1977 elections, especially in comparison with what was to follow. However, with riots of a racist nature all over the rest of the island, a new regiment was moved up to Jaffna since its predecessor was thought to owe allegiance to the SLFP. It found itself in a tense situation in which feelings were running high. Naturally it saw itself as having been moved into hostile territory with an obligation to assert a central, Sinhalese, authority. The government did little to discourage this attitude. No attempt was made to persuade the Sinhalese residents of Jaffna, who had fled when the riots began, to return there. Again, though the University of Jaffna, started by the previous government as a multiracial institution, had few Sinhalese students, their presence was at least a token of integration. When they withdrew in 1977, the new government was content to let the university function as a centre only for Tamils.

Parallel to the alienation engendered in the armed forces was the feeling of younger Tamils that they were being treated like inhabitants of a conquered land. As the years passed it seemed there was no real interest on the part of the government to alleviate grievances. The army stayed on and militancy increased. As a later army commander put it, hardcore terrorists in the Jaffna peninsula in 1977 barely reached double figures, but in a very few years the number had increased dramatically. Even so in 1981 militants inside and outside the TULF were not strong enough to insist on a boycott of the District Council elections. The killings of the two policemen at the election meeting alluded to above heralded a dramatic change in the situation. But, though they marked a development in the trend of violence, they need not necessarily have proved disastrous, as the attempt by other parties to continue the campaign shows.

What proved disastrous was the reaction of the government, the burning of the Public Library and other events associated with Mathew's advent in Jaffna; what amounted to official encouragement of an attitude of occupation was responsible for the exacerbation of hostility. It is true that terrorist action had been developing from 1977. But only two years after exposing the grievances of the Tamils, Jayewardene, having done little to relieve them, introduced in 1979 a draconian Prevention of Terrorism Act (PTA) that effectively suspended basic human rights and permitted arbitrary arrests and the brutal treatment of prisoners. A number of detailed studies, by Sinhalese, foreigners and Tamils, recount excesses committed during this period under these regulations, almost as though it were official policy to provoke as many young Tamils as possible into terrorism.

With regard to the excesses of the armed forces the role of the individuals involved is understandable. They were in a totally strange area with little to go on except awareness of their own power. The policy of education exclusively in one language or the other made it difficult for young servicemen to communicate with the young Tamils whom they perceived as the enemy. In the period in which they were sent to the north, they had no opportunity, nor any assistance from the civil administration, to build a reasonable relationship with the people amongst whom they functioned. Yet precisely because of the authority or rather licence that they were permitted, the state, which failed to advance a policy of reconciliation, was all the more culpable. The dispatch of Mathew to the north in May 1981 suggests that the whole process might have been deliberate: designed to provoke and then to crush.

Racial assaults in the south and the role of the Government

In consonance with this reading of events some even more bizarre developments took place soon after the mayhem of the elections. An orchestrated government campaign, even if its motive was not actually genocide, appeared to encourage those who wished to practice it. The process began when Amirthalingam gave notice in parliament of a motion of no-confidence on Cyril Mathew with reference to his actions during the elections. Instead of refuting the allegations, Mathew launched into a detailed catalogue of what he called the connivance of the TULF leadership in terrorist activity. The attack on the house of the Jaffna MP, for instance, was justified by the claim that he had close links with terrorists and had entertained them in his house. Official excesses were thus presented simply as legitimate exercises in Sinhalese self-defense. On the next day the cry was taken up by the entire media and the country was treated to an orgy of propaganda that Tamils were an anti-national group with Indian roots who were simply waiting for a chance to betray Sri Lanka.

Much of the material for this was provided by the government in a grotesquely unorthodox manner. The no-confidence motion on Mathew was disallowed on the grounds that the District Council elections had been challenged in the courts and therefore the substance of the motion was *sub judice*. That had not been an accepted principle with regard to Mrs. Bandaranaike's case, but questions of precedent and proper parliamentary procedure were now irrelevant. This became clearer when, Mathew's conduct having been consigned to oblivion, a back bench MP named Neville Fernando proposed a motion of no-confidence in the leader of the Opposition. This was allowed, and several speeches in this connection dwelt on the iniquities of all Tamils; these were given prominent coverage in the media. Apart from Thondaman and one solitary exception, all members on the government side, including the Tamil ones, supported the motion.

This barrage, sanctified it seemed by high authority, had its effect. Verbal assaults were followed by physical ones. In a subsequent interview Amirthalingam claimed that the violence had begun by deliberately inflammatory speeches of government politicians. In addition to those

The Proliferation of Violence 59

who specifically incited destruction, the entire government must bear responsibility for creating a climate of hatred.

The violence was less widespread than it was to be a couple of years later; at this time Colombo was not affected. This may explain why the period of actual terror lasted longer. Decision-makers were immune, so that it took time for a State of Emergency to be enforced and solid measures taken to stop the violence. In fact a concerted attempt to clamp down occurred only when an Indian tourist was murdered, and the Indian government made it clear that it might feel obliged to step in.

That the government's shock troops had played their part in the proceedings was scarcely doubted. Jayewardene's own later appeal-cum-sermon to his parliamentarians at a time when he was urging calm confirms Amirthalingam's allegation as far as individuals was concerned. Yet the conclusion that can be drawn is much more sinister. Far from individuals having taken the law into their own hands, both the prelude to the violence and the period during which it was permitted to continue unabated suggest that it amounted to concerted government policy.

The failure to conciliate

The incident with the Indian tourist however brought home to Jayewardene that things had gone too far, and that he had to make it clear to his cohorts that the carnival had to stop. The high point in this process was the expulsion from the UNP of Neville Fernando for having violated party discipline. This was followed by a motion for his expulsion from parliament. The government whips being out, Fernando resigned before the motion was carried; shortly afterwards he became a member of the SLFP. The TULF refused to participate in this charade and, together with the rest of the opposition, made it clear that this was simply another example of an authoritarian government imposing on members of the legislature.

That this was a token gesture was made clear because very little else happened. The Junior Minister for Regional Development, G V Punchinilame, member for the Ratnapura constituency where the violence had been especially bad and where the Indian had been killed, was removed from his post but soon accommodated elsewhere. No one else was affected.

Mathew enjoyed as much influence as before, and was indeed touted by Esmond Wickremesinghe as a possible successor to Jayewardene. Perhaps to further this possibility, he blithely issued more and more pamphlets describing the historical rights of the Sinhalese to the Northern and Eastern Provinces. These were particularly strong on the depredations of the Tamils and the emotive issue of the destruction they had wrought on Buddhist shrines in these areas.

An attempt to provide some relief with regard to entry to university proved abortive. An announcement that the merit quota for admission would be increased led to heated protests from government backbenchers, the adjustment was swiftly forgotten and the existing system continued.

Colonization by Sinhalese also went on as before while colonization by Tamils was dealt with firmly. Officials of the Gandhiyam movement were subjected to continuous harassment, and in time even arrested under the PTA. Of course there had been an increase in the number of Tamils, especially Indian Tamils, seeking land under their aegis in the north, and in particular in the Vavuniya District. But, given the assaults they had undergone and that land was available there in a context of more assured physical security, the motivation for such migration was clearly fear rather than a pernicious urge to fill up the land with Tamils before the Sinhalese could get to it.

Through neglect things were simply getting worse. Astonishingly, guided still largely by Wilson and Tiruchelvam, influential Tamils including the TULF leadership continued to take seriously the prospect of Jayewardene adopting measures to remedy the situation. The reason for this is that public life continued to be dominated by Colombo, and Colombo itself had been largely unscathed. The Colombo Tamils, who still constituted the most influential part of the community, had benefited from Jayewardene's economic policies. They still thought of the SLFP as chauvinist while the UNP appeared to them far more cosmopolitan; they were unwilling to read the signs. While attributing villainy to other members of the government, they could not accept that the man whom they had trusted had nothing to offer. His previous record seemed to count for nothing in their eyes. Instead, blindly, they continued to hope.

Chapter 5

Tightening the Reins

Advancing the presidential election

By 1982 doubts about the government's capacity to carry on its economic policies successfully had begun to grow. The immediate problem was the question of continued confidence in a country where the last six elections had all seen changes of government. Donors as well as investors were clearly nervous with an election due the following year.

It was advisable to settle the electoral question early. In addition, Jayewardene had during his long career observed that in Sri Lanka the unpopularity of a government in power increased dramatically towards the end of its tenure. Under the new constitution there was, of course, a new factor: two sets of elections were to be held, for the presidency and for parliament respectively. Thus a party that controlled both could continue to exercise power through one while elections to the other were being held. As things stood, parliament was due to be dissolved in July 1983, while a presidential election was due only a few months later, Jayewardene having elevated himself to the presidency as from February 1978 for a six year term. Such a gap would not have been enough to overcome the lame duck phenomenon.

The obvious course was to dissolve parliament early, and conduct these elections while Jayewardene was still president. But what he did instead was introduce yet another amendment to the constitution, to provide for an incumbent president to stand for re-election anytime after he had served four years in office, instead of going through with the fixed term of six years.

This absurdly *ad hominem* provision was challenged before the Supreme Court by the Civil Rights Movement, on the grounds that it affected the franchise adversely, and would therefore require a referendum. However, it was passed because the Court ruled that such an amendment required only a two-thirds majority in parliament. The election was fixed for October to give minimum time for nominations and campaigning. It seemed Jayewardene had realized that, after the initial splits in the SLFP, the party now seemed to be getting its act together. There was a possibility that under proportional representation the UNP would not get a majority in a parliamentary election, and even a slight possibility that the SLFP would defeat it. After that Jayewardene would have trouble at a presidential election and, if by some chance Mrs. Bandaranaike's civic rights were restored by the new parliament, he would probably be defeated. It suited him to get his own election over and done with while the parliament and the Cabinet that he dominated still continued in position; and the sooner the better in that it was just possible that the SLFP would be reunified in time to put forward a candidate who commanded wide oppositional support.

The SLFP and the election

Initially the split within the SLFP had been extremely bitter. It was exacerbated by rivalry between Anura Bandaranaike and his sister Chandrika. Apart from personal differences, the siblings differed ideologically. In the battle for the party hierarchy the left wing, supported by Mrs. Bandaranaike, seemed to be gaining dominance. Meanwhile the Deputy Leader of the Party, Maithripala Senanayake, and Anura Bandaranaike were working closely. The former was more sympathetic to the latter's right wing tendencies. When they found their position within the party difficult they withdrew and established their own group which they continued to call the SLFP because it held a majority in their tiny parliamentary group.

The moving spirit of the other faction was Chandrika's husband Vijaya Kumaranatunga, the most popular Sinhalese film actor of the time. Neither he nor the various former ministers of the 1979 government, who shared his ideological bent and still held important party posts, were in parliament. Those in the government parliamentary group, who stayed with this faction, had done so largely through personal loyalty to Mrs Bandaranaike and their main desire therefore, was to bring about a

Tightening the Reins

reconciliation. By the middle of 1982 the differences were well on the way to being resolved, and Anura Bandaranaike had been readmitted to the main party. Perhaps fearing that he would stake a claim for the nomination, the left, in line with the haste prescribed by Jayewardene, swiftly adopted as the party nominee the former Minister of Agriculture, Hector Kobbekaduwa.

Anura Bandaranaike did not then participate in the campaign, and his mother was unable to do so because of the legal position. Despite his age, Kobbekaduwa ran a remarkably energetic campaign, ably assisted by Kumaranatunga, who was its chief organizer. The campaign seemed to be going so successfully that some even thought that he would win. In the light of expectations the final result, in which Jayewardene won fifty three per cent of the vote, came as a disappointment to the SLFP. In actual fact it was remarkable that Kobbekaduwa, a figure suddenly thrown up out of relative obscurity and running against an incumbent president commanding practically unlimited official resources, should have won nearly forty per cent of the vote. Though the younger Ponnambalam, running as the TC candidate, did very well in Jaffna itself, Kobbekaduwa defeated both him and Jayewardene in the Northern Province as a whole.

The main reason for this is that the SLFP's protectionist agricultural policies won him the support of the Tamil farmers who dominated the other districts of the Northern Provinces, and in particular Vavuniya. Also, whereas the SLFP was still anathema to the Tamils of Colombo, in rural areas the elite Tamil view of the SLFP as a chauvinist party did not hold sway. It was a pity therefore that the TULF treated the election as a diversion for the Sinhalese and ignored it. If it had attempted to influence the choice of a common candidate and campaigned vigorously, it is conceivable that the result might have been different. Unfortunately, as with Anura Bandaranaike perhaps, the assumption seemed to be that the Presidential election was irrelevant, and the real test whereby the balance of power might be shifted was in the forthcoming parliamentary election.

The referendum to extend the term of parliament

What followed made clear how dangerous such complacency was in the political climate that Jayewardene had established. In less than a week it was announced that within two months there would be a referendum to extend the life of the current parliament with its massive UNP majority for a further six years. Jayewardene argued that, though the UNP would win a general election democratically, he did not want a number of undesirable left-wingers, by whom the SLFP was now controlled, to get into parliament under proportional representation, Posssibly his decision was based on Kobbekaduwa's unexpected good showing; but early in the Presidential campaign, when he seemed to be coasting home and the opposition looked in shambles, Jayewardene had boasted that he was going to roll up the electoral map of Sri Lanka for a decade, just as Napoleon had done for Europe. As the campaign progressed he realised the unpopularity of many of his party stalwarts in their electorates; he made it understood that he proposed to have a general election shortly afterwards to enable him to reorganize his administration. But the evidence suggests that, from the very start he had inclined towards this unexpected manoeuvre.

The term Jayewardene used in his rationalization to describe the dominant faction in the SLFP at the time was Naxalite. This term had originally been used for rural Marxist groups in India, and it had gained currency in Sri Lanka when it was used to characterize the JVP in 1971. But Jayewardene now transferred the opprobrious term Naxaiite to Kumaranatunga and his associates. That proportional representation had been prescribed by him since it better represented the will of the people was ignored by Jayewardene when he announced his obligation to preserve parliament from Naxalites.

Hand in hand went the announcement that there had been a plot by Kumaranatunga and his supporters to stage a murderous coup in the event of Kobbekaduwa winning the Presidential election. Accordingly Kumaranatunga was taken into custody and held until shortly after the referendum, when he was released; the issue died down with the suddenness with which it had risen. The police report on the subject, issued just before the destructive race riots of July 1983, insisted that there had been a plot but not much evidence about it was available. The investigator rather preposterously suggested that his failure to find evidence was because there had not really been much plotting, since those planning a coup after they have won an electoral victory did not need to plot too much.

Constitutionally, too, there were doubts about the whole business. At first Jayewardene had announced that such a referendum was perfectly legal, since the constitution permitted the extension of the life of parliament with a two-thirds majority and a national referendum. That this had been envisaged in terms of a parliament elected under proportional representation, so that it would happen only at a time of national crisis when a number of parties would be willing to make up the two-thirds majority, was not taken into account. However, the former Minister of Justice, Felix Dias Bandaranaike (a leading figure in both Mrs. Bandaranaike's administrations who had been deprived of his civic rights along with her) declared his intention of challenging before the Supreme Court the validity of the government's position, on the grounds that the present parliament existed under the transitional provisions of the constitution which laid down categorically that its term expired in July 1983.

The government accordingly shifted its stance and now proposed yet another amendment to the constitution, to substitute the date July 1989 for July 1983 in the transitional provisions. Felix Dias Bandaranaike challenged this amendment too on the grounds that the transitional provisions could not be amended, but four of the seven judges who sat held that the Court had no jurisdiction over a motion passed by two-thirds of parliament which was to be taken to a referendum. The reasoning behind the judgment was not given; the three judges who dissented also gave no reasons. Parliament went ahead with the amendment, and the referendum was announced for December 22nd.

Some senior members of the UNP were unhappy about the turn of events, but no one was willing to take a stand. With regard to members of parliament this was scarcely surprising. In announcing the plan to his parliamentary group, Jayewardene had reminded them of his commitment to tighten up his administration. Since he would not now be submitting members of parliament to an electoral verdict, he would perform the operation entirely by himself. Accordingly he demanded undated letters of resignation which he could date and activate at will, and his principal acolytes, most prominent among them Ranil Wickremesinghe, distributed the pre-prepared letters and had them signed. Once Jayewardene had these in his possession, he saw that it would be counter-productive to take any immediate decisions in case those who were deprived of their seats chose to campaign against him at the referendum. Instead, he could hold the letters in reserve to ensure loyalty, so he declared that the process of weeding out would take place after the referendum. It came to be rapidly understood that, instead of the corrupt or inefficient being expelled, it would be those who failed to ensure a majority in their constituencies at the referendum.

Though this explains the complaisance of members of parliament, it is still noteworthy that there were hardly any protests from elsewhere in the party. Many who had presented themselves earlier as devoted democrats, in particular in their opposition to Mrs. Bandaranaike's regime, now subscribed heartily to the new dispensation: Panditharatne, for instance, as Chairman of the party, presided over meetings of supporters at which he gave out the unequivocal message that the referendum had to be won at any cost. Others quelled their doubts on the grounds that Jayewardene knew best what was required by the country and the party, which could be considered synonymous. Yet so deep was the disquiet expressed in private, that it was only the tremendous power of his recent election to the Executive Presidency for a further six years that allowed Jayewardene's authority to go unquestioned. Rukman Senanayake for instance, who had succeeded his uncle Dudley in parliament in the bye-election after the latter's death in 1973, but had subsequently been expelled from the UNP by Jayewardene when he was consolidating his control of the party, was unwilling for fear of jeopardising his business interests, to branch out on his own. The lawyer A C Gooneratne, a respected authority in the party Central Committee, would not take a public stand without support, and found none amongst others of similar stature. The only exception amongst active party members was Chanaka Amaratunga, a youthful member of the party Propaganda Committee, who had been encouraged earlier to set up a Council for Liberal Democracy that was to be loosely affiliated to the UNP. Carried away by a concept of democracy that his erstwhile mentors no longer found acceptable, he moved the CLD into an oppositional role that it was to fulfill eloquently over the next few years.

Meanwhile there was confusion in the SLFP which was skillfully exploited by the government. Anura Bandaranaike was told that he was the intended victim of his brother-in-law's alleged coup; after a perfunctory statement against the referendum he left the country and did not return in time to make any valid contribution to the campaign. Maithripala Senanayake, who had still not been readmitted to the SLFP, announced that he would campaign in favour of the referendum. Despite these self-inflicted wounds, the wholesale arrests of several members of the other faction and the confiscation of party records and lists of supporters, the SLFP might still have made some impact, given that Mrs. Bandaranaike was not debarred from campaigning against the referendum, and her return to politics was inspiring to an otherwise faction-ridden party. However, resources were low; the SLFP was also prevented from holding meetings since the usual venues for public meetings had all been booked in advance by the UNP. This applied to all political parties including the JVP which, in attacking the referendum strongly, established itself for the first time in distinct opposition to the UNP, thus helping to nullify the claims of the SLFP and other leftwing parties, that it was a tool of the government.

The conduct of the referendum

Even when it was clear that the UNP had no intention of using the venues it had booked, the police refused to grant the necessary permits to other political parties for their campaigns. In the end these were largely confined to party political broadcasts on radio and television though even these had to be limited since, just before the referendum, the charge to each party for such programmes had been raised astronomically. The government meanwhile made full use of its control of the media.

The government benefited even more from its control of the security forces and their awareness that, whatever the result of the referendum, the government would continue in power. Not only were there restrictions on meetings and arrests of SLFP and other politicians who might have mobilized voters; there was intimidation of both political parties and nonpolitical organizations that were opposed to the referendum. The most celebrated case was the brutal suppression of a meeting of a multi-denominational organization called 'The Voice of the Clergy', when several thousand leaflets they had printed urging people to vote against the referendum were confiscated. The policeman responsible for the raid was charged before the Supreme Court with violating Fundamental Rights, found guilty and fined. The case was heard however long after the referendum was over. The return of the leaflets that was ordered was quite useless, and a triumphant government not only paid the fine but also promoted the officer Assistant Superintendent Udugampola to a full Superintendent.

In such a climate of violence and repression the government was bound to succeed at the referendum, and it was surprising, given too the manner in which the poll was conducted, that it obtained only fifty four per cent of the vote. The results were patently ludicrous. A district ravaged by floods at the time of voting had the highest voter turn out with a massive majority for the government; in several areas where many constituencies registered relatively evenly balanced votes for either side there was the occasional random constituency which gave a two-thirds or even greater majority to the government; in Mrs. Bandaranaike's own former constituency of Attanagalla, where the SLFP had, as in some other places, to withdraw its polling agents because of the threat to their lives, the government received a majority of over 30,000 whereas at the Presidential elections Kobbekaduwa had defeated Jayewardene there with a majority almost as large.

The only consistent results were to be found in the Northern Province, where the TULF had campaigned vigorously against the government, which in turn had neither the capacity nor perhaps the incentive to assert itself there. With regard to the rest of the country the University Statistical Unit, which studied the referendum as it had done the Presidential election, producing an instructive study of the latter, found itself unable to reveal its analysis of the former. The only sensible explanation of the extraordinary results it observed was illegality on an overwhelming scale – fraud, intimidation and impersonation (this last not, as in previous elections, individuals pretending to be others, but rather droves of UNP supporters and hirelings visiting polling stations and extracting, with threats backed by arms, ballot papers from officials and casting them on behalf of those who had not yet voted). The magnitude of the operation, obvious to those who studied the results, was officially confirmed by the report of the Commissioner of Elections which recorded a number of abuses and made clear his considered view that such an exercise should not be repeated if democracy were to be maintained. Unfortunately the report came out four years later.

Before that, in an unusual alliance of forces, Wijeweera had challenged the results of the referendum in a case prepared for him by Felix Dias Bandaranaike. However in 1983 the government proscribed the JVP and Wijeweera went underground; the case had to be dismissed. The JVP felt that this was the main reason for the proscription; its unremitting hostility to the referendum, on which unlike other parties it was prepared to take action, had worried the government sufficiently to take what in 1983 seemed an easy way of stifling opposition.

Selective by-elections

The referendum having been won, Jayewardene set about in characteristic fashion to fulfill his commitment to clean up the administration. Several months were spent in working out a scheme that might appear to be based on some principle: the main purpose was to have fewer seats at stake than would jeopardise the two-thirds majority. The final decision was that by-elections would be held in constituencies in which Jayewardene had not won in the Presidential election, which had also been lost by the government at the referendum, and in which the total polled by the government at the referendum was lower than that polled by the UNP in 1977. This last bizarre provision was so that those seats in the Eastern Province from which members of the TULF had crossed over would not be an issue. There were therefore just eighteen seats in the south and west of the country that were to be declared vacant. Eighteen letters were accordingly dated and activated. The rest Jayewardene continued to keep in his possession.

Under the 1978 constitution by-elections had been abolished so that there had to be yet another amendment to the constitution to permit them to take place when the party secretary failed to nominate a successor within a month to seats that had become vacant. Further absurdities proliferated before May when seventeen by-elections were finally held. The original assumption had been that the members of parliament who would be got rid of were those against whom there were serious complaints. As it happened, though in some cases failure to win majorities was a mark of unpopularity, in others it was due primarily to incapacity or unwillingness to resort to the violence and fraud that had characterized the referendum. It was no coincidence that the only two ministers to lose their seats under Jayewardene's special formula were amongst the few who were free from allegations of thuggery. One was Ronnie de Mel, the Minister of Finance, who had been elected to parliament from the SLFP in 1970, but had rapidly become one of the most effective backbench critics of that government before joining the UNP shortly before the 1977 election. He was now widely held to be one of the most able ministers in the cabinet and, given his familiarity with donor organizations and his skill at extracting aid from them, he was thought too precious to risk. Fortunately the member of parliament for the constituency from which de Mel's wife hailed lay ill. A nineteenth letter of resignation was accordingly activated, and de Mel was nominated to the vacancy and restored to his Ministry.

With regard to the rest, though the stated aim was to clean up parliament, and though the assumption of unpopularity had played some part in selecting candidates for removal, most were renominated when the final list was drawn up. Had this not been done there would have been a danger of the disgruntled working against the party; and, far from the earlier claim that a larger opposition was desirable, the by-elections turned into a battle for prestige which the government was determined to win at all costs.

Again, the reason only seventeen by-elections were held was that, just before the stipulated month had elapsed, a nomination was effected by the UNP for the seat from which Neville Fernando had been expelled the previous year. No explanation was offered for this singular exception from the stated formula. None was required. It was clear that Jayewardene was not prepared to tolerate his erstwhile disciple back in the house, and it seemed likely that no opposition party would contest him.

Elsewhere too the opposition was on the whole united, and the by-elections were seen as a tussle between the UNP and an informal association of all manner of opposition parties led by the SLFP, in which Anura Bandaranaike and Vijaya Kumaranatunga now maintained an uneasy co-existence. When the results were declared, the UNP had won twelve seats and the SLFP three. One seat went to Philip Gunawardena's son Dinesh, the leader of the MEP, which he had maintained distinct from the UNP since his father's death in the early seventies. The seventeenth seat was not announced at the time. This was the one contested by Kumaranatunga. The campaign had been a heated one, and on the day of the election his bodyguard had been shot dead while standing next to him in a moving vehicle. All indications were that the government was determined to keep him out of parliament, and the final result declared a few days later was that Kumaranatunga had been defeated by fifty votes. The result was challenged in court, but after much delay a procedural objection was upheld: the President had been cited as one of the respondents in the action, but in terms of the constitution the President is immune from suit as regards all his actions, not only those performed as President. The case was therefore dismissed.

Intimidating the judiciary

Meanwhile, flushed with its success at the referendum, the government embarked upon a policy of confrontation with those elements in the judiciary that still preserved some independence. The Chief Justice was hauled before a select committee of parliament, while three judges of the Supreme Court found demonstrations outside their homes after they ruled against the government in a Fundamental Rights case. This was after an organization of women engaged on a protest march was hauled in by the police. A leading protestor, formerly a Trotskyist member of parliament, alleged that she had been kicked and abused. The Court upheld her claim that her basic right of peaceful congress had been breached, and fined one of the policemen concerned. As was usual now, the government paid the fine and immediately promoted him. Meanwhile the three judges whose homes were surrounded got no response when they tried to contact the police on the telephone. Observation of the streets outside their houses revealed that most of the demonstrators had been transported in public buses; the numbers of these were given over to the police, but no action was taken.

In this instance, however, public indignation ran high and the government was widely blamed. An individual turned up at the offices of one of the government controlled newspapers and took responsibility for the incident. He claimed to be a former member of the JVP who felt that the verdict of the judges had dealt a serious blow to law and order: if old women were to be permitted to demonstrate at will, so could anyone, with the very unfortunate consequence that he had striven to make clear to the judges. The story as published was ludicrous enough, but fresh light was cast on it a couple of days later when the *Island*, a recently started independent newspaper, revealed that the attesting witnesses at this individual's marriage had been two cabinet ministers including Ranil Wickremesinghe. The public was not surprised at this revelation. The government took it in its stride and calmly allowed the matter to lapse.

In retrospect this incident was the turning point which demonstrated to the public that a government swept into power in 1977 on a wave of democratic feeling was now committed to authoritarianism, violent intimidation, malpractices and a brutal cynicism towards individuals or institutions that stood in its way. But this did not worry it in the slightest. It felt itself far too powerful to be threatened by the very different way in which the public regarded it, as compared to the enthusiasm of 1977.

The proposed all-party conference on the Tamil issue

It was from this position of presumed strength that Jayewardene decided, after the by-elections were over, to summon the all-party conference on the Tamil issue that had been pledged in 1977. The reason he gave for his refusal to hold it then still obtained, namely that a number of parties had failed to win representation in parliament; but perhaps by this time he was prepared to acknowledge that parliament was neither relevant to the issue nor representative of the population at large. Correspondingly the executive was so powerful now that it may have seemed that all parties would have no option but to respond positively to his call if they hoped to have any further impact on the situation.

The TULF was in an embarrassing position at the time. One of its parliamentarians had died the previous year and, lulled into security during the Presidential election by Jayewardene's hints of an immediate general election, its leaders had agreed to fill the vacancy by nominating a self-confessed terrorist called Kuttimani who was in jail. It was the militant wing of the party, most prominently Chelvanayakam's son Chandrahasan, that pressed for the nomination, perhaps to focus attention on Tamil grievances at a time when there were many political distractions, and when the Tamil elite was seen to be supporting Jayewardene. Conversely, the leadership of the party was not upset when the government refused to let Kuttimani out of jail to take his seat, since the seat could suitably enough be left vacant for the few months that were left till the next election. At this point the government sprang the referendum on them.

The nomination of Kuttimani provided potent propaganda material for the UNP during the referendum campaign. In the south it was used against the rest of the opposition as the TULF was associated with it in the campaign. Perhaps because of the embarrassment this caused, after the referendum the TULF swung to the other extreme and, though Chandrahasan now staked his own claims, nominated Neelan Tiruchelvam who was seen as associated with Jayewardene. Tiruchelvam himself was in an unfortunate position since he had been critical of the system of filling vacancies by nomination. However it was important to him and the cause for which he stood to keep Chandrahasan out of parliament.

Neither he nor anyone else in the TULF took advantage of the fifth amendment to the constitution to resign and promote by-elections in the north at the time seventeen by-elections were held in the rest of the country. This could have created a serious problem, in that the militants were now stronger and might well have stopped them from standing: in May for instance they were compelled to withdraw their candidates for local elections under pressure of boycott, which, given they had withstood similar pressures in 1981 with regard to the District Council elections, makes clear the shifting balance of power in the north. In addition it might have seemed to them that they had all the time in the world, to resign all together in July after their term, so as to focus attention on the situation by a general action.

The sixth anniversary of the election of 1977 fell on 22 July. It was for the week before that Jayewardene summoned the conference. To his irritation and surprise not one opposition party turned up, only his own UNP and Thondaman's CWC. It was clear that no one was willing to continue playing a game in which the President not only held the cards, but felt at liberty to change the rules as and when he wished.

So the all-party conference, summoned after six long years, seemed likely to prove an anticlimax. Jayewardene had set his heart on it and was not prepared to give in easily. He postponed the conference for a week. In the days that followed he made no mention of the political solution he envisaged, which the other parties had requested. Their position was that, since the problem had been exacerbated by him, he should make suggestions which they would consider. His technique was, having made clear his own continuing absolute power, to encourage them to put forward proposals from their positions of weakness which he could then modify. For the moment that technique seemed to have failed; aware of their limited strengths, the others were not prepared to participate until he placed an agenda before them for discussion. But Jayewardene saw no reason to alter his approach. It had after all brought him to a position of unparalleled power in what had previously been a democratic state. In the days that followed therefore all that seemed necessary to him was the mixture as before, but in even stronger measure.

Part IV

The New Dominion

India in the driving seat (1983–1987)

Chapter 6

The Bang and the Whimpers

The riots of July 1983

On Saturday 23 July thirteen soldiers were killed in an ambush in Jaffna. The newspapers next day gave prominent coverage to this without mentioning that the armed forces had promptly gone on the rampage where the incident had occurred, and killed over forty people. In fact this was never reported in the Sri Lankan press, although the President was to acknowledge the incident later in an interview to a foreign correspondent. What was reported therefore created the impression in the south of the country that Sinhalese youngsters were dying unavenged, and that something had to be done about this.

In addition to media presentation of the incident, the management of the funeral arrangements also contributed to what ensued. The bodies were not disposed of in Jaffna, which would have been the least inflammatory course of action. The alternative of handing over the bodies to relatives at different places in the country was also not considered. Instead it was decided to have a mass funeral at the general cemetery in Colombo on the evening of 24 July.

If all this can be attributed to insensitivity rather than deliberate policy, what happened next is even less easy to excuse. Demonstrations at the cemetery were followed on the night of the 24th by fires in the area round about, in view of the President's residence. The government took no action. Though the situation got much worse the next day, it did nothing until 5 pm, when a curfew was at last declared. By then containment seemed impossible. The curfew was hardly enforced over the next two days. Right through the 25th and the 26th mobs of well organized individuals, equipped with electoral registers so that they were able to distinguish which houses belonged to whom, swept through the streets burning Tamil homes.

They generally spared the occupants, ensuring in an almost disciplined fashion that there were no people in the houses when they set fire to them. Goods however went up in the flames, the explanation offered being that the Tamils had to be taught a lesson. But such discipline could not be maintained everywhere. Looting took place with increasing frequency; cars were stopped in the streets and the Tamils discovered inside were assaulted and sometimes killed. Even so, in the light of the tremendous damage inflicted on these two days, with the mobs and the mayhem unchecked, the number of actual deaths was comparatively small.

Truckloads of men kept coming into Colombo and its environs, to which the trouble was restricted on these two days, from areas where there was no curfew; they appear to have had no trouble in traveling through the areas under curfew to add to the mayhem. Later it was argued that the government was not confident enough of its authority to order the armed forces to put a stop to the rioting. Members of the armed forces however, who acted promptly once the order to shoot on sight was given, expressed surprise at the government's initial failure to act. Thus, whether it was due to culpable cowardice or to policy, for two days the government abandoned the capital to anarchy.

By the evening of the 26th the forces were ordered to quell anything in Colombo and, when they succeeded, the curfew was lifted on the 27th. At this point the scene shifted to the central areas where the Tamil population was largely of recent Indian origin. Over the next two days they too suffered in the same way, only now the violence was more brutal and the callousness more marked. Even more obviously the mobs were not indigenous to the areas they affected. Incidentally, this development nailed the canard used later by some government supporters to play down the enormity of what had occurred in Colombo – it was regrettable, but the Tamils of Colombo had asked for it in not openly expressing support for the government in its struggle against the northern terrorists. Since Thondaman had loyally supported the government over the previous five years, as had his supporters, it is difficult to see what more they could have done to avert the holocaust.

Official government reactions and further incidents

While the mayhem continued the government made no official pronouncements. The news rather was full of descriptions of how supplies to the capital were being maintained. Other aspects of what the authorities were doing to remedy the situation were left unmentioned. It was only on the evening of Thursday July 28th that Jayewardene finally appeared on television and radio to address the nation. To the bitter surprise of the many Tamils who had suffered, but who still looked to him as a responsible leader, hoped for some comfort from his pronouncements, and had awaited his address eagerly, he announced that what had taken place was an understandable Sinhalese reaction to the attempt to divide their country. He had been too lax with the separatists: the reaction of his government was to introduce legislation to proscribe any Party that advocated separatism and to make public servants and members of parliament take an oath of allegiance to a unitary state.

The newspapers that had meanwhile been stressing the hardships caused to the people by the disruption of food supplies reported that morning that several Tigers (as all terrorists were now called) had tried the previous morning to blow up the main railway station in Colombo in the Fort, and been killed in that attempt by vigilant public-spirited citizens. This was simply rumour. But the propagation of this story, combined with the President's speech that characterized as patriots those who had attacked Tamils in the interests of the unity of the country, had an irresistible effect the next day. Fuelled by the accidental discharge in the crowded Fort area of a soldier's shotgun, the rumour gained currency that the Tigers had arrived to attack Colombo. The mobs that ran riot on this occasion killed without quarter all Tamils they came across. The precise figures have never been established, but the loss of life in Colombo on Black Friday as it came to be called, probably equaled that of the previous few days put together.

With that the circus stopped. Curfew was declared fairly promptly, right through until Sunday, and in the course of the weekend and thereafter the ministers who appeared on television sang a different song from their leader's. Though hardly any expressed regret with regard to the suffering of the Tamils, they expressed their anguish at the deprivation the country had undergone through disruption of supplies. Most importantly they announced that what had occurred was the result of a Marxist conspiracy. It was not Sinhalese patriots, as Jayewardene had averred (though no formal correction was made of this lapse), but rather diabolical leftists who had planned the whole business to cause damage to the country. In addition to the TULF, proscribed in accordance with the wishes of those who, according to the President earlier, had been responsible, three leftist parties were now to be proscribed also.

Before long the ban on two of these, the Communists and the Revolutionary Trotskyists (NLSSP), was lifted and their jailed leaders released. The speech of the one Communist Member of Parliament refutes the allegation forcefully, in documenting what he characterizes as the racism of the UNP through its history, as opposed to the attitude of his own party. Instructively some of his statements are echoed in the speech made by Thondaman who made clear that he thought Mathew responsible for the outbreak. Meanwhile, though the JVP promptly went underground, and became a much stronger force there than it had ever been outside, it always denied the government's allegation. Certainly no concrete evidence was ever produced to connect it with these events.

Though some of the most active rioters and arsonists were arrested towards the end, most of them were released after the intervention of government politicians. Opinions differ as to the precise degree of government complicity in what occurred, but it was soon widely accepted that most of the damage, in the initial period, was done by the government's own storm troops: those forces that had been seen in action earlier with regard to the strikers of 1980, the elections in Jaffna and the riots of 1981, the referendum in 1982, and then earlier in 1983 in the demonstration against the judges. Equally certainly they believed they were carrying out a policy of which the government approved, which it had initiated, and which the public was encouraged to join or at least commend.

One of the main purposes of the exercise was to intimidate the Tamils, not only ordinary citizens who were made to see what the activities of the northern terrorists could entail for them, but also the Tamil politicians who would thus be driven to negotiate on Jayewardene's terms. Though the relatively mild lesson originally planned had got out of hand, Jayewardene's speech on 28 July suggests that he was not seriously upset. Since the violence had subsided and it was clear that the government could maintain control when prepared to assert itself, the TULF could be proscribed with the determination to put Tamils on the defensive. The government was to be seen then as representing the will of a majority now on the warpath.

The intervention of India

On this analysis the sudden change after Black Friday in pronouncements if not in policy needs explanation. Possibly there were radical elements opposed to the government that took advantage of the situation to create further disorder, and the government realized these had to be checked; again there might have been elements in the cabinet with humanitarian qualms who wished to be dissociated from the attacks; but most important of all, after the events of Friday, the Indian government made it clear that unless the situation was brought under control within a couple of days it would feel obliged to intervene, by an invasion if necessary. Since the explanation for the failure to maintain law and order offered by the government in response to foreign concern was diffidence as to the reliability of the armed forces, such an invasion would not have seemed unreasonable. If only to forestall this, the government had to take prompt action to prevent further incidents. Attributing the troubles to leftists was the surest way of making it clear that it was serious in its call for restraint.

There was a characteristic attempt at diversion in that Foreign Minister ACS Hameed was dispatched to London to find out whether the British government would respond positively in the event of Jayewardene invoking a long forgotten mutual defence treaty of 1947 in the face of an Indian invasion. The reply was definite that the British government would not. Help was also requested from the United States, which also responded negatively.

Anyway, whether because the pressure exercised by India could not be resisted, or whether it was because (once the riots had been stopped and the damage done to the Sri Lankan state in terms of perceptions had been properly assessed) it was thought the problem would soon be resolved and this could best be done with Indian assistance, there was in the next few months a great deal of diplomatic activity involving India. Certainly Indian involvement could no longer be dismissed as unwarranted interference. The TULF parliamentarians had fled to India at the first hint of trouble, and in effect thrown themselves on Indian mercy for a solution. Even Neelan Tiruchelvam was amongst this group. He had begun to dissociate himself from Jayewardene after he had been appointed to parliament, and it was clear that he could not be used in the future to impose half measures as a response to the problem. Interestingly, the other Tamil with whom Jayewardene had been accustomed to negotiate, the Canadian professor A J Wilson, had been in Colombo when the riots began. With touching presence of mind Jayewardene had telephoned and offered him safe passage out of the country, which he had promptly accepted. It was, for the author of *The Gaullist Constitution of Sri Lanka*, a fitting end to his aspirations in contributing through the hero of that book towards the welfare of the Tamils or of the nation.

Before negotiations with India began Jayewardene introduced another measure that gave reason for disquiet. While the government would provide financial aid for the restoration of damaged property, this was subject to the condition that such property would be vested in the government. Though the provision did not have any noticeably adverse consequences, a Rehabilitation Authority, with a retired admiral at its head, to monitor closely those who had been affected, seemed one of the least felicitous ways to restore confidence.

In the event a fair number of Tamils simply did not go back to their homes. Australia and Canada both opened their doors wider than before to Tamils, and while many went there straight away; over the next few years many more followed. Many also sought refuge in a number of European countries, such as Britain and in particular West Germany that had relatively liberal provisions. A vast number however simply went to Jaffna. For most of them, though they kept contact with connections in the area, it was a question of settling into a place and a lifestyle unlike anything they were accustomed to; but in the immediate aftermath of the rioting that seemed the safest place. Similarly, though on a smaller scale, there was an exodus back to the east of Tamils originally from that area. After a few months therefore it was largely Indian Tamils who were left in the refugee camps; they were relatively lacking in skills and the ability to exploit the enhanced opportunities for emigration; many were unwilling, without roots in the north or east, to make the break and move to those areas. Some of the younger amongst them did so and, together with the younger Ceylon Tamils who had moved from the south, bitter as they were about what they had suffered, added swiftly and substantially to the strength of the militants.

One more incident that took place at the height of the troubles needs to be mentioned; or rather two, for astonishingly enough it occurred in duplicate. On the morning of Monday 25 July about forty Tamil prisoners were massacred within the high security prison of Welikada in Colombo. Two days later twenty more were killed in the same way. Amongst those disposed of on the first day was Kuttimani, the terrorist who had been nominated some months earlier to parliament. Most of the others were also suspected or in some cases actually convicted of terrorism, but amongst the victims was also S Rajasunderam, the Secretary of the Gandhiyam Movement. There had been a suspicion that the Gandhiyam Movement was collaborating with the terrorists. Nevertheless, as Esmond Wickremesinghe put it afterwards, Rajasunderam's death had been an accident, because he had put himself forward when the others were being killed.

Sinhalese prisoners carried out the killings but there can be little doubt that they were officially instigated. Wickremesinghe claimed that allowing them to go ahead was a way of defusing tension. The repetition of the incident two days later suggests that the complicity of the authorities went deeper. So does the fact that at the inquiry no one could provide details of what had happened, and none of the murderers could be identified. Wickremesinghe's account of how an over-zealous magistrate who tried to question the prison guards more thoroughly had to be reined back substantiates the view that his description of the incident came from the perspective of those in authority, even if it did not represent official government policy. The massacre, in cold blood, of sixty prisoners of state within the confines of their jail, passes therefore into an act of statecraft, uninvestigated and unpunished.

The all party conference

In the aftermath of the riots Jayewardene traveled to India to hold consultations about solving the problem. The position of the government was complicated: the TULF having been in effect proscribed, Jayewardene could not very well summon it for negotiations. Nevertheless, with the Indian government acting as an intermediary, proposals were drawn up as a first step to a solution. At this stage Jayewardene said that he could take no steps unless an all party conference were held so that other parties could be consulted. Ironically, the man who now commanded practically all the seats in parliament (after the departure of the TULF members who refused to take the oath of allegiance to a unitary state, prescribed under a sixth amendment to the constitution that was rushed through) claimed that he needed the opposition parties he had treated so contemptuously. The gleeful talk in his party after the referendum about the next referendum suggested that there was an urge to outdo even Napoleon and avoid elections altogether. Now however Jayewardene seemed obliged to confess that there was more to the country than his own power.

Or perhaps it was simply that he wanted someone to pull his chestnuts out of the fire, if only for the purpose of allowing him the pleasure of flinging them back in again. When after he returned to Colombo an all party conference was summoned, the TULF was not invited. It was only after other parties, behaving more responsibly than the treatment that had been meted out to them warranted, attended and requested that the TULF too be asked to come that Jayewardene agreed. Its attendance had been essential for discussions to start if the conference were to mean anything. Jayewardene's manoeuvers suggested that all he wanted to do was dodge the responsibility, and not appear inconsistent with the proscription he had perpetrated and which he felt obliged to keep in force.

There were other factors that from the start vitiated the progress of the talks. Jayewardene had undertaken that Mrs. Bandaranaike's civic rights would be restored, to enable her too to participate in the conference. This did not happen immediately. The SLFP nevertheless attended the first session, at which it was decided that the TULF be invited, but by the time that was done and the TULF had accepted it was clear that Jayewardene was still determined to keep Mrs. Bandaranaike out. At the next session of the conference the SLFP stayed away, whereupon the other parties decided to adjourn and try to persuade it to attend. It gave in readily, but the point had been made.

There were other indications that the originator of the conference was not keen on any decisions. A further constraint was that the conference was not confined to political parties. Various religious organizations were invited, not on any clear basis. The result of such mass participation was a proliferation of views, some without any basis in political reality; this led to a consensus being impossible. The excuse of the government was that all sections of the community that might be affected should have an opportunity to express their views. Yet if that were the case a crucial omission was the terrorist groups. It was argued (until the inevitable retraction under pressure eighteen months later) that it would have been wrong to negotiate with them until they had renounced terrorism. Yet their exclusion meant that any decisions reached would have little validity. It is worth noting that none of the delegates to the conference belonged to the age bracket of the terrorists or the membership of the JVP. The conference was very much a case of Hamlet without the Prince.

Yet having cut away the younger generation and expelled Gertrude, Jayewardene achieved the impossible of leaving out Claudius as well. Though he appeared at the conference, it was very much in the role of the Ghost: the proposals that he formulated in India, and published in Sri Lanka on his return, turned up at the conference as a disembodied presence. They were put forward without any parentage, called merely Annexure C, available for comment but with no one acknowledging their origin. It is uncertain whether at this stage they would have been generally acceptable, as opposed to their being advanced in the aftermath of the rioting when the urgency was widely acknowledged. Nevertheless they would have provided a fruitful ground for discussion.

They appeared however without a sponsor, and understandably no one else was prepared to sponsor them. The result was that there was nothing concrete for the conference to proceed on. Instead the country was faced for the next year with a series of speeches that delved deep into history or rather legend. The nonpolitical groups played an ever increasing part in the proceedings as time went on, and the conference seemed no nearer to producing anything like a solution.

The result of the conference

This was scarcely surprising. It rapidly became clear that, as far as the UNP was concerned, the primary purpose of the exercise was delay. This strategy was based on the assumption that India was not especially interested in the problem but that, with a general election due, Mrs. Gandhi had to show willingness to assist in the face of pressures upon her from Tamils in the south. The aim therefore was to spin negotiations out until after the election had been held, and after that there would be no threat from India; Jayewardene could carry on as before.

Such an assumption could not be sustained for very long. But before considering the other incidents that affected the issue over the subsequent months it may be as well to follow the all party conference through to its preposterous conclusion. As the conference spun itself out, the number of people who actually attended grew fewer. The SLFP soon withdrew its delegation. TULF representatives kept going to India and returning to Colombo, but nothing new was offered. The visits of Mrs. Gandhi's personal representative, the veteran diplomat Parthasarathy, got an increasingly cold response and began to be represented in the Sri Lankan media as unwarranted interference. Before six months had passed the conference was considered a farce. Nevertheless it ploughed on and, a year after it had begun, a document was prepared that purported to be its conclusion.

It was this document, and what immediately happened to it, that led to the claim by a columnist in the *Island* that Sri Lanka had established a new record: it had held the first all party conference, the conclusions of which were disowned by all the involved parties. One after another all the organizations represented at the conference picked holes in the proposals. The criticism of the Buddhist organizations was almost as contemptuous as that of the TULF.

One drama however, despite the general uselessness of the proceedings, the conference did produce. When the final document emerged, Cyril Mathew weighed in with a comprehensive critique that was circulated to the press. Not immediately, and reportedly only after pressure had been applied by other moderate ministers, Jayewardene decided that this was a breach of the doctrine of cabinet responsibility and announced that Mathew's public pronouncement amounted to resignation. Mathew's deputy was immediately appointed in his place and, by a few judicious promotions, including that of Mathew's son, any disaffection that might have arisen was promptly nipped in the bud.

The efficient way in which Jayewardene dispatched Mathew suggests that, had he wanted, he could have got the remedies proposed in the document, weak though many of them were in comparison with what had been set out in Annexure C, accepted by parliament. Instead, following upon Mathew's dismissal and the rejection of the proposals by the TULF, Jayewardene declared that there was nothing more to be said about them, and consigned them and the all party conference to oblivion.

Chapter 7

Raising the Stakes

Government relations with other forces

Despite the impetus given to the Tamil cause by the events of July 1983 and the ongoing negotiations, there was no change in the government's attitude to crucial issues. No attempts were made to enhance opportunities in the public sector for education or employment.

With regard to devolution, far from there being any advance, the District Councils in the north and to some extent in the east, were rendered virtually defunct by the enforced dismissal of TULF members, who were unwilling to take the oath of allegiance to a unitary state prescribed under the sixth amendment to the constitution. Since the JVP, the only other party to contest the elections in 1981, had been proscribed, District Councils throughout the country, far from being an alternative repository of authority, became rubber stamps for the government. This situation was exacerbated by the government; using its powers under Emergency Regulations that were renewed without remission month after month, it postponed elections to these Councils when they were due, so that members elected in 1981 held office for over seven years.

The government did not explain why it was necessary to postpone these elections for the entire country. It was not due to the security situation for, continuing with its window-dressing operation, it held by-elections to a few select seats over the next few years. These were selected usually where the UNP's previous majority was large. Despite this, at first the opposition parties participated in them. In time however the SLFP realised that there was no point in this and announced that it would not contest any more such elections.

Opposition unity on this score was interrupted when one more by-election was contested by the Sri Lanka Mahajana Pakshaya (SLMP), a breakaway group set up by Kumaranatunga and his wife Chandrika. . Kumaranatunga's personal differences with his brother-in-law had contributed to the decision to leave. After Anura Bandaranaike's elevation to the post of leader of the opposition in parliament (following on the expulsion from it of the TULF), his supporters gradually took control of the party, apparently with Mrs. Bandaranaike's blessing. Kumaranatunga's personal charisma continued but the SLMP as a party did not do too well, and it moved into close association with the CP and the LSSP. They too soon decided as a group to boycott the UNP's by-elections, and there developed an opposition agreement to press for a general election as a prerequisite for a solution to the problems confronting the country.

Developments within the UNP

More important than what was going on outside the UNP during this period were developments within. Disagreement with regard to the question of colonization surfaced within the party soon after July 1983. In particular problems arose over the attempt to settle Sinhalese on the borders of the Eastern Province, in the Maduru Oya area, in connection with the Mahaweli development scheme. Though this was mainly associated with the Dimbulagala priest, it was suspected that Dissanayake and Panditharatne were providing active support. Thondaman voiced strong criticism of what was going on, and in the aftermath of the riots he wielded tremendous influence as the principal token of the government's good faith towards the Tamils. Jayewardene felt obliged to act and a board of inquiry was set up to look into the matter. Its brief included investigation of Panditharatne's actions. Panditharatne waited for the the board's report which came out over a year later and exonerated him; then, on the grounds that the board's brief indicated a lack of confidence in him, he resigned both as Chairman of the Mahaweli Board and as President of the UNP.

The impact of all this has to be considered in the light of the fact that both Dissanayake and Panditharatne belonged to the wing of the party that was closest to Jayewardene, the wing to which Mathew also belonged. Very distinct from this group was Premadasa, whose social origins and caste might have precluded him from ever succeeding to the leadership. Dissanayake however was young and Panditharatne had never been a public figure, though at an early stage even he was mentioned by the elder Wickremesinghe as a possible successor. In time that wing of the party decided on Mathew; because he too belonged to a minority caste, though a comparatively large one, his profile was built up through his championship of the Sinhalese.

The events of July 1983 put paid to Mathew's chances. His own performance in parliament immediately after, when he quoted at length from *The Malay Dilemma* by Mahathir Bin Mohamed (who expounded an aggressive policy of positive discrimination for the Malays, and subsequently became Prime Minister of Malaysia), indicates that he had his own ideas about the future. Jayewardene however was at this stage committed to conciliation and, though Mathew remained in the cabinet for over a year, on some issues a line had to be drawn.

It was in this context that Jayewardene turned to Lalith Athulathmudali, previously seen very much as his own man. He was made Minister of National Security, a position he occupied for the next five years and which strengthened his claims as a possible successor, even though, unlike Premadasa or Dissanayake, he had no great backing from any group within the party.

National Security under Lalith Athulathmudali and the connection with Israel

Athulathmudai's tenure began well; though nothing very positive came of it, this can be attributed to the chaotic nature of government policy in the years that followed. The most that Athulathmudali can be blamed for is his failure to impose some sort of coherence, to use the expertise he gained to convince his colleagues in the cabinet that what would emphatically not work was half-hearted negotiations at intervals, interspersed with attempts at military domination that India was bound to oppose.

With regard to minor aspects of the problem, Athulathmudali's appointment certainly saw a change for the better. He got to the spot to offer condolences when servicemen had been killed by terrorist activity or when retaliatory or other aggressive action by servicemen had caused casualties among Tamil civilians. Casualties amongst Sinhalese, servicemen as well as civilians, were minimized in the media, while retaliatory actions were also noted. Thus there was no room for the feeling that the deaths of Sinhalese had gone unavenged. Those who claimed that the violence of July 1983 was spontaneous had argued that the public had risen up because they felt that Sinhalese soldiers were being killed and the government was doing nothing to avenge them. Evidence suggests that that had little to do with the uprising of 1983 in comparison with what the government contributed deliberately. Whether through more balanced reporting of news, or through the government realizing how counter-productive its actions had been, there has certainly never been any mass uprising against minorities after 1983, despite much more violent acts of terrorism than the incident that was claimed to have provoked that pogrom.

Leaving aside public relations, Athulathmudali was less successful with regard to what was increasingly considered a war effort, though he became one of the most prominent hawks in the process. Following the failure of the West to live up to expectations, it had been decided (with American blessings and encouragement) to seek Israeli assistance. In exchange Israel was permitted to set up an Israeli interests section within the American Embassy.

Given that diplomatic relations with Israel had been severed in 1970, this concession from a country that had chaired the Movement of Non-Aligned nations could be perceived as the thin end of the wedge. Whether Israel was especially gratified or not, Arab nations certainly were not, and problems arose over the issue of visas to Sri Lankans to work in certain Arab countries; this had been an important source of revenue for the country over the previous decade. The problem was down-played and finally did not prove serious, but the original blithe announcement of the Israeli connection by the government was rapidly followed by marked diffidence.

On the field of battle not even the assistance of the Israelis was enough to help. The lesson Sri Lankan troops had to learn was to not alienate the local population. This was what they had accomplished most successfully over the last few years, and in the crucial period after July 1983 Israeli training did nothing to improve the situation. On the other hand one feature attributed to Israeli strategy, that of decimating areas where acts of terrorism had occurred, appeared to have been indiscriminately adopted; it led to even greater ill feeling.

After Athulathmudali took over there were attempts to improve discipline, including the creation of a special education unit to inculcate the need for good relations with the Tamils, but it was difficult to change attitudes completely. As the terrorists gained strength after 1983 and mounted more and more successful attacks, the army reacted against civilians in specific areas, and rationalized decimation. Swiftly and more markedly than before, the army was seen as an army of occupation throughout the north.

In December 1984, just before the collapse of the all party conference, a new dimension was introduced with a security zone declared round the coastline. This was to prevent ready access to and from India, where training camps had been established for the terrorists by the Indian government's secret service, the so-called Research and Analysis Wing (RAW). These camps explain the total failure of the strategy outlined above, in that the terrorists were able to make a quick getaway to India after any burst of activity so that, when the army took forceful action in response, it was rarely that any guilty party suffered. The security zone was intended to make some sense of the strategy that had been adopted but two major attacks immediately afterwards provided conclusive evidence that, despite it, the government had little actual control in the Jaffna peninsula or even further south.

The expansion of terrorist activity and government responses

The most obvious consequence of the security zone was to prevent fishing by those who earned their livelihood from it; this furthered the economic hardships the area was already facing. It was partly in response to this that there occurred a brutal attack on a fishing village just south of the Jaffna peninsula, where Sinhalese fishermen spent several months each year on the generations old pattern of migrating from south west to north east and back again, according to the monsoons.

Even more startling was the first attack on Sinhalese civilians, which occurred just after the imposition of the security zone and rigid control of movement within the Jaffna peninsula. The attack on settlers on farms in the Vavuniya district, in the south of the northern province, made clear the breadth of the area in which the terrorists could operate. The claim made in mitigation of that attack, brutal as the massacres were, was that the settlers were prisoners, some of them participants in the slaughter of Tamil prisoners at Welikada in 1983, and that they had been planted on the farms by the government as part of its policy of colonizing the area with Sinhalese. Even if these allegations had some truth, the brutality of the deed detracted from the argument that Tamil activists were militants, not terrorists, inasmuch as they only attacked servicemen or Tamil civilians who were collaborators. That Sinhalese now suffered made clear the limitations of the state's capacity to protect its citizens.

Even more worrying was that the area of active conflict was now spreading. The most marked development in this occurred in the Eastern Province. From about the beginning of 1984 there were increasingly frequent incidents of terrorist activity there, usually with reference to Tamils held to be anti-social elements, sometimes with reference to servicemen. These last had led to retaliation, and there came a stage in which the government withdrew much of the army and confined those elements of the security forces that remained in the area to their camps. Security was handed over, the police having proved inadequate for the task, to the Special Task Force (STF), a new breed of police commandos that had been specially trained to deal with terrorists.

Though one aspect of this training was to preserve good relations with the population of the area, by the beginning of 1985 relations had reached a new low and in some quarters it was even hoped that the army would be permitted to return. Terrorists had continued to find victims, and the response of the STF grew increasingly oppressive.

At the same time the phenomenon of individual Muslims being killed for informing became more common. The Muslims in the Eastern Province are largely Tamil speaking and constitute about a third of the population. They had not been associated initially with the demand for a separate state and had tended to support the Sinhalese parties. Following upon the announcement of the new relationship with Israel however there were a number of Muslim demonstrations against the government. Though they were played down in the media, the force with which they had been quelled had left bitterness. There was fear therefore that the terrorists might establish some sort of common ground with the disaffected Muslims.

This fear appeared to be put to flight in April 1985 with the outbreak of riots between Muslims and Tamils in the southern coastal areas of the Eastern Province. Over ten thousand Tamils were made homeless and the impact on those who suffered was similar to that of 1983 elsewhere. The media devoted little attention to the subject, though several interesting points had emerged during the few days that the news was highlighted.

The main reports suggested that the attacks were due to resentment over the increasing number of Muslims being killed by terrorists. This was not the version of events presented soon after the riots began by the government's own ministers. Both Thondaman and a senior UNP Tamil minister, whose electorate lay in the affected area, announced that outsiders had gone into the area to create trouble and that the STF too had been involved. This led to an independent Tamil newspape, the *Virakesari* that had reported Thondaman's remarks, being censored, though Thondaman was not reprimanded in public. Instead he went to India until the crisis subsided.

The official line however scarcely carried. The general belief was that the STF was behind the incident, with agents brought from elsewhere to inflame the situation. And, though the government was satisfied for the time that the Tamil speaking Muslims of the east had been conclusively divided from the Tamils, there was less complacence elsewhere. The Muslims had suddenly been equipped with arms and there was no guarantee how these would be used in the future. Even amongst Muslims in Colombo there was a suspicion that the violence had arisen from a policy inspired by the Israelis, Muslims being dispensable in Israeli eyes, the more important aim being to set two minorities against each other.

Spurs to negotiate

There occurred, less than a month later, an attack by terrorists in what might be termed quintessential Sinhalese territory, the sacred city of

Anuradhapura in the North Central Province. There had been some attacks before in Sinhalese areas, but they were relatively minor. What happened at Anuradhapura however was on too large a scale to be dismissed. Having driven through the city, the terrorists opened fire in the area of the bus stand and killed about two hundred people. The armed forces were unable to stop them. Then the terrorists drove off to the west, to the wild life reserve of Wilpattu, where they killed several employees before vanishing into the jungle in a vehicle.

In some quarters it was alleged that the increased reach of the terrorists sprang from even greater Indian support. With no other way of dealing with this, the government had to seek closer contact with India at the highest levels over the weeks following. This led in mid June 1985 to a cease-fire followed by negotiations between the government and the various terrorist groups, held under the aegis of the Indian government in Bhutan.

Before that relations with India had deteriorated considerably, even though things had turned out as anticipated by those who argued that the Sri Lankan government simply had to see things through until the Indian election, after which the pressure would be off. After Mrs. Gandhi's assassination in October 1984, the Congress Party under Rajiv Gandhi won an overwhelming majority; he was clearly less susceptible to pressure from the Tamil south than his mother's government had been. As if to confirm this Mrs. Gandhi's special envoy Parthasarathy was sidelined, with the new Prime Minister relying more on the new Foreign Secretary Romesh Bhandari. Unlike Parthasarathy who was a Tamil himself, Bhandari came from north India and could be expected to be less sympathetic to the Tamil cause.

Yet though Bhandari did pay a visit to Sri Lanka a few weeks before the outbreak in the east, little was achieved, and the tensions that had been mounting found even more aggressive expression in Sri Lanka in the period immediately following. The terrorist bases in Tamil Nadu seemed a fundamental problem to the Sri Lankan government, and it was suggested that the central Indian government had a responsibility to eradicate these. Until this was done, the Sri Lankan government could not be expected to alleviate Tamil grievances.

Relations with India were complicated further early in 1985 by the leasing out of land to the Voice of America (VoA) to establish a broadcasting station near Trincomalee. The agreement gave responsibility for the security of the area to the VoA, which could be interpreted by India as the provision of facilities for American defence personnel in general. This was highly contentious in that India was deeply concerned about the involvement of other countries in Sri Lanka. They were particularly concerned about the area around Trincomalee, which is a fine natural harbour. Earlier in the eighties they had protested when old oil tanks constructed near Trincomalee during the Second World War had been leased to an American company. The lease was cancelled, but an agreement was later reached with another company which opposition members of parliament alleged was simply a front for the first. That agreement too fell through, arguably under Indian pressure. The provision of facilities then that included absolute rights of defence to the VoA were construed as a threat to Indian security.

The debate over a possible unit of devolution acceptable to everybody depended to a great extent on the position of Trincomalee. By this stage it was apparent that the Sri Lankan government, for all its denials, would finally have to accept the principle of Provincial Councils. The north therefore would be governed by Tamils, while the east would be controlled by a coalition that would include Sinhalese and thereby have a closer relationship with the central government. The Tamils however insisted on the north and the east being joined into one unit that would be dominated by Tamils; the reason advanced was that this was their traditional homeland, but the control of Trincomalee would mean a more viable economic unit, and therefore more real autonomy than the north by itself would allow.

The government's argument was that such a situation would allow domination of Trincomalee by a foreign power, by which was meant India. The Indian position was that that was preferable to domination by any other power. In the context of such mutual suspicion, and India's own relations with America at the time of the Cold War, a long lease granted to the VoA would not inspire confidence. The Sri Lankan government meanwhile made a formal protest against the speech of the Indian Deputy Minister for Foreign Affairs who had referred in the Indian parliament to discrimination against Tamils in Sri Lanka. As a more forceful token of its resentment, the government decided to boycott the meeting of the South Asian Association for Regional Cooperation (SAARC) to be held in Nepal.

The commencement of negotiations

After the personal intervention of Rajiv Gandhi and other South Asian leaders, Jayewardene sent a representative to Nepal, namely Esmond Wickremesinghe, whose close personal association with him had survived his alienation from their mutual friends, Mathew and Panditharatne. During Bhandari's visit to Sri Lanka Wickremesinghe had established a personal rapport with him and, on the way back from Nepal, he stopped in Delhi for what turned out to be very fruitful discussions, though it is unlikely that things would have gone further but for the jolt given by the killings at Anuradhapura. After that, Jayewardene himself went to India for talks with Gandhi, and shortly after that a ceasefire was announced. In July the first negotiations between the government and the terrorists began in Bhutan.

From the very beginning of the negotiations there was little reason for optimism. The terrorists began by reiterating four points they regarded as basic: recognition of the Tamils as a distinct nationality, recognition of the fact of a Tamil homeland in Sri Lanka, recognition of the Tamil right to self determination, and full citizenship rights for all Tamils who looked upon Sri Lanka as their home. While the second and third of these might have been difficult for the Sri Lankan government, its own proposals were denounced as no better than those advanced at the discredited all party conference. The unit proposed for devolution for instance was still the district rather than the province. After a week of fruitless discussion the conference was adjourned until mid August, in the hope that talks behind the scenes would produce some softening on both sides.

The composition of the government delegation had left room for doubt as to how serious Jayewardene was about the whole business. No politicians were included. Instead the leader of the delegation was the President's brother Harry, a successful Colombo lawyer whose only other claim to distinction was his unquestioning loyalty to his brother. The rest of the delegation consisted of other lawyers and civil servants. This may have been suitable had the purpose of the negotiations been to work out legislative formulas and methods of administrative implementation for an agreement; the problem was that the political principles underlying such an agreement had scarcely been approached by the main partners in the talks.

Wickremesinghe was not included. Though he fell ill after his visit to Delhi, and was to die at the end of September, in July he had expected to attend the talks in Bhutan. As the possible reasons for omitting politicians did not apply to him, that he was left out is particularly significant. He had shown himself able to get on with his counterparts in Delhi and was obviously able to achieve results. The implication is that Jayewardene was not especially interested in results.

Chapter 8

Holding the Centre

The failure of negotiations

The negotiations in Bhutan gradually collapsed, as violations of the ceasefire by terrorists on the ground were met with corresponding violence from the Sri Lankan army. As violence escalated, so did the acrimoniousness of the remonstrations on either side.

The Sri Lankan government was perhaps encouraged in its uncompromising attitude by the perception that Rajiv Gandhi was displeased with the intransigence of the terrorists. Even when they withdrew from the talks, the ceasefire was not renounced, and the impression was that the Indian government was keeping the groups in line and would help to produce a solution. The pot of gold at the end of the rainbow was to emerge after discussions between Jayawardene and Gandhi at the SAARC meeting for heads of government to be held in Dhaka in early December.

In accordance with this the government produced a draft paper that represented a distinct advance on what had been proposed before. Though the unit of devolution was still to be District Councils, provision was made for the amalgamation of these into Provincial Councils. However, the union of the Northern and Eastern Provinces was ruled out, while the Provincial Councils were allowed more limited powers than were likely to be accepted.

It was not surprising that by the beginning of December the pot of gold had begun to look more distant. While the TULF put forward alternative proposals, the most powerful Tamil group at the negotiations, made up of four terrorist organizations, rejected the government's proposals and refused to put forward any of its own. Significantly, at this time the Indian Foreign Minister was critical in Parliament of the Sri Lankan armed forces. This happened before the meeting in Dhaka and also afterwards, at which point Gandhi too, though critical of the terrorists as well, made a similar observation. Corresponding to this shift perhaps was Jayawardene's reiteration in an interview with *India Today* of his determination to crush terrorism. If this seemed a reversion to his position before he agreed to meet with the terrorists in Bhutan, the suspicions of the terrorists were justified by a response he made when asked if the ceasefire was only to buy time for both the government and the militants. His response was, "Yes, we were not ready earlier. Now we are acquiring arms and getting our soldiers trained. We are getting ready for decisive military action if nothing comes out of the negotiations."

In the same interview Jayawardene sidestepped the question as to why he was seeking military aid from Pakistan while apparently relying on Indian help to solve the problem. As though to underline the change in hopes and expectations, the pot of gold that Jayawardene brought back from Dhaka was not a basis for agreement, but rather President Zia of Pakistan.

With nothing having emerged from Dhaka except a reason for heightened Indian suspicion, Jayawardene predictably tried to consolidate his domestic position. In January 1986, two measures were announced that earlier might have enhanced his claim to be a representative democratic leader opposed only by marginal forces of violence. On 1 January he pardoned Mrs. Bandaranaike and restored her civic rights, while a few weeks later he announced that all stateless Indian plantation workers would be granted citizenship. But both positive acts were seen simply as concessions made under pressure.

Domestic Strategies

In the case of Mrs. Bandaranaike's civic rights, international pressure had mounted. In December 1985 Sri Lankan papers carried reports of a motion of the Liberal International, instigated by Amaratunga's CLD (the first Sri Lankan political organization apart from Marxists to establish such international links), calling both for the restoration of Mrs. Bandaranaike's civic rights and for an immediate General Election. Though the International itself was not influential, a number of its constituent members, all of whom supported the motion, belonged to governments that had hitherto been amongst Jayawardene's strongest supporters. The German Free Democratic Party for instance held the portfolios of both Foreign and Economic Affairs in a government that supplied Sri Lanka with substantial aid. Jayawardene admitted to having been influenced by this first critique from an international body of a sort he affected to have affinities with.

Equally important were domestic considerations. Having been placed outside the political process, Mrs. Bandaranaike was a focal point for dissent that went beyond party considerations. Earlier she had not exploited this, but in response to the talks in Bhutan she set up, together with some prominent Buddhist monks, a 'Front for the Motherland' that was designed to prevent too many concessions to Tamil Separatists. On hindsight this proved inessential, but Jayawardene was worried enough to stamp down hard to prevent any demonstrations or protests in this connection. In restoring Mrs. Bandaranaike's civic rights, he was also anxious to show that there was still democratic space in the country for opposition to be expressed.

The increasing hollowness of his authority was exemplified by the manner in which the decision to grant citizenship to the stateless Indians was forced upon him. When he procrastinated, Thondaman announced that CWC members would embark on a prayer campaign about their civil status during working hours. Within a couple of days it was clear that this withdrawal of labour was having a crippling effect on the economy. Jayawardene gave in and announced that the stateless would be granted citizenship within eighteen months.

In itself the step may be seen as merely a just restoration of what had been taken away unfairly in the forties. Yet amongst planters, who were responsible for the management of the estates, it struck hard at morale which was already low. They had already suffered the previous year when, on another demand from Thondaman, the workers were granted a wage increase with a guarantee of six days work per week. The planters thought this impractical, since there are long periods in the year in which there is no need for so much labour on a tea estate. Initially Jayewardene had accepted their argument that labour should be paid basically in terms of seasonal requirements but, after a meeting between Thondaman and Jayawardene, that position was reversed, and what amounted to a guaranteed regular wage, whether labour was needed or not, was granted.

The planters' conviction that their authority had been disastrously undermined gained credence in the month after the prayer campaign, when riots broke out in the hills. This time it was planters in their isolated bungalows on the estates, together with the Sinhalese villagers in the areas round about them, who were placed under siege. When some terrorist groups from the north began to make headway in the plantations too, the original claim made by some Tamil separatists, that their traditional homeland included parts of the central hill country also, no longer seemed absurd but a reason for genuine apprehension.

Fortunately for Jayawardene these disturbances were relatively easily contained and the opposition Sinhalese parties did not try to make capital of the issue. The old left wing parties welcomed his move to grant citizenship. Their approach had been cosmopolitan before and their moving spirit now was Kumaranatunga whose attitude towards the Tamil question was markedly liberal. Again, though the SLFP criticized the act, they concentrated on Jayawardene's inefficiency in implementing the pacts Mrs. Bandaranaike had negotiated previously, instead of attempting to rouse racist feeling. But the dangers that lay ahead became apparent when the most aggressive reaction to the move came from the JVP.

Proscribed in 1983 with its leader Wijeweera under threat of arrest, the JVP had seemed dormant; but, having worked underground effectively, it emerged once again as a force, precisely because of its willingness to occupy the ground that had been opened up by the prominence of Tamil extremists on the other side. Though it did not advocate a clearly racist line, its argument was that divisive measures were being taken at the behest of India. That this approach allowed it to appear as the champion of overtly racist forces was not a reason for worry. On the contrary there seemed every willingness to exploit this factor. Characteristically, Jayawardene's attitude to the JVP remained incoherent. Despite their fostering a possible chauvinist backlash, Jayewardene became shrill in his insistence that there were links between the JVP and Tamil terrorists.

Divisions amongst the Tamil terrorists

In 1986 divisions between the various terrorist groups in the north took on a crucial significance. Four groups had come together for the negotiations in Bhutan. The main one was the Liberation Tigers of Tamil Eelam (LTTE or the Tigers as they were commonly known), who were concerned with what they saw as a racial struggle. For the talks they had come together with three other groups that laid greater stress on ideological objectives: the Eelam People's Revolutionary Liberation Front (EPRLF) which had a Marxist-Leninist bias, the Tamil Eelam Liberation Organization (TELO) and the Eelam Revolutionary Organization of Students (EROS).

With the breakdown of the talks at Bhutan however, the union of the four groups collapsed. That the ceasefire continued may indeed have owed less to pressures on the terrorists by India than to the fact that the Tigers wanted to devote their energies to other things. A couple of months later they launched operations that effectively destroyed the TELO and EPRLF presence in the north. Amongst the casualties was Sri Sabaratnam, the leader of TELO, who was thought to be the terrorist leader closest to India.

Spurs to negotiate seriously

The attitude of the Sri Lankan government at this stage suggests a belief that dissension amongst the terrorists could work to its advantage. Its response in January to the almost derisory rejection of its previous proposals was once again to rule out a merger of the Northern and Eastern Provinces. It was only in April that it submitted a revised list of proposals, and these did not go much further. Though they were sent through an active politician, it was only Foreign Minister Hameed, who went to Delhi for a meeting of the Co-ordinating Bureau of the Non-Aligned Movement. The use of the lightweight if amiable Hameed, his relative unimportance heightened by the fact that as a Muslim he would have to be extremely wary of entering into commitments the Sinhalese might take amiss, underlines the procrastinatory nature of Jayawardene's strategy.

Events however soon overtook this complacent approach. P Chidambaram, a Tamil Minister in the central government known to be close to Rajiv Gandhi, was sent to Colombo with quite far-reaching proposals in reply to those conveyed by Hameed; a series of destructive explosions followed in Colombo and other especially vulnerable places. Instructively, though not all these actions could be attributed conclusively to EROS, there was sufficient evidence of the active involvement of its cadres; and, with Sri Sabaratnam dead, it was EROS that was known to be closest to RAW, the arm of the Indian establishment that had the least patience with the Sri Lankan government's dilatoriness.

The Sri Lankan government did not cave in quite at once. There was a sudden flurry of military activity in the north; a fresh set of proposals followed that went much further towards satisfying the demands of the terrorists in finally accepting that Provincial Councils should be the basic unit of devolution. These emerged after a great deal of low key but high powered diplomatic activity involving J N Dixit, the experienced Indian High Commissioner in Colombo. In June the Indian government, having moved from facilitation of talks to mediation, forwarded the proposals to the Tamils, while Jayawardene unveiled them to other political parties at another conference. The TULF did not attend. It now worked through the Indian government, which made clear that India was involved in a bilateral negotiation on behalf of people for whom it was responsible rather than assisting two parties in confrontation with each other.

Fortunately for Jayawardene the other Sinhalese parties did not attempt to make political capital by condemning his proposals. At the same time he received no support, which was scarcely surprising, since he made it clear that he was not consulting them, but rather asking for suggestions for enlarging their scope. This was astounding, for they went far beyond anything he had previously advanced. Though merger of North and East was still not considered, the proposals provided for the institutionalization of arrangements for consultation and co-ordination between the two Provincial Councils. Whereas previously devolution had been presented as a concession that could be readily abrogated, now it would come about through a constitutional amendment requiring at least a two-thirds majority.

The Indian Government seemed satisfied and in the period that followed it made efforts to ensure that these proposals were accepted by the terrorists, at least as a basis for further negotiations. This did not reckon with the personality of the leader of the Tigers, Velupillai Prabhakaran. He had first come into prominence over the killing of the mayor of Jaffna during the SLFP regime. In the years that followed the election of the UNP to power he had broken with his erstwhile ideology inclined comrades and had pursued an aggressive single-minded approach that enabled him after the crisis of 1983 to emerge as the strongest terrorist leader. He was popular because he represented liberation for his peers: the northern peninsula had been dominated for generations by the Vellala farmer caste, so Prabhakaran's emergence was seen as an achievement not only for his own fisher community, but also for a variety of other groups that had hitherto been discriminated against and even despised.

Such sensitivities and satisfactions somewhat explain the enthusiastic favour accorded to the Tigers, both initially and when, in the latter part of 1986, they took over effective control of the peninsula. Given such success, Prabhakaran saw no reason to compromise. He was a man of solid determination, and his reaction to the proposals which the Indian government had managed to coax out of Jayawardene was that these were no substitute for Eelam, the homeland that he had fought for.

For its part, the Indian government could perhaps have compelled some one else to accept the proposals. With Prabhakaran however they were helpless; unless they were willing to use violence on him. This, in 1986 at least, they were not prepared to do.

Further concessions from the government

Amongst the further concessions coaxed out of Jayawardene in the months that followed was the proposal that the Eastern Province be divided into three, with each section termed a province in itself. Thus the Sinhalese, the Tamils and the Muslims could each have their own area, and the Tamil one could set about aligning itself closely with the north. Then, at the end of the year, he suggested the detachment from the Eastern Province of the markedly Sinhalese Amparai District (known now as Digamadulla), and offered that institutional linkages between the Northern and the new Eastern Province could be further developed. Yet even this astonishing negation of earlier intransigence failed to convince Prabhakaran.

One reason may have been that by now there was an added complication, in that this last suggestion was bound to upset the Muslims. Muslims constituted a substantial proportion of the population in the Eastern Province and, had that been the unit of devolution, they might well have exercised considerable power. A tripartite division too may have suited them but, under the new scheme, they could see themselves dominated by Sinhalese in Digamadulla, and by Tamils elsewhere, especially if the other areas were allowed to combine with the north.

Even on their own they were likely to oppose the new plan. There were however other factors to be considered. Recently a Sri Lanka Muslim Congress (SLMC) had been established, the first political party set up in Sri Lanka by Muslims, on the grounds that they could not expect their interests to be looked after by any national political party. Though the SLMC was strongly critical of Muslims within the UNP, it was close to some government forces, notably to Lalith Athulathmudali. The forthright condemnation of the new plan by the SLMC, the impetus for which came largely from the east, roused suspicions that the situation was similar to that of two years earlier, when Jayawardene had either used Cyril Mathew and the forces he represented or, on a generous view, been genuinely unable to control them.

The alternative approach

The Tigers, no longer bothering about the government's proposals, declared at the beginning of 1987 that they had effectively taken over the Civil Administration of the north. The government response was once again to go on the offensive. The military aspect of this was perhaps less forceful than Athulathmudali would have wished, quoted as he was in the government press in early February as claiming that Jaffna would be retaken 'within days'. Enough was accomplished to put the Tigers back on the defensive in other areas, and to some extent in their stronghold in Jaffna.

It became clear that the unilateral usurpation of authority by the LTTE had been a mistake. They had no experience in administration and, while previously they had been seen as providing protection against an oppressive government, their authoritarian approach, once they took over government, alienated the population. When the Sri Lankan government imposed a fuel embargo and what amounted to an economic blockade, this did nothing to make the government more popular, but the deprivation contributed to resentment against the Tigers.

The concentration of resources by the Tigers in the Jaffna Peninsula together with their decimation of other groups through the previous year made things easier for the army elsewhere. In the Eastern Province in particular, the operations conducted during this time against the Tigers proved remarkably successful, largely because of information supplied to the security forces by members of the other terrorist groups that the Tigers had struck against.

The response of the Indian government to such developments was a formal message sent through Dixit on 9 February that it would suspend its good offices with regard to negotiations until the Sri Lankan government stopped military operations and the violence against Tamils in the north and east, lifted its economic blockade, and affirmed its commitment to its earlier proposals as a basis for negotiations. In reply to this, four days later, Jayawardene declared that the government would call a halt to its legitimate defensive actions only if the Tigers stopped their hostilities and abandoned their attempt to set up their own administration. He added that the Sri Lankan government expected India to underwrite the implementation of any agreement.

This last was surprising, as it seemed a voluntary abnegation by the Sri Lankan government of its own sovereignty in the event of a settlement. The immediate implication was that Jayawardene expected the Indian government to compel the terrorists to come to the negotiating table, while remaining unwilling himself to make any further concessions. The Tigers categorically rejected Jayawardene's demand for a cessation of hostilities while the Indian government declared that it would remain inactive until Jayawardene made an unconditional commitment to stand by the earlier proposals. Jayawardene's subsequent offer, to send Gamini Dissanayayake to Delhi for further discussions, was not seen as an acceptable substitute.

Developments in domestic and international politics

India next applied pressure on Sri Lanka at an international forum. A motion critical of Sri Lanka was passed on 12 March at the United Nations Human Rights Commission at Geneva. It contradicted Jayawardene's assertion after the terrorist violence of 1986 that international perceptions of the crisis had shifted, and were no longer critical of the Sri Lankan government as they had been after July 1983.

The motion was passed by consensus after Sri Lanka realized that it could not be defeated. It drew attention to reports highly critical of the Sri Lankan government, on torture and on enforced or involuntary disappearances. The government was invited to intensify cooperation with the International Committee of the Red Cross in "the field of dissemination and promotion of international humanitarian law"; and also to take up the offer of its services to "fulfill its functions of protection of humanitarian standards".

Meanwhile India had conveyed to Sri Lanka that it should provide assistance and relief on humanitarian grounds to the suffering people of Jaffna. On the very next day the Sri Lankan government announced that it would review the fuel embargo, and soon fuel was allowed into Jaffna on ration. Before that, on 14 March, Rajiv Gandhi sent yet another special envoy to Colombo, the former Minister Dinesh Singh, after Jayawardene had taken the initiative to telephone Gandhi and offer to clarify issues if an envoy were sent.

Jayawardene's initiative may have come because India was now in a position to take full advantage of the opening created for "humanitarian assistance". At first sight nothing much seemed to come from Dinesh Singh's visit except the announcement of elections to the parliamentary seats that the sixth amendment to the constitution had forced the TULF to vacate. This was soon forgotten when violence escalated. On 23 March the Tigers successfully stormed a small army camp near the Jaffna Fort, which still continued in government hands as a stronghold. The reported backlash was indiscriminate, and in various attacks that included artillery and aerial bombardment over the following week civilian targets suffered considerably. Resentment against the army was overshadowed when Kittu, commander of the Tigers in Jaffna, was critically injured and two of his associates killed in an ambush. Rival groups were held responsible, the Tigers went on a rampage and slaughtered over a hundred members of the EPRLF and TELO.

Perhaps because of such dissensions and the relative demoralization of the Tigers after Kittu's incapacitation, perhaps because the rank and file in the forces wanted to return home for the holiday period, the government declared on 10 April that it would unilaterally cease hostilities for ten days, longer if the gesture was reciprocated. The ten days covered the Sinhala and Tamil new year period and also Good Friday, a conjunction of public holidays on which business and work would stop.

The first few days of the ceasefire passed calmly. Though the Tigers expressed scepticism about it, they claimed they would not engage in hostilities if the forces remained confined to their camps. On 17 April however, Good Friday, a number of buses proceeding between the North Central Province and Trincomalee were stopped, the Tamils in the buses asked to get down, and the rest of the passengers massacred. The ceasefire was at once abrogated, and forces in the east embarked on what was described as a mopping up operation of Tigers in that area.

Then, on 21 April, a bomb in Colombo claimed over 200 lives. Prompt action by the government prevented any backlash, once again proving that the 1983 riots had been possible only because of government inaction or support. More tellingly, the reaction of at least some Sinhalese, as indicated by a march by Buddhist monks on the President's residence, was anger not against Tamils but against the government.

Offensives in Jaffna and Indian reactions

To assuage the feeling that the government was powerless against the terrorists in the days following the explosion at the bus stand, it was announced that terrorist outposts in the Jaffna peninsula were being bombed. The Indian reaction was a direct grant of cash to the Tigers from the Chief Minister of Tamil Nadu.

The significance of the move could not be ignored. Though it had long been known that the terrorist groups had offices in Tamil Nadu, and that they had training camps on Indian soil, though it was generally accepted that the Indian government and the Tamil Nadu government were aware of all this, there had previously been no open aid to the terrorists from any official source. Now the message was clear, that in preference to the Sri Lankan government it was the terrorists who were to be treated as the official representatives of the Tamil people.

This perception may have strengthened the hardliners in the Sri Lankan cabinet. Alternatively, it might have been thought that action had to be taken before the money, though in theory for humanitarian aid, was converted into arms. Whatever the reason, in the last week of May Athulathmudali flew up to the peninsula to launch his long awaited offensive. There was heavy resistance. However the Vadamarachchi section to the north east, the stronghold of the fisher community, was brought under control, as were a couple of other strategic points. Morale was high in the army which had known all along that the going would be tough and slow.

Then India intervened again. A week after the offensive had begun, the central government declared that relief had to be provided to the starving citizens of the north. This time they left no room for misinterpretation in that money was not handed over to acknowledged terrorists. Following a line delineated by the motion at Geneva, the Indian government announced that a flotilla bearing food would be sent to the Jaffna peninsula. Representatives of the Indian Red Cross would be on board, and the Sri Lankan government was advised to send representatives of the Sri Lankan Red Cross to Jaffna to receive the provisions.

Jayawardene replied that such aid was not essential, but if proffered could be accepted once modalities of distribution had been worked out. India thereupon blandly thanked Sri Lanka for accepting its offer, and the flotilla set off for Jaffna. At this point the Sri Lankan government claimed it had been misunderstood. It added that its navy would ensure that the territorial waters of the country were not violated, the flotilla was intercepted and turned back. But the next day the supplies were airlifted with an escort of fighter planes, the Sri Lankan government having been warned not to interfere. Thus claiming to have acted on humanitarian grounds, the Indian government made it clear that it reserved the right to supercede the Sri Lankan government and arrogate to itself responsibility for the situation of some Sri Lankan citizens.

In such an eventuality Sri Lanka had neither remedy nor refuge. Newspapers around the world criticized the action but hardly any government openly condemned India. The West merely regretted that relations between the two countries had deteriorated, and even Pakistan was cautious in its comments. In short, the situation that had obtained in 1983, when Sri Lanka had sought vainly for aid against a possible Indian invasion, was repeated at a more public level. It was a handy lesson, at a time when the military assistance and training extended by Pakistan and indeed others, which had contributed to the recent relative success, had once again led to a failure of perspective.

Attempts at defiance and their failure

Though the media urged defiance in the aftermath of the Indian action, the general reaction of the populace was less emotional. While the country seemed ready to acknowledge political and international realities Jayewardene and his associates were not. On the same day as the Indian airlift, terrorists massacred a number of Buddhist monks who were traveling in a bus in the Eastern Province. The next week a monk close to the government organized a demonstration outside the Indian High Commission, to protest against the airlift and the massacre of the monks. At the government parliamentary group meeting the previous day Jayawardene was reported to have exhorted his followers to be present and Harry Jayewardene joined the demonstration along with several UNP politicians.

Far from being cowed the Indians returned to the fray asserting that more relief was required. Unwilling to provoke another airlift or worse, realizing that it was useless to try to rouse public feeling against India, Jayawardene agreed to let Indian food ships dock and food to be distributed under the supervision of the Red Cross associations of the two countries. The first ship arrived before the end of June and was greeted ecstatically by the inhabitants of the Jaffna area. In one respect there was some satisfaction for the government in the demonstration that celebrated the occasion: the Tigers who tried to control the populace and take charge of the area and the distribution of supplies were swept aside.

Ironically, the Civil Servant who was sent up to oversee the unloading of the Indian ships was Lionel Fernando, the Sinhalese Government Agent who had been immensely popular in the area in the period just before 1977. He too was greeted with satisfaction, but he had arrived too late to compensate for earlier deprivation. It was India that was seen as the relieving force; and, in a development that can be seen as a culmination of what had gone before, a memorandum was submitted to India from amongst the citizens of the area, asking for direct intervention to solve the continuing problem, if necessary even with annexation.

With the Indian government an object of adulation for the people of Jaffna as the number of food ships increased, it was reported that there were military personnel too amongst the representatives of humanitarian organizations working in the area. In addition calls came, from the TULF amongst others, for humanitarian relief to be extended to other areas, specifically to the east.

Difficult as it was to resist such pressures, Jayawardene could not have done so unless he was prepared to accommodate his domestic opponents. This he was not prepared to do: the power he had accumulated at the centre was more desirable than areas at the periphery, if something had to be relinquished. In that light the sudden abandonment of the principles and policy of the preceding decade becomes understandable.

The Indians took pains to suggest that they had not initiated anything. However, while it was common knowledge that they had insisted on an advance on previous proposals, it was also apparent they had shown the way forward. On this occasion, perhaps because they knew that Jayawardene alone was liable to backtrack on any undertaking he gave, the plan was made public after a meeting of all important members of the cabinet, except Premadasa who was abroad.

The most important feature of the plan was that the north and the east should come together in one Provincial Council. In short, the single linguistic region which the Tamils had fought for and which Jayawardene had strenuously resisted, was to be created. There was a qualification in that the east would have a referendum to decide whether it wished to be joined to the north; but it was specified that this should be held not in advance but after a year of government by the Provincial Council which would have a substantial Tamil majority.

Reports from the start made clear that many senior cabinet ministers were unhappy with the proposal. In the end no decision was taken, since Ranil Wickremesinghe proposed Premadasa's views should first be ascertained. Wickremesinghe's contribution was interesting in that it might have been inspired by Jayawardene to avoid confrontation and allow the new idea to sink in but conversely, perhaps Wickremesinghe's hitherto unquestioning support for his kinsman could no longer be taken for granted.

Premadasa provided no comfort for the President when immediately afterwards he declared in Japan that the Indian attitude provided grounds for suspicion. While he professed himself unaware of recent developments, he expressed confidence that no action would be taken that would harm the "sovereign unity, independence and territorial integrity of the country".

Jayawardene's response was pre-emptive. Ignoring the cabinet consensus, he announced on 23 July to the government parliamentary group that accord had been reached and that Rajiv Gandhi would be flying to Colombo to sign the agreement. He also made it clear that, if this were not accepted by his party, he would dissolve parliament straight away and hold a general election. Naturally criticism at this point was muted. Once again refuge was sought in the suggestion that the opinion of the Prime Minister should be ascertained before any decision was taken.

Far from awaiting Premadasa's return, on the 24th Jayawardene announced that Gandhi would fly over on Wednesday the 29th to sign the agreement. On the same day an Indian helicopter came over to Sri Lanka to take Prabhakaran to India to obtain his consent. This was not immediately forthcoming, but Gandhi made it clear that he was coming over anyway. In Sri Lanka Premadasa returned and expressed his reservations and declared that he would not attend any ceremonies related to Gandhi's visit, but as far as the UNP went Jayawardene had a free hand for his Accord.

On Tuesday the 28th it was reiterated that Gandhi would be in Colombo on the following day. A demonstration against the Accord was immediately called, at the site of the bomb blast the previous April, and was attended by Mrs. Bandaranaike and other leading members of the SLFP as well as several prominent Buddhist monks. Rapidly the demonstration turned violent and, in trying to quell it, police opened fire and killed at least twenty persons and injured over a hundred.

The signing of the Indo-Sri Lanka Accord

The government promptly clamped a curfew which lasted four days. Rigorous censorship was also imposed so that the Indo-Lankan Accord was entered into in a context of absolute repression in Sri Lanka. Despite this over seventy people were shot dead in various uprisings; it is clear that such a curfew was the only context in which the Accord could have been signed. The implication was that the government had no qualms about continuing with the authoritarianism it had displayed over the previous decade, which had done so much to bring it to the present crisis. At one level therefore there was a danger that opposition to the Accord, having thus been repressed, would go underground and burst out in more dangerous forms, just as Tamil feeling had done. More significantly, the refusal to consult or deal responsibly with opposition political groups made it inevitable that common cause would be made with those who relied on other means to express their opposition.

The full text of the Accord, revealed only after it had been signed, indicated that in order to win peace Jayawardene had gone far down the road he had tried to avoid. It had already been let slip the previous week that the President would have discretion to postpone the referendum whereby the east could break free from the north if the union proved unsatisfactory. Apart from this and an agreement to appoint an interim administration for the area (which would allow immediate power to the terrorist groups), there was also an appendix to the Accord that, in dealing with Indo-Lankan relations as apart from the internal conflict, made clear that Sri Lanka had formally accepted Indian suzerainty over the region.

In this appendix, which took the form of an exchange of letters of intent, Jayawardene agreed to "reach an early understanding about the relevance and employment of foreign military and intelligence personnel", that "Trincomalee or other ports in Sri Lanka will not be available for military use by any country in a manner prejudicial to India's interests", that "the work of restoring and operating the Trincomalee oil tank farm will be undertaken as a joint venture between India and Sri Lanka" and that "Sri Lanka's agreements with foreign broadcasting organizations will be reviewed to ensure that any facilities set up by them in Sri Lanka are used solely as public broadcasting facilities and not for any military or intelligence purposes".

Perhaps there had been little gain to the country from Jayawardene's manoeuvres over the past few years and the letters of intent did no more than enunciate what should have from the start been accepted as a cornerstone of any realistic foreign policy for a small country situated so helplessly at the tip of India. Yet that this should have been set down in writing was indeed a triumph for Gandhi.

At the guard of honour before he left a soldier attempted to attack Gandhi with his rifle butt but the blow was mistimed and he escaped unscathed. The soldier was handed over to the Indians for questioning. That pathetic action seemed a suitable symbol for the efforts of Jayawardene's government to flex its muscles over the last few years.

Part V

Changing the Guard

Premadasa's Emergence (1987–1989)

Chapter 9

The Accord in Action

Political consequences of the Accord

Immediately after the signing of the Accord over 6000 Indian troops arrived in Sri Lanka, a number that grew tenfold by the end of the year. The reason was ostensibly to ensure the surrender of arms by the terrorists. However, as the presence of a couple of Indian frigates anchored off the coast of Colombo for a few days after the Accord indicated, it was felt that Indian forces would also provide security in case demonstrations against the Accord turned dangerous. Indeed some saw their presence in the north as a safeguard against disaffection over the Accord among Sri Lankan forces. Later, since such disaffection did not prove dangerous, the gradual takeover of security responsibilities in Tamil areas by the Indians released Sri Lankan forces to be deployed elsewhere. For the moment the greater threat to the Accord seemed to come from the south. In the north, after holding out for a few more days, Prabhakaran came back from India and, though claiming that it was only the method of struggle for the cherished separate state of Eelam that had changed and not the goal itself, he ordered his followers to turn in their arms.

The proliferation of Indian troops indicated the reversal of Athulathmudali's approach, and he did not attended the signing of the Accord nor the reception for Gandhi though he slipped into the official dinner for which only a few ministers had been invited. Premadasa meanwhile kept away from all official functions. His strategy was to claim that he had been right all along in asserting that there was no point in seeking a political solution until the terrorists had laid down their arms, and until India stopped assisting them. He also indicated that the Accord itself was only a letter of intent, and it was open to anyone to challenge the proposed legislation in the Supreme Court.

The differences within the UNP about the Accord found their parallel in the opposition on a larger scale as many different parties were involved. The SLFP opposed the Accord, as did in their different ways the JVP, the MEP, Amaratunga's recently formed Liberal Party and the United People's Party (ELJP), which had been set up recently by Rukman Senanayake and some others who had finally broken with the UNP. On the other hand the Accord was welcomed by the Tamil parties and the SLMC (albeit with grave reservations), and also by the old left parties as well as the SLMP. A consequence of the attitude adopted by these last was that they suspended their call for a general election. Enthusiastic for a settlement of the racial question, and believing that it required time to be accepted, they were willing to put up further with the regime whose legitimacy they had recently questioned. This was also the attitude of some human rights groups that had earlier been highly critical of the government's increasing authoritarianism. Delighted that the devolution they had long advocated was at last to come about, they ignored the high handed and dangerous manner in which this had been achieved.

Ignored too was the cynical joining up of the Northern and Eastern Provinces. Jayawardene's constant assertion had been that the people of the east did not want to be joined to the north. He continued to assert this after the Accord had been signed, and to declare that the merger would be rejected at the referendum that was supposed to be held within a year. This made it obvious that he had consented to the twinning under compulsion. Worrying therefore was the clause in the Accord that provided for the President postponing the referendum at his discretion. The way was in effect left open to preclude self determination if sufficient pressure was exerted.

Meanwhile, though in Colombo and most areas where the war had been fought the Accord was welcomed, elsewhere the government was in difficulties. Soon after the Accord was signed a government MP from the Southern Province was shot dead by a mob that stopped his vehicle as he was heading back home. State property and the property of government politicians was attacked, including Jayawardene's holiday retreat on the coast a hundred miles south of Colombo. Rampant threats introduced some uncertainty as to whether Parliament would pass the legislation required by the Accord.

The growth of violence as a reaction

In the middle of August a couple of grenades were flung into a meeting in Parliament of the government parliamentary group chaired by the President. Only one District Minister and an official were killed but amongst the injured were Premadasa and Athulathmudali. It was coincidence that those most prominently against the Accord were injured, but all sorts of plots were suspected and Dissanayake thought it necessary to explain publicly why he had been late for the meeting.

Over the next three months there was no single incident of similar importance but rather an exponential growth in disregard for the authority of the state. This was most obvious in the Southern Province where the JVP had always been strong, but it steadily spread to other Sinhalese areas. The most startling form this took, on the pattern earlier of terrorist activity in the north, was the carefully targeted shooting of members of the ruling party. No one of political significance was killed but over the next few months on average one minor UNP functionary was killed somewhere in the country every day. The danger became so intense that before long, in the most affected areas, a number of party officials resigned.

The JVP did not take responsibility for many of the actions and stratagems that were generally associated with it in the public eye during this period. Instead there sprang into prominence an organization known as the Patriotic Front for the Motherland (DJV), which was unashamedly chauvinistic in its approach, but rapidly managed after July 1987 to command considerable support, in part because other political outlets for opposition to the Accord had been precluded. Predictably, as the violence worsened, the government's response was to set up what were termed Green Tigers, private militia units under the control of government members of parliament or other UNP worthies, provided with arms and otherwise supported by the state.

Renewed tensions in the north

In the north and the east all seemed peaceful at first, given the relief the population felt at the cessation of hostilities. Under the surface however violence and resentment were brewing. These found most obvious expression with regard to the east, the final decision as to the joining of which to the north was to be the subject of a long delayed referendum. Both sides began promptly to treat the whole business as a race in which it was important to be first off the ground.

The most vital area for action in this regard was the District of Trincomalee, not only because of its strategic value, but also because it had a relatively high proportion of Sinhalese compared both with the Northern Province and the Batticaloa District that lay just south of it. As soon as the ceasefire was in operation the government turned its attention to the colonization schemes that had been set up in the area. The argument was that Sinhalese who had been dnven away by terrorist action had to be restored to their homes, but there were suspicions that new settlers were being brought in.

Correspondingly the terrorists, on the argument that previous colonization had already upset the original demographic balance of the area, began to exert pressure, often violent and sometimes brutal, to drive the Sinhalese away. Unfortunately the brigade of the so-called Indian Peace Keeping Force (IPKF) that was stationed in Trincomalee was predominantly Tamil, and its members seemed naturally to sympathize with the Tamils against the Sinhalese. In addition the Sri Lankan security forces that still remained in the area were resentful of the Indian presence. Reports were rife of clashes between the police and the IPKF, and tensions came to a head in late September when a Sinhalese monk, who had been agitating against terrorist action and what he alleged was Indian support for it, was shot dead in the course of a demonstration, almost certainly by Indian fire.

The Indian authorities proved conciliatory and a crisis was avoided; but perhaps only because more critical developments elsewhere led to turmoil on a wider scale. Soon after the Accord there emerged yet another Tamil militant grouping that was an amalgamation of some members of groups that had opposed the Tigers. This had clearly been set up by the Indians. The Tigers on the other hand were still wary about the Accord, and now they felt that India had set up a rival group to inherit the region that had only come into being because of the protracted struggle waged by them. They reacted violently, and throughout August and September reports multiplied of internecine warfare, mainly between the Tigers and one or more of the other groups.

In Colombo predictably there were those who rejoiced at the idea that Jayawardene's skill at manoeuvre now kept Sinhalese soldiers safe, while the terrorists proved to their former Indian paymasters how violent and irresponsible they were. What was ignored until the Indians were compelled to take account of it was how effectively the Tigers dominated the region. This did not apply to the Sinhalese and to most Muslims, but the ordinary Tamil population seemed to favour the Tigers.

The success of moral pressure by the Tigers

Despite this, with so many interests ranged against them, a gradual but long war of attrition might have worn them out, had not the Tigers launched yet another initiative that was one of the most remarkable during the whole decade of crisis. In September Thileepan, the head of their political wing, announced that he would carry on a death fast until various demands that the LTTE felt were due under the Accord were granted. In addition to the unconditional release of all political prisoners and a stop to colonization, the Tigers demanded that rehabilitation work be stopped until the interim administration for the north and east that had been pledged under the Accord was established before elections to the Provincial Council. Their understanding was that they would be allowed control in such an administration, and they wanted their authority in the region to be formally established before lengthy delays allowed others to usurp it.

For the Tigers delay in setting up the interim administration went against the provisions of the Accord they had been dragooned into accepting. Equally the government claimed that the establishment of such an administration was subject to the surrender of arms by the terrorists and this the Tigers had not done. The Indians should have ensured the surrender of arms within a few days of the Accord but, though the number of their troops in the area had been increasing, they had not succeeded in this.

All this might only have seethed under the surface but Thileepan's fast changed all that. It was a classic case (as an American diplomat put it, in exulting over the difficulties the Indians had to face in their attempts to establish themselves as the new regional superpower) of Gandhian methods being used against the country Gandhi had created. Dixit tried to arrange a compromise but Thileepan remained adamant. He slid into a coma, and Dixit had to give in. Alongside the news of Thileepan's death, even the government newspapers making clear that the decision had been made by Dixit and the Tigers without reference to the Sri Lankan government, it was reported that the Tigers had got practically everything they wanted. An interim administrative council was to be established straight away in which they would have seven of the twelve places, including that of the Chief Executive. All Prabhakaran had to agree to in return, and that only before the Indians rather than any Sri Lankan representatives, was that he accepted the unitary nature of the Sri Lankan state.

That seemed a small price to pay for control of the entire north and east, and in Colombo initially there was despair. Such despair however took no account of the room still left for manoeuvre. When the list of appointments to the administrative council was made public, it was found that all seven of the LTTE nominees were from the north. This roused resentment in the east, not only amongst the Sinhalese and the Muslims who were in any case unhappy about these developments, but also amongst the Tamils, since the appointments seemed to indicate the determination of the Tigers that the north should dominate the merged region. What had not been made clear was that the Tigers had submitted through Dixit a list of twelve names, at the head of which had been three persons from the east, including their preferred candidate for the post of Chief Executive. It was Jayawardene who, as he was entitled to do in terms of the agreement Dixit had made with the Tigers, had chosen all seven representatives from the north.

The breakdown of relations and the Indian attack on Jaffina

At this time of heavy tension a boat heading towards the east coast of the country was intercepted by the Sri Lankan navy. In it were thirteen Tigers transporting weapons. The government announced its intention of bringing them to Colombo for interrogation. The Tigers declared that under no

The Accord in Action

circumstances would they agree to being taken to the capital, and appealed to the Indians to prevent this. The Indians advised against the transfer but did not insist, and the Sri Lankan government had its way.

Prior to being flown to Colombo the arrested Tigers were permitted visitors. The cyanide capsules that Tigers usually carried, but which had not been found on them at the time of their apprehension, must have been conveyed at this point for, on the tarmac, before they could be put on the plane, they all swallowed cyanide. Eleven died straight away.

Whether what followed was due to rage or bitter distrust or simply incapacity to control cadres that had fought so long for Eelam and resented any compromise may never be known. Eight servicemen who had been in the custody of the Tigers for several months were cut up into little pieces. The same was done to two Sinhalese officials of the Cement Corporation who were on duty at their factory in the north, where their relations with the local labour force had been excellent. Four Sinhalese members of a state television crew were killed while they were traveling to drop a Tamil colleague home. In the east, two Sinhalese villages were attacked and over two hundred men, women and children slaughtered.

May be the Tigers hoped for a backlash elsewhere that would have made partition inevitable. The response however was muted, with the only intense reaction coming from opposition parties opposed to the Accord, who demanded that the IPKF should be told to withdraw since it had manifestly failed to fulfill its function. This strengthened the hand of the government in asserting to the Indians that they had no option now but to act. Jayawardene indeed issued an order to this effect, and displayed it on television, to make it apparent to the nation that the Indian army was under his control.

Insistence had not been necessary. Not only in terms of their obligations under the Accord, and correspondingly in terms of world opinion, but also in their own interests, the Indians clearly had to take on the Tigers. Reinforcements poured in, increasing exponentially over the next couple of months, as it became clear the task was not an easy one. On the 10 October the march on Jaffna began, as a prelude to the eradication of the Tigers, or rather of their independent ambitions in the region.

Newspaper accounts of what happened indicated that, while the Tigers proved a formidable enemy, civilians suffered immensely from the Indian offensive. The slow retreat of the Tigers contributed to this, though it also made them unpopular, as reported by Qadri Ismail, a journalist generally considered objective – 'Initially, the tigers received widespread popular support as a result of their actions and the counter-actions of the IPKF. In the non-war zones, this remained high. As the conflict wore on, however, it abated somewhat in the battle areas. Once it became clear that the LTTE were retreating, people could not understand why this was not done fast enough so that they could get back on the path to normalcy… .

The Tigers cleverly manipulated public opinion with stories of Indian atrocities. Actually, they didn't have to. The fact that the IPKF was attacking the Tamils and civilians undergoing harsh suffering was enough. But the Tigers spiced things up anyway. The best instance of this was with regard to the events in Jaffina hospital, where the story went that the IPKF massacred 60 patients and staff and raped the nurses. The first survivor to come out, the young son of an ambulance driver who could not have understood the meaning of the word, said the nurses had been raped. Upon close questioning, he said he had been asked to say so and a different story emerged - from him and others.

It was the LTTE that provoked the incident by occupying the back wing of the hospital. They didn't listen to the doctors who pleaded with them. The staff assembled in a two story building, fearing shelling. Then, the LTTE fired upon the advancing Indians who entered the hospital with guns blazing. Most of the deaths occurred in this crossfire, though later the Indians killed some of the wounded who were groaning and, according to one account, also shot all the young men who were warded in the hospital. Clearly, both the IPKF and the LTTE did not care how many civilians lost their lives during the confict.'

The Indian army displayed rigour that was typical of any army dealing with a ruthless enemy in territory to which it has no allegiance. Certainly the vigour of the Tiger resistance forced the Indians to be implacable: placing Iandmines that took a great many Indian lives before they learned caution, and the massacre of troops caught out of line (a detachment of

Gurkhas was dropped in the wrong place behind enemy positions and promptly massacred) and the willful use of civilians as shields. But apart from this understandable rigour, there was a total absence of accountability. The war was distant from the people whose reactions were relevant to the army, and the Indian press, that exulted in detailing the misdeeds of Sri Lankan soldiers, was blind to the peccadilloes of the Indian army.

Other developments in the Tamil areas

Yet at the end of the year the struggle was still not over. Though it was claimed that over a thousand Tigers had been killed, the general impression was that casualties amongst combatants amounted to only a fifth of that figure. Correspondingly Indian casualties were acknowledged as at least a couple of hundred, with many more wounded. Of course, given the relative numbers involved, there was no doubt that this was a war the Indians could not lose. That it was causing them concern however was apparent from the fact that from the middle of November there was talk of further negotiations. These were sponsored to a great extent by RAW which had not been entirely supportive of the Indian strategy which it thought too indulgent to the Sri Lankan government. Unofficial contacts led to a ceasefire, but with the Tigers adamant the struggle continued. By the end of December Jaffna and the area around it seemed to have been taken, but there was no question of any settlement.

Despite the limited area of the Jaffna peninsula hostilities had continued openly for long; it was only to be expected that elsewhere the Indians found it more difficult to establish ascendancy. This was certainly true of the east where they also had other problems because of the ethnic mix. For instance a report of a massacre by Indian troops of several persons in a mosque prompted an immediate outcry in Colombo that, given their conditioning, all Muslims were enemies to Indian soldiers and to be eliminated. Soon afterwards the Indians appointed a Muslim commander to the region

Conversely, in an area where the Tigers had been more active, there was a report in the *Sunday Times* of Indians sorting out Tamils from Muslims and killing the former indiscriminately. With reports towards the end of December of some Sri Lankan forces too getting in on the act with the support of Indians, there was a renewed crisis in public confidence in the forces of authority imposed on the area.

As the reports mentioned above suggest, relations between the Sri Lankan and the Indian authorities continued satisfactory through this period. Certainly the brutality of the assault on Jaffna had made it impossible for opponents of the Accord to claim that India supported the Tamils in their struggle for Eelam, though that did not preclude continuing charges of hegemonism. Again, though the Indian press at one stage declared that an interim administration for the north and east was once more to be set up as required by the Tamils, the Sri Lankan government was confidently able to deny this, and state that no further steps would be taken in this direction until elections to the Provincial Council had been held.

The passing of the Provincial Councils legislation

The required amendment to the constitution was passed in the last week of November. A majority of the Supreme Court had ruled that no referendum was required and very slight changes would allow the proposed legislation to be carried with just a two-thirds majority in parliament. The changes were made and both the required amendment, the thirteenth to the constitution in less than ten years, and the Provincial Councils Bill itself, were carried in parliament with the required majorities.

The legal process gone through on this occasion led to more bizarre conduct on Jayawardene's part regarding the Supreme Court. A couple of years earlier, the then Chief Justice had been hauled before a parliamentary committee to answer charges of making improper remarks concerning the government at a public function. His replacement, the next most senior justice at the time, a Tamil, had been the chairman of the Special Presidential Commission that had found Mrs. Bandaranaike guilty. His tenure of office, which lasted till early 1988, had been quite satisfactory for the government, and after his retirement he was appointed governor of the Western Province under the new Provincial Councils Act. The next judge in line of seniority was Justice Wanasundera, who had been one of those who thought the Provincial Councils legislation required a referendum. His determination had gone in detail into questions of history and ethnicity which the President characterized as tosh a few weeks later.

The Accord in Action

To make matters worse, when the post of Chief Justice was about to become vacant a few months later, he summoned Justice Wanasundera and told him that he was prepared to appoint him if he would leave his resignation in the President's hands to activate when required. The tactics that had worked with UNP parliamentarians proved inappropriate on this occasion, and Justice Wanasundera made clear his contempt for the offer by walking out. Another judge who had worked formerly in Harry Jayawardene's chambers was appointed instead, which led to protests from the Bar Association and others since never had a junior judge previously been elevated over the most senior.

To return to the Provincial Councils legislation, almost all government MPs voted for the acts. Premadasa was out of the country when the bills were introduced and, though they had originally been gazetted in his name, those gazettes were withdrawn and a revised version appeared with the bills in the name of the acting leader of the house. Premadasa however came back in time to vote, and made much of the fact that the measures had been examined and passed by the Supreme Court.

The only actual vote against the measures from the government ranks was that of Cyril Mathew, against whom no disciplinary action was taken, since he already had a court action in train challenging his suspension from the UNP. The Communist member of parliament voted for the measures, while the SLFP voted against the constitutional amendment. It did not vote at all on the bill that established the Councils, having together with the MEP member staged a walkout to protest against the manner it was rushed through. The government suggested that this was a convenient way of dodging the issue, perhaps a reasonable charge, in that subsequent pronouncements from Mrs. Bandaranaike as well as the party suggested that it was not Provincial Councils that they were against, but only the merger of the north and the east.

There were hardly any major instances of violence in the country at the time the measures were carried from Sinhalese chauvinist groups, contrary to earlier expectations. The only substantial incident, a bomb blast in a business area that claimed thirty lives, was the work of Tamil extremists. As far as the JVP and its supportive organizations were concerned, while there were a number of minor incidents, nothing dramatic occurred.

At the same time the equally serious if less obviously noticeable incidents mentioned earlier, namely the steady killing of UNP functionaries, continued. In December the range of that sort of activity expanded, with the daylight shootings in Colombo first of the police officer responsible for investigating the JVP, and then three weeks later of the Chairman of the UNP. This was Panditharatne's successor, a purely functional General Secretary of the party, whose main claim to distinction was his total devotion to his President and his party.

Chapter 10

The Façade Cracks

The assassination of Vijaya Kumaranatunga

In this context of increasing violence, on 16 February 1988 Vijaya Kumaranatunga was assassinated. The JVP, functioning through the DJV, was widely believed responsible. Kumaranatunga was the lynchpin of the alliance between his own SLMP and the old left. They had welcomed the Indo-Lankan Accord and had just the week before been recognized by the Elections Commissioner under the title of the United Socialist Alliance (to be known, ironically, as the USA). The new party had made clear its intention of putting forward candidates for the elections to Provincial Councils that were now thought to be imminent.

Such a stance was bound to weaken the position opposition parties had jointly adopted earlier, of agitating for a general election as a prerequisite for the restoration of normalcy. But the USA could not refrain from contesting the Provincial Council elections since they had welcomed the Accord as a just solution that could, through substantial devolution, satisfy the grievances of Tamils.

Had the USA meant only the parties of the old left it would not have been so significant as they had little public support. The charismatic matinee idol Kumaranatunga however, married to Chandrika Bandaranaike who was held to embody the radical tradition of that family, would clearly provide a source of electoral strength. The following week the USA was due to sign a joint programme which might have been seen as filling the gap caused by the drift of the SLFP to the right. It was likely that under Kumaranatunga's leadership the USA would inspire a strong following in the Provincial Council elections. Since that would suggest wider popular support for the Accord than its opponents alleged, it could be argued that

Kumaranatunga's approach helped the government by easing the pressures on it.

Apart from this there was no love lost between the JVP and the old left. In aligning himself so forcefully with the latter, Kumaranatunga too had become a target for recrimination, while he himself had not been slow to condemn what he saw as regressive chauvinistic attitudes. So he fell victim to the climate of escalating violence that throughout his brief political career he had striven to defuse; that those responsible for his assassination should have seen him as a tool of government was doubly ironic, given the manner in which he had been imprisoned and ill-treated during the referendum, the event that exemplified most brazenly the government's authoritarianism. At that time, when the JVP on the one hand and Mrs. Bandaranaike on the other were both permitted, albeit under repressive conditions, to campaign against the referendum, Kumaranatunga, who was considered the most potent threat to the government, was held in custody.

Nominations for the Southern Provincial Councils

On the day after Kumaranatunga's death nominations were called for elections to seven Provincial Councils, excluding the joint one for the north and east. The USA, in spite of the trauma it had suffered by the death of its leader, decided to contest. The only other parties to contest were two that had also received recognition just the previous week: the Muslim Congress (SLMC), in nine districts in four provinces, and the Liberal Party (LP), in the three districts of the Western Province only. The latter, long having advocated devolution even though it objected to the manner in which it had been brought about, was fortunate in that the postponement of nominations for three provinces to mid-April enabled it to cobble a list together, although it had as yet no organization to speak of.

The former had come a long way since the time it had been patronized by Athulathmudali as a counterweight to Tamil claims in the east. The SLMC had distanced itself from the government as one aspect of the Accord could be interpreted as a handing over of the Muslims of the east to a regional administration dominated by the Tamils of the north. In addition, reports of harassment of Muslims in the area by Tamil militant groups, which the Indian forces were unable or unwilling to prevent, reached a high point in April; the SLMC's assertion of the need for an independent Muslim voice increased support for it at all levels of the community. It polled very satisfactorily at the elections, almost exclusively from the Muslim community, making it apparent that the government would have to be wary for the future about a section of the population that had hitherto been thought supporters of the UNP.

The SLFP decision to boycott and its consequences

No other opposition party contested these elections. Most significant was the decision of the SLFP to boycott, given its opposition to the 13th amendment. However there were those within the leadership who were in two minds about contesting, given that, with the SLFP not contesting, anti-government votes would go to the USA, and enable it to present itself in the future as a viable alternative to the two major parties.

The disastrous consequence of the SLFP stance only became apparent later. For the moment both the UNP and USA derived considerable benefit from it, but for the SLFP there was consolation in the aggression against their nominees and their supporters. This was initiated by the DJV, that took up the position that supporting the Accord by contesting the elections was treachery to the nation and deserved capital punishment. Some SLFP supporters seemed to approve of this approach. Certainly the violent activities of the DJV began from this point on to take on epidemic proportions, indicating a considerable increase in grass roots support. What the SLFP hierarchy did not appreciate was that such tendencies would be difficult to check when it re-entered the democratic process. Conversely, the success of an alternative approach was evident when in one constituency in the Western Province where the SLFP party organization supported Liberal Party candidates, they came within striking distance of the UNP, and polled better than the USA.

The conduct of the Elections and the results

This particular result served to confirm the view that the otherwise creditable performance of the USA owed much to the absence of other major opposition parties from the poll. But that performance was in itself remarkable. The USA had been plunged into disarray by Kumaranatunga's death and his widow Chandrika, made leader in his stead, went abroad for security reasons before the poll. Apart from that, the USA had far fewer resources in terms of men, money and materials than the government. It campaigned like the UNP under threat from the DJV, with less protection, and more USA candidates were killed or injured in the course of the campaign than UNP ones. Given this, and the particularly ruthless individuals Jayawardene had selected to lead the campaign, as candidates for Chief Minister of the first four provinces contested, it was astonishing that in many districts the USA ran the UNP very close, and in several constituencies commanded a majority.

The government adopted very different tactics for the elections that remained. Though there were allegations of malpractice in the first round, by and large distortion was limited. In the case of the election to the Western and Central Provinces, held on 2 June, things were very different. As in the case of the referendum, no holds were barred to achieve a victory.

On the day before the election there began a concerted campaign of intimidation. Shops were asked to shut, ostensibly by the JVP, but in fact notices to this effect were distributed in the presence of the armed forces; police vehicles careered through the city asking citizens not to panic, which of course led to offices closing early; the Minister of State appeared on television exhorting people to vote even at the risk of their lives, which suggested to many that they should wait and see what the situation was like before venturing out to vote, if at all; and the next morning the *Daily News* led with a graphic account of mass violence in the environs of the city, though in fact little of note had occurred.

The consequence was that polling in Colombo was extremely low on the morning of 2 June. By noon UNP candidates moved in with masses of thugs, extracted ballot papers from polling officials, threatening them with knives or guns, and stuffed the ballot boxes. Citizens who turned up to vote in the afternoon found at several polling stations that their names had been ticked off already. In some cases presiding officers wrote detailed complaints in their record books but the Elections Commissioner was unable to pursue these without authority. He claimed the investigation into problems in the previous round of elections had been stifled on instructions from the Presidential Secretariat. The most revealing comment was made by a police constable alone on guard duty at a polling station: in explaining his failure to hold back the mob brought to cast quantities of votes by the UNP candidate for the area, he said that they would have shot him and claimed that it had been done by the JVP.

Yet in the Western Province the UNP obtained only 52 seats while the combined opposition won 50. Given that this happened on a poll of less than 60 per cent, the implication was that, if a general election were held shortly and the SLFP participated, the government was likely to lose its absolute majority.

Although it had control of the administrations of the six provinces where elections had been held, there was little reason for the government to be sanguine. The elections to the Southern Provincial Council, which were held on 9 June, put the lid on the situation. In this instance, capitalizing on the disruption the government had contributed to the preceding week, the JVP was able to show its strength. The ease with which authority had appeared to collapse on 2 June allowed it to step up its campaign. The consequent increase in the number of assassinations, not only of UNP or USA candidates, but also of families and supporters, suggested that the threats that accompanied the call for a boycott might well be implemented. Despite attempts to repeat the illegalities of the previous week, polling in the south as a whole was only thirty per cent, and in the Hambantota District less than seven.

Deliberations within the UNP about Electoral Strategy

The suggestion that had gained currency earlier in the year, that immediately after the Provincial Council elections and prior to the Presidential election due in December Jayawardene would spring a general election, died away. In fact one was not necessary until the following July. The argument for an early general election was that a victory for the UNP, however slim, was bound to enhance its chances for the Presidency. This was considered essential at this stage, because Jayawardene seemed to want to be nominated again as the UNP candidate. Constitutionally no president could run for a third term, but the argument was that Jayawardene's first term did not count as he had not been elected, but simply elevated from the post of Prime Minister.

Premadasa could not be denied the nomination by anyone except Jayawardene himself. Premadasa's assertion that he would only accept the UNP nomination if it were unanimous served to make it quite clear that no one else could hope for the nomination: Premadasa, seeking the nomination himself, obviously would not support them, which would make clear the paucity of general support for anyone other than himself. But Jayewardene had no desire to give up the reins to Premadasa. Though it was possible that as the months passed his unpopularity would reach such a low ebb that he would be forced to yield, he was not likely to go willingly since Premadasa was quite likely to disown his predecessor once he had come to power. For the sake of continuity alone therefore, it was necessary for Jayawardene to carry on. This seemed to be the view of the party hierarchy when its new Chairman-cum-General Secretary Ranjan Wijeratne declared that it was desirable that Jayawardene be nominated again. Wijeratne, a party loyalist turned administrator, distinguished as much for ruthlessness as for honesty, wielded significant influence since he had been prepared to take on the post of General Secretary when no one else would, after the assassination of the previous Chairman in December and the General Secretary in the middle of the year.

The decision as to the candidate for the presidential election still lay in the future, since an early election was not possible in a president's second term. At the time of Provincial Council elections, in June 1988, room for manoeuver lay only with regard to the parliamentary election. After the results were declared however it was clear that the popularity of the UNP was low, so there was no likelihood of further elections in the south until after the Presidential election due in December.

In the north and east meanwhile, far from the Indians having brought things under control, the situation had become even more confused. There was talk at intervals of an agreement with the Tigers, but it was apparent by July that that was not likely. Instead the Indians had embarked upon what seemed yet another forceful military effort, though clearly no final military solution was likely, either because the Tigers were too solidly entrenched in their strongholds or because at the end of the day the Indians were unwilling to be too brutal.

On the political front the Tamil militant group now thought to be closest to India, the EPRLF, had been officially recognized in February, so it could contest the PC elections when they were held. However it became evident that any group that contested them would be running a grave risk. The TULF made it clear that it had doubts about coming forward, and there was no assurance that the EPRLF might not feel the same way.

The government position was that conditions in the Northern and Eastern Provinces made it impossible to conduct elections there. For a long time this position went unchallenged; those opposed to the Accord did not want elections anyway, while those in its favour felt that they should not rock the boat and embarrass the government. Around August however many of those concerned realized that Jayawardene was taking advantage of the situation for his own ends.

The tremendous success of the hartal that was called by the DJV on 29-30 July to commemorate the anniversary of the signing of the Accord was telling. Shops were shut, workplaces deserted, private bus operators failed to function, and in general the country came to a halt. In the Southern Province the government bowed to the inevitable and declared a curfew, but elsewhere it made a desperate attempt to keep things going, only to find that the people observed their own curfew. The government's failure seemed a sure sign of things to come; but when it began to talk of its desire to hold elections were it not for the terrorism, suspicions rose that Jayewardene would once again take advantage of the situation to stay in power without any election at all.

Soon afterwards, Dixit let slip in discussion his rising suspicion that Jayawardene was manipulating the situation in the north and east to put off submitting himself to the democratic process in the rest of the country. He may have been provoked by a sanctimonious remark that it was unfair on the citizenry of the north and east for anyone else to ask for elections when it was impossible to hold them there. A further indication of the way the wind was blowing may have come to Dixit when the government press headlined Gamini Dissanayake's statement that the Indians had failed to fulfill their obligations in the north and east. The implication was that it was this failure that hindered the implementation of the democratic process. Perhaps it was only at this stage that India fully appreciated the implications of the clause that Jayawardene had inserted into the Provincial Councils Act that precluded the President from proclaiming the merger of the Northern and Eastern Provinces unless he were satisfied that all arms had been surrendered.

Pressures towards Elections

India decided that it had to be firm. Continuous military activity allowed for consolidation to an extent that enabled it, by the end of August, to inform the Sri Lankan government officially that conditions were such that an election could be held. Soon afterwards an amendment to the PC Act was gazetted under emergency regulations, allowing the President to proclaim the merger if he were satisfied that "operations have been commenced to secure the complete surrender of arms". Jayawardene had no further excuse for putting off the election unless he were willing to defy the Indians openly. That, they knew, he would be unwilling to do.

In such a climate of widespread political dissatisfaction it was announced, in early September, that Wijedasa Liyanarachchi, a lawyer from the south who had been active in defence of those arrested as JVP suspects, had been arrested. When *habeas corpus* was filed, he was reported to have been brought to Colombo from the Police Station in the south where he had been interrogated. On the day before he was to be produced in court he was pronounced dead.

Government papers stressed that he was a ranking member of the JVP politbureau and had been amongst those responsible for ordering a number of political assassinations. This however did not make up for the fact, revealed at the inquest, that he had suffered over a hundred injuries, internal and external, in the course of interrogation. The general sense of indignation found expression through another hartal suddenly called for 12 September. The almost total collapse of all services, including the closure of even the commercial sector of Colombo, made clear to the government and to its most determined supporters that public feeling against it was mounting.

It was in such a context that there occurred Premadasa's great coup that prompted the definitive closing of ranks in the UNP against its leader who had brought the party so much power but also such unparalleled disrepute. For some weeks before there were rumours that Jayawardene's birthday, the 17 September, had also been declared by the JVP as a day of mourning, when everyone should stay at home. But the 17th was a Saturday, when government institutions did not function anyway, so a hartal made little sense. Later the JVP was to declare that it was not interested in mocking individuals; on the 17th itself, in at least one area it publicly accused the government MP of being the force behind the hartal.

After September 12th the rumour spread round the country that the 16th as well as the 17th were to be days of mourning, and people should eat only dried fish and pumpkin with their rice, the traditional food at funerals. The government issued a number of stringent emergency regulations that included giving the forces the right to break open shops that remained closed. Though all was not normal on the 16th it was certainly nothing like the almost total shutdown that had occurred four days earlier.

The point however had been made. The exercise cannot be attributed entirely to Premadasa. Perhaps there were elements in the government that had, as the JVP hierarchy thought at first, evolved this scheme for reducing the popular appeal of the JVP and diminishing the impact of the tactics they had hitherto used with such success. Certainly there must have been elements within the JVP as well as the SLFP which relished the opportunity of making a personal point against the President. The proliferation of the rumour however had much in common with what had happened on 1 June, when the dirty tricks department of the UNP had come to the fore. On this later occasion it was made clear, not least to Colombo's business community and to foreign donors, who had seen how effectively the economy could be paralysed, that a change was required. Jayawardene had to go. Since it had been made clear by Premadasa that no one else could stake what would amount to a controversial claim ahead of him, there was no option but that he take over.

On 16 September, while Colombo wondered whether a hartal were taking place or not, Jayawardene announced to a meeting of the UNP parliamentary group that a Presidential election would be held, on 19 December. The date for nominations would be 10 November, and Premadasa would be the UNP candidate. His name was proposed by Jayawardene, and seconded jointly by Athulathmudali and Dissanayake. The UNP as a whole rallied round, even Ranjan Wijeratne. It was obvious that everything had to be put into the campaign if the party were to stay in power; despite the onerous nature of this challenge, for the UNP as much as for the country, Jayawardene's announcement came as a relief. At last the claustrophobic atmosphere that had enveloped the country could be dissipated.

Chapter 11

The Last Hurrah

The Democratic People's Alliance of Opposition Parties

Mrs. Bandaranaike was Premadasa's chief opponent. Finally nominated by the SLFP under its own symbol, she ran as the common candidate of five parties which had come together under the title of the Democratic People's Alliance (DPA) on a manifesto prepared by them and three others, including the JVP and the SLMC.

The grouping had begun in February through an initiative of the MEP, led now by Dinesh Gunawardena, who had entered parliament in the by-elections of 1983, after an electoral alliance with the SLFP. It was thought he owed his victory to the refusal of his UNP opponent to allow the fraud and thuggery rampant elsewhere; that opponent was now the Secretary of the ELJP, set up by Rukman Senanayake.

Gunawardena had called together leaders of opposition political parties to take a stand on the violations of human rights and the disappearances of persons in the south, following the government's offensive against terrorism there. The same strategy that had led to disaster in the north was being applied, with similar results in terms of increasing militancy. Whereas the Tamil Liberation groups had a well established information network that kept the issue alive internationally, abuses in the south received little publicity, and only roused indignation when they were as gross as in the case of Liyanarachchi.

The parties that came together on Gunawardena's initiative could do little except issue statements, but they decided to meet regularly to discuss issues of common interest. The constituent parties of the USA had initially declined to attend, but all other interests were represented. Those representing Tamil interests, the TC and the DWC, commanded minimal support amongst Sri Lankan and Indian Tamils respectively, but it was significant that they were engaged in ongoing dialogue with parties seen as primarily Sinhalese in inspiration, such as the MEP, the ELJP and even the SLFP. This last dominated the group in terms of size, but was constrained by the need to accept a consensual approach to broaden its racial appeal. Apart from these the SLMC was bound to be an important factor, as became clearer with the results of the PC elections; and the LP, though tiny, was the only one that from the start possessed a coherent programme, and so exercised a disproportionate influence, also because it functioned as secretary to the group and performed an important task in keeping the initiative alive.

Among subjects discussed was a common approach to elections; a common candidate for the Presidency became an urgency towards the latter part of the year. It was generally accepted that Mrs. Bandaranaike's candidacy was to be supported, but some parties were keen that shared policies should be formulated, while others were more concerned that she contest under a common symbol as distinct from that of the SLFP. This last was also the position of the JVP which sent a representative to the group towards the end of September.

Shortly afterwards, Mrs. Bandaranaike announced that she was willing to contest under a common symbol. Though recent legislation made it possible for the Elections Commissioner to recognize new parties at any time (thus making it. possible to attract more Tamil parties to contest the elections in the north), there was an embargo on this between the opening of nominations for any election and the close of polling. By this time the government had called for nominations for the long delayed election to the North-Eastern Provincial Council, and these were to be held the week after the date for Presidential nominations. Thus the recognition of any new political party was effectively precluded; to forego the privileges such recognition entailed would not be easy for Mrs. Bandaranaike in what promised to be an uphill struggle.

Elections to the Provincial Council of the north and east

In the Tamil areas the situation was calmer than in the rest of the country, and the Indians could claim that they had fulfilled their obligations to

The Last Hurrah

enable an election to be held. Indeed they went one better, and removed the need for an election in the north altogether. The nod of approval having been given to the EPRLF, it emerged uncontested in the bulk of the Northern province, including the Jaffna District; a couple of the smaller districts went similarly uncontested to the group that had sprung up under Indian patronage after the Accord. The TULF left the field clear for the younger groups, perhaps because an understanding had been reached under Indian auspices that participating groups would join together under its banner in the forthcoming general election, The TC and the Tigers did not contest, being opposed to the Accord. EROS did not because, having accepted the Accord, it leaned now towards the Tigers rather than the Indians, and there were allegations that their attempts to nominate independents were threatened by IPKF cordons. The UNP was content to give India's selected militants a free run under the circumstances. The only possible opposition therefore, and that only in the Mannar District where there was a significant Muslim population, might have been the SLMC, which found itself without transport to submit its list.

Contrarywise in the east, where there was less risk of the Tigers disrupting an election, the SLMC was given aerial transport by the Indians, which enabled it to submit lists for all three districts. The EPRLF and its allies did the same, while the UNP submitted lists for two; whether its failure to submit a list for the all important Trincomalee District arose from negligence or from desire to prevent violent repercussions was not clear.

Campaigning was low key, but the Tiger threat of disruption did not materialize. The Indians had by now armed EPRLF cadres, who not only provided security for their candidates but also went on the offensive. By the time the election was held, in the east they were in a position of dominance. That in a relatively high poll they secured 17 of the 35 seats in the three districts allowed them to claim popular backing. The SLMC also won 17 seats. To their surprise, far from being treated as hostile by the Indians, their supporters were given every encouragement to canvass and to vote. From the Indian point of view this made sense, since the higher the poll the more convincing their claim to have restored normalcy:

there was no threat to EPRLF control of the Council, given its uncontested victory in the north.

It was in the Sinhalese areas that the poll was lowest, the percentage being in single figures in the Digamadulla (Amparai) electorate where most Sinhalese were concentrated, just as it had been in the Hambantota District as a whole in June. The UNP thus won only one seat in the Digamadulla District, and none in Batticaloa. It was bizarre that, after so much blood shed on either side, the elected government of the Tamil speaking unit that the separatists had demanded should be dominated by a group that had not played a large part in the struggle, either militarily or ideologically.

Increasing anarchy before Presidential Nominations and the attitude of the JVP

That aspect of the Sri Lankan crisis was not however of much interest any longer to the Jayawardene government which was struggling to cling to its authority in the rest of the country. The sense of relief at Jayawardene's announcement of his retirement and a definite date for an election was immense; but it was dissipated almost immediately by another act of wanton destruction.

Gruesomely tortured bodies of three youths were discovered. They had been abducted by a paramilitary group affiliated to the son of the Chief Minister of the Sabaragamuwa Province, the Junior Minister who had lost his position after the racist violence of 1981. The government press again made much of the fact that all three murdered were members of the JVP, as though this made up for the brutal manner in which they had been tortured and killed. Public indignation was so great however that the son was remanded, and Jayawardene compelled to accept the father's resignation as Chief Minister.

The evidence that this incident provided of the brutality of instruments of state contributed significantly to spiralling anarchy and the increasing polarization of society. Over the six weeks before nomination day institutions broke down all over the country: officials resigned from their posts under pressure, services collapsed, transport services were chaotic,

The Last Hurrah

and it was clear that the writ of the government ran hardly anywhere. The climax came on the 7 November when there was a stoppage of work at the main oil refinery a few miles outside Colombo, and fuel supplies broke down, so that the capital too came close to a standstill as much of the rest of the country had already done.

In this respect the JVP had displayed tremendous organizational skill and what seemed widespread public support, though some of this derived from other disgruntled forces that owed allegiance to political parties with which the JVP was now negotiating. Their strategy was to bring the government down by their activities; they suggested to the other parties therefore conditions that would have exacerbated the polarization that was already fast verging on the absolute: their suggestion was that the Presidential election should be boycotted unless parliament was dissolved, and the President too resigned and handed over power for the period of the election to the Senior Supreme Court Justice (namely Wanasundera, who had become a folk hero amongst those deeply against the Accord).

Reactions from other parties and the submission of Presidential Nominations

The other parties however knew that Jayawardene was not likely to accept these terms. Besides, he could correctly claim that constitutionally they were not possible. In such a context, given their image as democratic forces committed to the rule of law, they could not threaten to boycott the election if extra-legal conditions were not met. Having made the elections their principal demand over the preceding months, to boycott them now would be to provide the UNP with an excuse to stage an election with USA participation, as had happened over the Provincial Councils, and then repress all opposition. While this might appeal to the JVP in terms of creating a revolutionary situation in the long term, it would certainly destroy the democratic opposition as a political force.

The JVP's assertion however, that a fair election was impossibile while the government continued so powerful, was valid. The Alliance therefore asked for parliament to be dissolved and an interim administration consisting of all parties established. In his anxiety to ensure that Mrs.

Bandaranaike did contest the election, and that total polarization was avoided, Jayawardene agreed to these conditions at a private meeting on the 5 November to which he invited her.

A couple of hours after she had left him he telephoned to say that Premadasa had protested vehemently, and threatened to boycott the election himself on the grounds that he would have no chance at all of winning if parliament were dissolved beforehand. To the disappointment of the JVP, despite Jayewardene's repudiation of his pledge, Mrs. Bandaranaike did hand in her nomination on the 10th, together with Premadasa and Ossie Abeygoonesekera, who had taken over as leader of the SLMP after Chandrika Kumaratunga (as she soon began to style herself, omitting a syllable that perhaps was deemed inauspicious) had gone into exile. In some parts of the country therefore the JVP turned on the SLFP as well.

Reactions of the JVP

A number of strands within the JVP emerged, disconcerted as it was by Mrs. Bandaranaike's candidature. In spite of its disappointment a substantial body within the JVP still wanted a victory for Mrs. Bandaranaike, which would open up further the democratic process in the election that would follow, in which the JVP would be able to participate.

There were also those who, having relished the impact of their recent revolutionary tactics, wanted to continue with that sort of campaign. Though many of these were amongst the younger cadres, in the pattern that had earlier characterized developments in Tamil militancy, there were also senior members who saw such a strategy as preferable; a Premadasa victory and the consequent marginalization of the SLFP would prepare the ground for revolution more satisfactorily.

There was some risk in this approach, since a Premadasa regime following a contested election would have more authority than Jayawardene had exercised over the preceding year. Aspects of what could happen were already visible in that the armed forces had begun to move more forcefully against the JVP after nomination day, which had indicated that there was no identity of interests between the SLFP and the JVP.

The Last Hurrah

In addition, Premadasa too may have commanded some support amongst those whose primary allegiance was to the JVP since his populist approach, together with his caste and social background, could be seen as some sort of triumph against the elite that had dominated Sri Lankan politics. Elements in the JVP may have been influenced in this direction by their continued contact with the ELJP, which had also dropped out of the DPA since Mrs. Bandaranaike would not be contesting on a common symbol. All the other parties, including the SLMC that had also been keen earlier on a common symbol, had accepted that legally this was not possible. The intransigence of the ELJP could have arisen from Senanayake's close association with Premadasa which had survived his split with Jayawardene. Certainly Premadasa himself in his election speeches, where he distanced himself as far as possible from his present leader, made great play on the bond that had existed between himself and Dudley Senanayake. It was likely therefore that, whereas the ELJP had joined the DPA in the conviction that Premadasa would never be nominated by the UNP, it was glad of a reason to withdraw after he was. It continued to keep up its contacts with the JVP, which appeared to provide Premadasa too with a link; unlike Jayawardene he was careful not to criticize the JVP, insisting rather that the SLFP was responsible for the anarchy that gripped the country.

The continuation of disruption and the involvement of the State

It is not easy to attribute precise responsibility for the disruptions that continued over the following weeks. Despite the relief that the announcement of one election had provided, the disruptions had some sort of continuing public support as a perversely unrepresentative parliament still continued in existence. Continuing violence, as well as the urgent pleas of independent interest groups including the business community, made clear the intensity of feeling. Finally, with the nation limping more and more helplessly from day to day, Jayawardene declared on the 3 December that parliament would be dissolved on the 20th, immediately after the Presidential Election. This seemed to put paid to whatever sinister designs Premadasa had for legislation requiring a two thirds majority.

The pressure eased after the proclamation, but at this stage another element in the process of disruption began to assert itself, This was the perception within the UNP that a low poll was its best means of ensuring victory, as had happened during some PC elections; and the best way of ensuring a low poll was to capitalize on the JVP threat.

Tactics used included the creation of another variation on the Green Tigers, a People's Patriotic Revolutionary Army that went about attacking suspected subversives it claimed were hindering the democratic process. This led to a massive increase in the number of dead bodies that were a common sight now in the fields and roads of the deep south; and in general a massive insecurity in those areas where the SLFP might have polled strongly. Perhaps as a result of a perception by less radical elements in the JVP about the reasoning behind these tactics, posters appeared in the Southern Province purporting to come from the JVP on behalf of Mrs. Bandaranaike's candidature. Ranjan Wijeratne however, who had swiftly emerged as the strong man of the UNP campaign, immediately called a press conference to assert that these were the work of the SLFP itself; and in his instructions to his cadres he made clear the need to create and capitalize on confusion if the UNP hoped to win. Thus although SLFP meetings had not generally been disrupted, on the last day of campaigning a bomb was flung at a meeting in Colombo which Mrs. Bandaranaike was to address. The perpetrators were taken into custody, but it was soon discovered that they had UNP connections; after the election the matter was allowed to lapse. Even more significant was the shooting of the SLFP organizer in Dambulla in the Matale District, which must have contributed to the extremely low poll there, paralleling the very low turnout in certain areas in the deep south and in the Moneragala and Polonnaruwa Districts. That this was not primarily due to JVP activity was suggested by the fact that Premadasa polled relatively well in those areas; though on a limited poll, he had significant majorities, whereas earlier voting patterns had suggested the government would do badly in such places.

Premadasa's victory and its causes

On a very low poll by Sri Lankan standards, as was noted in the critical report of SAARC observers, 55% as compared with 80% at the previous

Presidential election, Premadasa scraped through with just over 50% of the vote. The SLFP did not accept this result, and challenged it in court. Apart from the low poll that had resulted in UNP majorities in areas of strong anti-government feeling, the high government majorities in almost all the electorates of the Sabaragamuwa Province, where the government had fared worst in the first round of PC elections, were also suspicious. Right through the period preceding the election complaints had been made of additions and omissions to the voters' lists that benefited the government. Lacking organizational capacity the SLFP was unable to present these complaints coherently; its resentment at the final result was increased by the realization that advantage had been taken under the aegis of the new Provincial Administration to prepare a new voters list after the PC elections. A number of the additions may however have been legitimate in the light of the legislation the government had put through to enfranchise the Indian Tamils. Thondaman had come out strongly for Premadasa, and the majorities in Sabaragamuwa could have been due to the solid support he received from the plantation workers who were able to vote. Certainly this was a perfectly acceptable explanation of his 30,000 majority in the predominantly tea growing Nuwara Eliya District, which accounted for more than the 20,000 that was his nationwide plurality over both his rivals.

Similarly, Premadasa's other massive majority of 30,000 in his own Colombo Central seat (though in the rest of the Colombo District as a whole he ran behind Mrs. Bandaranaike) was understandable; though support for the government had been eroded in neighbouring once solidly UNP electorates, the large Muslim population in Colombo which had turned to the SLMC at the PC elections swung back to the UNP at the behest of the SLMC, or rather of its charismatic leader M H M Ashraff.

At the last moment the SLMC had dropped out of the DPA because of a dispute over the division of symbols for the forthcoming election in case the DPA were not recognized as a party in time. In such an eventuality the agreement was that the SLFP would include candidates from other parties on its lists for most districts, but that a few districts should be allocated to other parties which would adopt the same principle. The SLMC had originally asked for the Colombo metropolitan zone, one of the three into which Colombo District was to be subdivided, as well as the three districts of the Eastern Province. In negotiation Ashraff had agreed to concede the Trincomalee and Batticaloa Districts to the SLFP, but he hung firm on Digamadulla and the Colombo zone.

The SLFP, ignoring the fact that as a national party it should seek representation at the periphery, while it was equally important that a party of the periphery such as the SLMC should feel secure at the centre if it were not to slide towards separatism, agreed to grant the whole of the Eastern Province to the SLMC but insisted that it should retain the Colombo zone. After protracted negotiations Mrs. Bandaranaike did give in, and made Ashraff understand that she had conceded his point. Next morning however, as he was preparing to come to her residence to sign the agreement formally, he was told that she had changed her mind.

For the SLFP this was to prove a fatal error, indicative of the inconsistencies that had plagued the party for the last decade. There had been those within the party who had from the start suggested that the concept of the DPA was a mistake, and that the SLFP would do better to go it alone. That this was an erroneous assumption could be deduced from the previous record of the SLFP, in that it had only come to power previously when allied with other forces. The reduction of its vote at the subsequent general election when it did go it alone suggests that the strategy it adopted for the Presidential election was the more sensible. That strategy had involved accepting policies to attract the votes of the minorities. It was extraordinary that it sacrificed Ashraff's proven vote-getting potential on a purely symbolic issue, for Ashraff had conceded that almost all the candidates on the list could come from the SLFP, and that its leader could be the sitting SLFP member from the area. The SLFP's decision was even more extraordinary for of all the other parties left in the DPA only the SLMC had any notable electoral appeal.

Ashraff, bitter about the way in which he had been treated, responded positively to Premadasa's overtures. He felt he could at this stage only ask for little, which Premadasa granted. He at once rushed legislation through parliament to adjust aspects of the electoral system that were of particular concern to the SLMC: the cutoff point for parliamentary elections was lowered from 12 ½% to 5% in each district and, with supreme irony, the system of zones that had been recently introduced by the 14th amendment to the constitution, and which had caused the split between the SLFP and the SLMC, was abolished. Thus the entire Colombo District became once again the polling unit, so that the SLMC, which anticipated winning a minimum of 5% in the district as a whole, was confident, even contesting on its own, of at least one seat.

Ashraff was overwhelmed by such attention, and issued a statement urging his supporters to vote for any candidate for the presidency except Mrs. Bandaranaike. To ensure that Premadasa benefited from his advice, he was provided by the government with transport to the east, from where he came and where, as the PC results had indicated, his influence was especially strong. His energetic campaigning contributed to Premadasa's extremely good showing there in comparison with the pitiful result for the government at the PC elections the previous month. That result, and the result in Colombo, suggest that Ashraff exercised substantial influence over the Muslim vote in the nation as a whole. Even assuming he influenced just a quarter of the Muslims in the country, that made the difference, since had such voters swung the other way Premadasa's majority of less than 300,000 over Mrs. Bandaranaike would have vanished.

There were other factors that affected the result. One was Premadasa's pledge that he would provide a monthly grant of Rs. 2,500 ($75 then) to recipients of welfare. Since this was more than twice the average wage, and it was only those who received less than Rs. 500 per month who were entitled to welfare on the existing scheme, the pledge was at first seen by the opposition as an economic absurdity. Premadasa however insisted that his plan, which was to be called the Janasaviya programme, would go ahead and the UNP included it in its manifesto, though modified with references to a compulsory savings component in the sum, and restrictions on the number of recipients. Certainly the SLFP seemed to be of the view that it had made a difference electorally in that, in the new manifesto it issued on its own for the parliamentary election that followed, it advanced a similar scheme.

The vote in the north

In the Northern Province Premadasa's support was limited as had been expected; both Mrs. Bandaranaike and Abeygoonesekera did better. The poll however was low, either because the people of the north were not especially keen to vote in an election they did not think concerned them, or because the Indian army which provided security at the polling booths was determined that there should be a low poll to prevent large opposition majorities. Given how well Kobbekaduwa had done in 1982, and also that the DPA programme included measures that the LTTE were reported to have thought more satisfactory than the Accord, a better performance had been expected from Mrs. Bandaranaike.

The DPA programme was accepted by both the TC and the SLMC after lengthy negotiation. The former had submitted the proposals, which included provision for separate Provincial Councils for Tamils and for Muslim majority areas in the north-eastern region, to the LTTE for consideration before acquiescing, and to the MEP and the JVP, which had both been thought to be opposed to devolution. Though it was not specified in the manifesto, it had been agreed, as Ashraff explained in a public statement just before the manifesto was signed, that the delimitation commission appointed would be empowered to detach Sinhalese majority areas contiguous to other provinces, and join them as required to other Districts. This provision was not clear; with Ashraff's departure and the TC wary of drawing attention to it, the DPA failed to put it across convincingly. Thus there was room for the UNP to insist that its own merger of the entire east with the north was temporary, and to accuse the DPA of selling out the Sinhalese. Even Cyril Mathew was brought out of retirement to attack Mrs. Bandaranaike on the subject. Given that the TULF was reported in the government press to claim that the DPA would withdraw from the Tamils some concessions the Accord had won them, it is clear the government was anxious to exploit whatever communal tensions it could in order to win the day. The results however, which registered clear majorities for Mrs. Bandaranaike both in Jaffna and in the areas of the deep south where polling was reasonable, suggested that such tactics no longer had major impact.

The General Election and its aftermath

The SLFP thought otherwise. It had been embarrassed that the DPA manifesto pledged to restore article 29 of the 1948 constitution, which banned positive or negative discrimination with regard to race or religion. The UNP alleged that this implied that Mrs. Bandaranaike would repeal the article her government had introduced into the 1972 constitution, and which it had kept on in the 1978 constitution, making Buddhism the principal religion, and enjoining upon the state the responsibility of fostering it. The DPA did not think the two articles were incompatible, and Mrs. Bandaranaike issued a statement to this effect, but after her defeat, elements in the SLFP that had opposed the Alliance regained control. The SLFP adopted the stance that she had lost because the SLFP had neglected the Sinhala Buddhist constituency that was its primary base. Accordingly it fought the general election that was held on February 15th on an entirely different, markedly populist, manifesto.

The reasoning behind this may have been that it was not looking for Tamil or Muslim votes on this occasion (and did not indeed contest any districts in the Northern Province); but the strategy did not win it any further Sinhalese support; it received only 31% of the vote whereas at the Presidential election Mrs. Bandaranaike had received over 44%. It thus won only 58 seats to the 110 won by the UNP, which received nearly 51% of the vote. In addition, of the 29 seats available on national lists, the UNP won 15 and the SLFP 9; as a consequence of its resentment of the DPA, the SLFP did not nominate to parliament the leaders of the DWC and the LP, nor the former Secretary of the SLMC, all of whom had been led to believe that they would be nominated if the SLFP won a reasonable entitlement.

The other major casualty of the shift in perspective within the SLFP was Anura Bandaranaike, who had been given to understand that he could continue as leader of the opposition while his mother would be content to take a back seat. He had been closely associated with the negotiations that led to the formation of the DPA and as a result found himself out of favour; Mrs. Bandaranaike took over the post of leader of the opposition.

The big surprise of the election was in the northeast, where the coalition that contested under the TULF banner won only nine seats, with none of its former parliamentarians elected (though Amirthalingam entered parliament as the TULF nominee for its national list seat). More seats, and by far the majority in the Northern Province, were won by an independent group put forward by EROS. Their aim had been to provide an alternative to what was seen as the TULF list of Indian proteges, and EROS had accordingly hoped for LTTE support for this move. At first this was not forthcoming, and the group tried to withdraw in accordance with the Tiger demand for a boycott. A couple of days before the election the Tigers changed their strategy, perhaps in a bid to show just how much popular support they had, and urged the people to vote for the EROS list. The result made clear how hollow the view put forward by the Indian and Sri Lankan authorities was, that the power of the Tigers was waning and the EPRLF would soon have effective control in the region.

If in the north then the situation seemed no nearer a satisfactory solution than before the Accord, in the south it continued to deteriorate. A few days after the Presidential election, though Premadasa had tried to sound conciliatory, the JVP made clear its determination to renew the struggle, and proved surprisingly capable of doing so with the same intensity as before. Its first goal was to disrupt the general election that Jayawardene had fixed for 15 February when he dissolved parliament on the morning of 20 December, and to accomplish this it turned its guns on the SLFP as well as the UNP. There were allegations that some of the violence against the SLFP came from the UNP, in its attempt to fulfill Premadasa's expressed anxiety that he secure another two-thirds majority.

Despite various pressures the UNP exercised against it to maximize its own electoral advantages, in contesting the general election after Premadasa's victory the SLFP recognized that it had set itself against the JVP strategy of denying the existence of democracy and encouraging revolution. It accepted that the JVP was against it, and in some areas indeed, such as the deep south, it found itself making common cause with the UNP.

The Last Hurrah

Immediately after the election Premadasa reconstituted the cabinet. Athulathmudali and Disanayake were given relatively unimportant portfolios, but both were excited by Premadasa's announcement that he would let the UNR parliamentary group elect the Prime Minister. The rivalry between the two became so intense however, that Premadasa was able to appoint D B Wijetunge instead, a remarkably colourless politician whom he had made Minister of Finance. His determination to devalue the post of Prime Minister, and thus prevent the establishment of an independent identity such as his own, was clear. Wijetunge's most prominent characteristic was his unquestioning loyalty to him; but he also indicated that he planned to rotate the post of Prime Minister amongst members of his cabinet.

Both Athulathmudali and Dissanayake were disappointed; their resentment at what could be construed as a general insult could even have led them to make common cause with each other against the president if an opportunity arose. Premadasa however had taken care to conciliate the rest of the establishment, in that Ranjan Wijeratne became Minister of Foreign Affairs and Deputy Minister of Defence, while Ranil Wickremesinghe received the portfolio of Industries and was made Leader of the House. At the same time Premadasa's radical changes with regard to administrative methods as well as senior personnel made clear his rejection of a lot of what Jayawardene had initiated and developed. If things went wrong Premadasa was unlikely to receive much sympathy from the UNP establishment; this was the more risky for him as it was apparent that he would have to act very fast in other respects given the situation in the country.

Part VI

Using the Executive Presidency

Premadasa in Action (1989–1993)

Chapter 12

Controlling the Country

The southern problem

Though the SLFP suffered more from the JVP during the 1989 general election, that the long term threat from the JVP was to the UNP became clear in the few weeks immediately after 15 February. There was a rapid escalation in violence and a couple of hartals that proved as successful as those at the height of the agitation for elections.

Premadasa however was slow to react. Before the election he released many suspected JVP detainees and revoked the state of emergency that Jayewardene had maintained. Though violence increased dramatically Premadasa did not shift his stand about opening up negotiations with the JVP.

The JVP did not respond. Since they had so soon brought the country to boiling point again, even though elections had been held and therefore the main reason for public discontent mitigated, they thought complete success just round the corner. The first new hartal they called on 22 March proved remarkably successful. This may have been because of resentment on the part of other political parties at what seemed the stealing of the election by the UNP. In addition fear played a great part in the continuing success of JVP demands over the next few months, a psychosis born of the habit of obedience ingrained when JVP tactics seemed the only way to ensure elections.

With Ranjan Wijeratne at their head however, the security forces were in no mood to yield. They resumed the strong arm tactics used previously to suppress the JVP which had been muted during the election period. Cordon and search operations in JVP strongholds began on a large scale, and death squads were systematically set up to punish suspects when the ordinary resources of the law seemed inadequate.

Meanwhile Premadasa announced a week long ceasefire in April to give the JVP a chance to enter into negotiations. The JVP ignored this on the grounds that the security forces were not sincere about it. Though Premadasa set up a monitoring committee, chaired by the very judge the JVP had wanted to head an interim government, suggesting that he himself was sincere, the JVP thought that meaningless in a situation in which the forces had other views.

In May the universities closed because of a strike by minor employees. The government began negotiations with the JVP led students' union, since they were behind the strike. These proved fruitless and a couple of months later the Ministry of Defence insisted on the closure of all universities. This furnished a pattern that recurred over this period as a range of unions, through conviction or under persuasion and threat, went on strike, paralysing essential services such as transport, hospitals and schools.

As the country slithered towards anarchy Premadasa continued to exercise restraint. In addition, believing that one reason the JVP continued to command support was resentment at the presence of the Indian army, he formally requested in June that the IPKF be withdrawn completely by 29 July, two years after its arrival. The Indian government had shown some understanding of the situation in announcing the withdrawal of a couple of battalions in January. After that however nothing more happened, and now, in response to Premadasa's request, the Indians insisted on discussions before a decision could be reached. Premadasa agreed, and managed to convince the Indian government that he was not hostile and that his approach was largely dictated by domestic difficulties. Indeed, as Wijeratne took on the role of baiting India, Premadasa, aided by capable High Commissioners he sent to India during his tenure of office, managed to project himself as more moderate. Though Premadasa's relations with India could never be described as cordial, he reached a satisfactory *modus vivendi* with the Rajiv Gandhi government, further cemented when a new government under V P Singh took office in India later that year.

Controlling the Country

With that flank covered, the security forces fought back with incredible ruthlessness. They were helped by public opinion veering towards them. Hartals were proving extraordinarily effective, even in Colombo, with days on which there were scarcely any vehicles on the roads except those of ministers and the security vehicles they thought essential. In the country there were large areas where the government's writ had ceased to run. At the same time there was no clear idea as to what all this was to achieve, except the replacement of what could pass as an elected government by one that seemed far more rigid.

As the government counter offensive took effect extreme censorship was imposed. The JVP responded by killing the competent authority appointed for the purpose and threatened newscasters, most of whom withdrew in terror. For a few months therefore the security forces had to take charge of the radio and television stations, and the news was read by hastily trained service personnel.

The turning point came when the JVP announced that it would eliminate the families of security personnel unless they deserted. The JVP itself realized that this was a desperate measure: in the face of the onslaught the services had launched, it was bound to lose. The announcement then only made the onslaught more relentless. There was one more ceasefire proposed, which the JVP again ignored, though some of its cadres had begun to surrender. By the beginning of October the JVP was in full retreat.

Meanwhile Premadasa had been able to establish his legitimacy fairly clearly; political parties including the LTTE attended an all party conference he summoned to find a political solution to the conflicts, and unanimously issued an appeal to the JVP to attend. When Premadasa began his Janasviya programme, the handouts for which he had secured World Bank assistance in return for structural adjustments in the economy, he was able to attract support in areas that had hitherto been almost wholly dominated by the JVP.

By November the curfew that had been imposed almost every night for several months was lifted; and on the 13th and 14th the government announced the deaths of Rohana Wijeweera and Upatissa Gamanayake, the leader and the general secretary of the JVP. The former, reportedly killed while trying to escape, had been in custody for some time. It was the revelations extorted from him that facilitated mopping up operations. Gamanayake, deemed the more dangerous of the two, was killed in a shoot out by the police party sent to arrest him.

Credit for crushing the JVP was in the public perception due largely to Wijeratne, who had provided the necessary ruthlessness and the backing the hardliners in the military required. Premadasa himself was seen, as he set about picking up the pieces of a shattered country, as having vacillated. At the same time, when it became obvious to him that the JVP would not negotiate, he gave Wijeratne the go-ahead to proceed without due process. The question he now had to face was whether the monster that had been created could be brought under control so that orderly government could be restored for him to proceed with a positive agenda.

Restoring normalcy

Over the next three months the death squads continued to operate with impunity. What finally brought the process to a halt was the murder of the journalist and human rights activist Richard de Zoysa in Colombo. He was taken away from his home in the middle of the night by a posse led by Senior Superintendent of Police Ronnie Gunasinghe, long known as a hatchet man, not only for the Jayewardene government, but in Mrs. Bandaranaike's time too. He had been responsible for what was claimed to have been accidental deaths at a Tamil cultural rally in Jaffna in 1975, the incident commonly thought to have given birth to the separatist movement. Later, in 1982, he was identified by the wife of an SLFP supporter as the man who had taken her husband away in the middle of the night. The husband had never been seen again, but with threats to her family and herself the wife had allowed the case to be dropped.

It was not so easy however to dispose of de Zoysa's case. He was socially the most exalted figure to be thus eliminated, but that was not the only reason. He was a close friend of Lalith Athulathmudali and had indeed done some confidential propaganda work for him while he was Minister of National Security. De Zoysa's abduction in fact occurred shortly after that of a minor UNP politician, also close to Athulathmudali, who had produced a play that sharply satirized Premadasa. He was never found. De Zoysa's body, cast out to sea after he was shot, came floating back. It was found by a fisherman who recognized it and stood guard so that it could not be disposed of before a magistrate had recorded the finding, and de Zoysa's mother, who had been present when he was abducted, had identified it.

Despite threats against her own life de Zoysa's mother, divorced and with no other children, refused to let the matter drop. Having categorically identified Ronnie Gunasinghe after she saw him on television, she was able to demand specific action. Her statements received a great deal of publicity. De Zoysa's journalist colleagues, both local and foreign, gave full coverage to the incident. The government held firm. But the contortions it went through, which included palpably illogical opinions by the Attorney General so that Ronnie Gunasinghe was not produced in court as the inquiring magistrate had ordered, made clear that the government had been responsible and was protecting its own.

The investigation then ceased. Yet de Zoysa's death helped the country to return to normal for, in the furore it caused, those who wanted the carnival to stop were able to assert themselves. The week after the murder the death squads were disbanded at a party presided over by Wijeratne. There the message was given out that the emergency which had justified their actions was over, and the impunity with which they had acted thus far was no longer available. The reign of terror, that had helped to destroy the JVP but continued long after any such justification was available, was halted.

To what extent Premadasa was responsible for the terror, or its cessation, is open to question. With regard to those marked for elimination, Wijeratne is held to have passed him a list for authorization, which was returned without specific comments and a blanket instruction to go ahead as necessary. The furore over de Zoysa's death however shocked Premadasa. Both Athulathmudali and Dissanayake attended the funeral. Athulathmudali went personally to the airport with de Zoysa's closest professional associate to ensure that he got out of the country safely. Dissanayake raised the issue in cabinet and demanded a full investigation since the country was entitled to know what had happened. Both later closed ranks in parliament in voting against an opposition motion to set up a select committee of inquiry; but it was clear that the incident had pushed them to the limit.

Yet this in itself could not have swayed Premadasa. He felt himself quite capable of dealing with opposition within his own party and made this clear when, less than a month later, he dropped Dissanayake from his cabinet. Had he wanted the terror to continue it is unlikely, given the centralized control he had established, that external pressures would have changed his mind. What is more likely is that he wanted a shift. Over a year had been spent on reacting to the situation that he had inherited. It was time now to move on to the programme for which he saw himself as having been elected President.

The Tigers on Trial

Premadasa's attitude to India, when he took office, was a function not of a foreign policy, but of what he wanted to convey to the local population. His main target was the Sinhala audience. However the Tamils too had nothing to respond to except this approach. Thus the militant groups allied to India viewed him with suspicion, whereas the Tigers saw in him, if not an ally, someone with similar interests who could be used to their advantage. Premadasa naturally felt the same about them, and over the next eighteen months contacts between the two developed apace.

It was during this period that, as was later alleged by his opponents in charging Premadasa with treason, arms were given to the Tigers by the Sri Lankan forces. This may not have been on Premadasa's instructions, but it would be myopic to suppose that he was not privy to such practices. The charge of treachery however is one that could only have been made on hindsight. At that time, since Premadasa was projecting himself as a national leader whose domestic agenda required that the Indians leave, such actions made sense. One reason that the Indians left relatively readily was that they realized that the war against the LTTE was unwinnable, and the casualties they were suffering were no longer acceptable to their own citizens. The arms supplied by the Sri Lankan government to the Tigers helped to achieve this. In the long term of course the action was unwise, given that the arms were likely to be used against the Sri Lankan army in turn. But that may not have seemed important in comparison with the crisis that confronted Premadasa at the time he took office.

Soon after the election it became apparent that Indian protection for its chosen government in the North-East could not be taken for granted on a permanent basis. In January 1989 steps were taken, as permitted under the Accord, to set up a regional security outfit to supplement the Indian forces. This was clearly intended by the provincial administration, run by the EPRLF, to be a Tamil paramilitary organization, and the SLMC therefore refused to take their seats in the Provincial Council. This was the more serious in that the SLMC constituted the largest and practically only opposition there.

The anger of the SLMC at the attitude of the North-East Provincial government, which saw itself as a government of Tamils for Tamils, was grist to Premadasa's mill. Not only did he help the Muslims to build up their own voluntary security organizations, but he also facilitated recruitment of Muslims to the army and the police; the proportion of Muslims serving in the East, side by side with Sinhala colleagues, increased considerably. In a context in which Muslims who spoke Tamil might have sided with Tamils such tactics were crucial to develop new alignments. All this cemented even more thoroughly the relationship between Premadasa and Ashraff who became one of Premadasa's closest supporters over the next couple of years.

In April 1989 the Tigers declared their willingness to talk with the government. In the previous month the pro-Tiger independent group elected to parliament had had discussions with the government, having refused to take their seats until this happened. The talks evidently proved successful, for they entered parliament and in May the Tigers formally began negotiations. With Premadasa's demand the following month that the Indians withdraw by July, the Tigers issued a joint statement with the government on the cessation of hostilities.

The EPRLF, with the withdrawal of the Indians imminent, announced the establishment of a Tamil National Army that was clearly set up with the assistance of the Indian Peace Keeping Force. This however did not worry the Tigers unduly, for they felt confident they could deal with that sort of opposition. Characteristically, what concerned them more was the TULF. Although their performance at the polls had made clear they counted comparatively little in the eyes of the people whose sole representatives they had earlier been, the TULF still commanded a great deal of attention and respect internationally as well as in Colombo. Amirthalingam had once again emerged as the most effective public spokesman of the Tamils through his performance in parliament in Colombo, though for any settlement it was necessary to involve his senior colleagues too. The most prominent amongst these were Party President Sivasithamparam, and the Colombo lawyer Neelan Tiruchelvam who had by now managed to get over his earlier reputation as an adherent of the urban establishment and hence a pawn in Jayewardene's hands. Since the Tigers were pressing for the dissolution of the Provincial Council in the North-East, they were irritated by parliamentarians and seasoned negotiators who could argue against such actions and object to any mechanism whereby power in that area was handed over to the LTTE.

Towards the end of July these three leaders of the TULF were due to attend a meeting at the Colombo house of the former MP for Jaffna, Yoheswaran, the most militant of the former TULF parliamentarians. Shortly after the appointed time gunmen entered the house and shot them. Tiruchelvam being ill had not attended the meeting; Sivasithamparam was injured badly. Amirthalingam and Yoheswaran were killed instantaneously. There was some talk later that Yoheswaran had been involved in the plot and had been killed by accident; more likely he had been deceived into thinking that genuine negotiations with the LTTE were possible.

A few months later the Tigers gunned down the most effective new entrant to parliament, Sam Tambimuttu from Batticaloa in the Eastern Province. He was part of the umbrella coalition the Indians had put together and had been prominent earlier as a human rights activist. His associates claimed that the motive for the killing was to prevent him publicizing Human Rights abuses on the part of the LTTE, about which he had been compiling a dossier. His murder led to a downgrading of the role of the Tamils elected to parliament through the TULF slate. The majority of those left were seen as young militants with little public standing; the assassinations established that there were no Tamils of importance compared with the Tigers, with whom the government needed to negotiate.

The commencement of discussions

Meanwhile, with the withdrawal of the Indians, the government resumed the central role in negotiations that it had abdicated three years previously when the Indian government was required to mediate between the various interests. Now in addition to the Tigers, both major Tamil parties opposed to them, the EPRLF and the TULF, came without demur to the all party conference summoned in September 1989. In that very month the IPKF officially suspended its operations, whereupon the Tigers declared that they would reciprocate. The TNA still continued, and it was known that the Indians had helped to establish it; but with the Indians officially withdrawing both the government and the LTTE were confident that they could deal with residual problems.

Just as with the south, nothing came of the initiatives with regard to the north that the government embarked on through the conference. As far as the south went the JVP did not attend; and the major opposition parties withdrew, refusing, in the absence of the JVP, to participate in the committee set up to explore options for peace there. With regard to the north, the Tigers categorically refused to sit in committee with the EPRLF. Their position, which they reiterated over the next few years, was that it was absurd to equate them with the other Tamil groups, which had backed the Indian army in its war of oppression and were no more than Indian puppets.

Premadasa may have sympathized with this argument but, given his delicate relations with India, he could scarcely accept it openly. He had to face opposition in his own ranks, in particular from the military that had no love for the Tigers. The LTTE later claimed that Premadasa had initially been more sympathetic to them but Wijeratne, himself influenced by the forces, had persuaded him not to trust them.

Despite their intransigence over the round table negotiations Premadasa had wanted, relations between the Tigers and the government continued cordial over the next six months. As the IPKF withdrew, beginning with the Amparai District, the TNA and the Sri Lankan army moved into the vacated areas. The Tigers confined themselves then to attacks on the TNA, in some areas it seemed with the support of the Sri Lankan army, and soon forced it onto the defensive. By November the TNA actually attacked government police stations in Muslim majority areas but could make little headway. In predominantly Tamil areas, where the battle was between them and the LTTE, it was not on equal terms. By the following March it was clear that the EPRLF writ ran practically nowhere in the province.

Premadasa had by then held talks with Mahattaya, the deputy leader of the LTTE, who on the strength of the understanding they reached, set up a political wing of the party to contest the election to be held shortly. All this prompted Vartharaja Perumal, the EPRLF Chief Minister of the Province, to threaten a unilateral declaration of independence; this gave the Sri Lankan government an excuse to try to take him into custody. He fled to India in March 1990, just as the IPKF completed its withdrawal. Premadasa thereupon dissolved the Council and imposed direct rule. This meant that the administration was in the hands of the governor, a former army commander with a reputation for moderation, who had been appointed to the post in 1988 after several civilians had turned it down.

For three months the LTTE and the Sri Lankan army were in joint control of the two provinces. The LTTE was preponderant in the North, where they had long been dominant and had opposed the Indian army so effectively; the Sri Lankan army confined itself to its camps there. In the East the situation was evenly balanced, with the army prominent in the Sinhala and Muslim areas. But the way the wind was blowing became apparent as early as January, when in the course of its manoeuvres the LTTE abducted 450 Muslims.

In April the LTTE leader Prabhakaran emerged from hiding for the first time in months, evidently feeling safe now from the Indian threat to his life. The government's chief negotiator, sent up to Jaffna to talk to him, was the Muslim Minister Hameed who chaired the All Party Conference, as it attempted to fulfill the limited mandate given it after the opposition parties had withdrawn. The particular crisis that had been its initial focus had been resolved but Premadasa was unwilling to dissolve a useful sounding board; he asked that it produce proposals for devolution that could supersede those imposed under the Indo-Lankan Accord. The main participants left were the SLMC and the minor Tamil parties, so this was particularly appropriate, even if it was understood that they could actually decide nothing without the major players. To satisfy the Liberal Party, which also remained, and to suggest to the international community that he was interested in political reforms, Premadasa also asked for drafts for a new media policy and constitutional amendments to strengthen human rights.

Despite Hameed's reputed skills, the crucial negotiations he chaired proved fruitless. This was not accidental; his charm and careful attention to detail were designed on occasion to delay a solution. This became obvious some months later, when a fairly solid agreement between Tamil and Muslim parties on the vexed question of the North East merger fell apart under his relentless probing and hypothetical questions. His defense, when criticized for this approach, was that he did not want to broker a solution that contained the seeds of failure. In other areas, as when he negotiated with university staff, he was quick to reach decisions that his successors found embarrassing. It seemed that he knew from the start when a solution was needed, and when it was not. Thus the elaborate 17th amendment to the constitution about Human Rights was never put forward; the draft on media policy remained a draft, and most important of all the discussions on the ethnic question faded into obscurity.

The LTTE concluded that negotiations with Hameed would prove fruitless; the government was not sincere in wanting a solution. They in turn provided the government some justification for its own position of intransigence about the administration of the North-East being given to them pending an election. The government claimed this was impossible, given all the other interests involved, and the uncertain state of the linkage between the North and East. This linkage, long resisted by Jayewardene, had seemed to Tamils the most important concession the Indians had obtained on their behalf through the Accord. Though it was in theory conditional upon a referendum, Jayewardene had kept postponing this and Premadasa was to do the same. Actually handing over both provinces to the LTTE without a poll was not something he could contemplate.

The resumption of war

In June war broke out again with attacks by the Tigers on police stations in the Eastern Province. A number of these were captured and held for some time, and several policemen were killed. Attacks on army camps were less successful. The government tried to renew the ceasefire, but the LTTE held to the view that negotiations were useless. Finally the government declared war on the LTTE, and moved fairly quickly and effectively throughout the entire East. Meanwhile a mark of Indian government support was provided by the arrest of Tigers in Tamil Nadu.

By July the government could claim that it had liberated the East. Though this was not quite the case, since pockets of LTTE resistance continued, it was on a diminishing scale. The East had always been an area in which the LTTE had not been especially powerful; many Tamils in the area were anxious about maintaining close links with the North and therefore supported the LTTE, but its attacks on those opposed to it, Tamils as well as Muslims, led to a consolidation of forces against it. Meanwhile Premadasa changed horses and began to cultivate the other Tamil groups. This was less arbitrary than it looked, for they had already responded to his overtures in attending the all party conference and also the hangover from it. The brunt of government hostility had initially been directed towards the EPRLF, which seemed a threat in view of the independent stance the North-East Provincial Council had tried to take. Now the EPRLF had been rendered powerless, and its leaders had fled to India where a number of them, including the leader of the party and an MP from the Jaffna District (though not Perumal, the former Chief Minister), were assassinated by the Tigers. The Sri Lankan government therefore could be indulgent, while the other militant groups also fell into line. Though some residual distrust remained over the next year, with a resolute attempt by Premadasa to win over the minorities, by 1992 the other Tamil militant groups were almost all on his side, in opposition to the LTTE.

Controlling the Country 171

In the North, given the public support the LTTE enjoyed after its resistance to the Indians, things were tougher for the government. The army did manage to gain ground in the Mannar District, where there was a substantial Muslim population. Over the next year it also moved into Vavuniya town, the capital of the extensive district of that name. That was in the very south of the district, and elsewhere in the North, except for a few military outposts, it had virtually to give up. Even those outposts proved vulnerable. The historic Dutch fort in Jaffna, the headquarters of the army there, though defended keenly for a couple of months, had to be evacuated in September and was blown up by the Tigers. In the Jaffna District itself then, in the Kilinochchi District just to the south, and in the Mullaitivu District to the southeast, just to the north of the Trincomalee District, the army maintained just a few strategic outposts, which were subject to constant attack.

At the same time the LTTE, reacting to incidents in which Muslim groups in the East had attacked Tamils, engaged in what amounted to ethnic cleansing by asking Muslims to abandon the areas in the North which it controlled. Nearly 50,000 Muslims thus expelled had to be housed in refugee camps in the rest of the country. Intense as was their suffering, the episode could also be seen as a tragedy for the LTTE; their action signified the collapse of the initial Tamil demand for an autonomous Tamil speaking region consisting of both the Northern and the Eastern Provinces. Such an extensive region was essential if it was to be a viable entity, for the Northern Province was inadequate by itself. If Trincomalee and its magnificent harbour were included however, as well as the fertile and productive areas on the east coast and its hinterland, a very prosperous unit could have developed.

Whereas the North had a massive Tamil majority, the East was divided fairly equally between Tamils, Muslims and Sinhalese. Given that the Muslims spoke Tamil there was a Tamil speaking majority in the area. The original demand of the Tamils had referred to a Tamil speaking homeland. Since the rights of Tamil speakers had been eroded by successive governments, with a concomitant reduction of employment opportunities for them at the centre, the demand had been a rallying cry.

By 1989 however the Tamil language had been given its due place constitutionally, and the government did not see this as merely a cosmetic measure. In fact with the desire for internationalism under the new economic dispensation the heyday of Sinhalese linguistic nationalism had passed; English was in demand, as in the days when Tamils shone because of their better command of that language. So in the recent past, instead of a community of interests arising from claims based on language, political tensions had developed between Tamils and Muslims. These may have been exacerbated by government action, but they were also fanned by hegemonic Tamil assumptions, similar to those they had resented on the part of Sinhalese. Thus it now did not make sense to class all Tamil speakers as a unified political entity. Despite this, negotiations over the past few years had still been based on the assumption by Tamils that Tamil speaking Muslims had more in common with them than with the Sinhalese. Now, having expelled Muslims from the North, the LTTE enabled its opponents to claim that it sought dominion rather than partnership.

At the start of hostilities the independent groups the LTTE had supported stopped attending parliament and shortly afterwards they resigned their seats. Parliament was no longer of consequence to the Tigers and they were quite content to leave electoral politics to Tamils who they felt had no claims at all to be considered representatives of the people.

But there was still a role for parliament to play with regard to the ethnic issue: an SLFP MP known for his moderate views proposed a select committee to suggest alternatives to the prevailing system of devolution. After the collapse of the residue of Hameed's conference this seemed a way to indicate a continuing willingness to compromise, and a parliamentary committee was set up with the proposer of the motion as its chairman. In 1992 both major parties were reported to have agreed to a federal constitution, a concept hitherto too emotive to be accepted. Fleshing this concept out, an MP called Srinivasan had proposed a compromise whereby the North and East would be delinked; the separate councils that would be established would have greater powers so as to satisfy some complaints about the ineffectiveness of devolution. In the end both major parties bowed to pressure and did not accept the measures suggested. No agreement was reached, and the select committee collapsed in a welter of recrimination.

The idea of a negotiated settlement had long lost credibility owing to the continuation of hostilities between the government and the LTTE, both of which seemed to think victory was imminent. The reasons the government was confident had a great deal to do with Premadasa's increasing capacity to conciliate the Tamil population in areas where the government was in charge. Though pockets of Tiger resistance continued in the East, by 1991 the area was well under control and Premadasa was able to embark on a number of developmental programmes that brought more in real terms to the province than successive governments had provided over the previous few decades. Again, though the area the government commanded in the North was minimal, Premadasa was swift to act there too with his mobile secretariat that seemed to make government more accessible to the people. As part of his programme Vavuniya for instance, a backwater for many years before, found itself by the end of 1992 with a university college as well as a couple of garment factories, providing employment on a scale the area had not known before. The Janasaviya programme too, Premadasa's monthly grant of Rs 2,500 to welfare recipients, implemented in such areas, created positive feelings towards the government. So when the government militarily extended its control northward, the population actually welcomed it in view of the anticipated benefits that this programme would provide to deprived sections of the population, in effect most people in such areas. This was a great change from earlier responses to army activity.

A great deal of the credit was due to General Kobbekaduwa who had been appointed commander of the crucial northern region after an earlier successful stint at Trincomalee. He was one of the most able and popular officers in the army; and his popularity extended to all communities for he was indefatigable in assisting with civilian life in the areas in which he served. Professionally, he planned operations carefully and implemented them systematically. He was successful in mopping up activities in the East, offensives in the North to extend control of its southern regions, and even sorties from the bases the army still held further north, to fight off threats and improve communications.

Tiger assassinations

Over the first two years of the war the Tigers were on the defensive though this did not preclude a number of attacks on army bases as well as civilian targets. Their successes that kept even the balance between them and the government came through assassinations that marked them as an effective terrorist organization.

Their first major success was the elimination of the military commander in Trincomalee who had followed Kobbedakuwa and done a successful job of conciliating the local population while extending the area under government control. Three months later, in March 1991, Ranjan Wijeratne was killed by a car bomb in the heart of Colombo. There were suspicions that his opponents in the government had been responsible, or else foreign casino owners whose operations he had recently banned; but the Tigers made no bones about accepting responsibility.

A few months later they achieved their greatest success when Rajiv Gandhi was killed by a suicide bomber in the closing stages of an Indian general election campaign he was expected to win. He had turned into a figure of hate for the Tigers for setting up the Indo-Lankan Accord which was implemented in a manner detrimental to their interests and culminated in the attack on Jaffna by the Indian army. Though the subsequent Indian government and the one in Tamil Nadu state had adopted a similar approach, and tried to limit Tiger activity, Gandhi remained their principal bugbear. What they saw as his personal animosity to them, as well as his assertive personality, could have led to more forceful joint activity against them on the part of the two governments if he came back to power. Eliminating him (the most important world leader to have been assassinated in a quarter of a century), emphasized their power and their reach.

A month after that, another suicide bomb went off at the headquarters of the Joint Operations Command in Colombo, killing 22 people. A meeting of senior commanders had been due to take place that day, but the bomb was mistimed so there were no major casualties. The incident led to enhanced security, and there was a lull in this sort of activity for a while. Instead over the next twelve months the government scored some notable victories, which seemed to put it ahead in what was a protracted war of attrition. But then, in August 1992 Kobbekaduwa and his principal lieutenant for the Jaffna offensive and also the admiral in charge of naval support operations in the area were killed when their jeep exploded a land mine on the island of Kayts. Once again there were rumours in Colombo that it was an inside job, with Premadasa's opponents suggesting that he was behind it, from jealousy of Kobbekaduwa's popularity. The circumstances under which the bomb went off, with so many officers travelling together contrary to normal procedure on a road that had not been cleared, involved too many coincidences for a plot to seem plausible; again the LTTE took credit for the incident and decorated those it recognized as responsible.

There was one more successful offensive after Kobbekaduwa's death, which he had himself planned. After that the army went on the defensive. Meanwhile the LTTE also eliminated the navy commander through another suicide attack in Colombo, so that the operations he had implemented, to limit their supplies and their operational capacity, suffered similar decline. By early 1993 then, just as the deliberations of the parliamentary select committee came to naught, the Sri Lankan government had no real prospect of achieving a military settlement.

Chapter 13

Reforms and Reactions

The new Cabinet

It took Premadasa a little over a year to take control of the country, since he had first to quell the JVP insurrection in the south and ensure the departure of the Indians. Thus he had just about three years to carry out whatever programmes he intended. That period can be divided into two sections, distinguishable through a change in the structure of Sri Lankan politics.

The monolithic structure of the UNP broke up along with the overwhelming power of its leader, which Jayewardene had built up and which Premadasa had unashamedly used. This occurred because Dissanayake and Athulathmudali led a revolt against Premadasa from within the UNP. This did not receive as much support as they had expected but it made quite clear the resentment against Premadasa's one-man show.

The charge was to a great extent true, as he had sidelined the two most distinguished and effective members of his parliamentary group. The process began with the 1990 cabinet reshuffle, which took place in March, less than a month after de Zoysa's murder. When he appointed Wijetunge as Prime Minister in 1989 Premadasa had claimed it was only for a year. A year later, with his position secure, Premadasa could now make his real views about the other claimants clear. Dissanayake was dropped from the cabinet, a startling innovation in Sri Lankan politics where reshuffles rarely involved anyone being removed.

Athulathmudali received in the reshuffle the portfolio of Education as well as Higher Education, brought together now under the same Minister for the first time since 1980. However, with Dissanayake removed, since

Wijetunge was kept on as Prime Minister, it was clear that Premadasa had no intention at all of promoting him. Besides, Hameed was kept on as Project Minister of Higher Education, and it was evident that, supported by Premadasa, he was to be in charge there.

Such treatment, shortly after what had happened to de Zoysa, seemed to Athulathmudali a warning, which the dismissal of Dissanayake reinforced. It made clear Premadasa's willingness to use the absolute powers of the Presidency without any sense of accountability to his peers. Increasingly therefore Athulathmudali began to consider his own days in government as numbered.

Some other cabinet changes also reflected Premadasa's determination to stamp his distinctive mark on the government. Wijetunge continued as Minister of Finance, which meant that policy decisions were left entirely to Premadasa, working through his former Permanent Secretary Paskaralingam, now Secretary to the Treasury, the top post in the Civil Service. Premadasa also showed himself anxious to run foreign policy. Wijeratne, though continuing as Deputy Minister of Defence, was moved to Dissanayake's post at Plantations; the Foreign Ministry was given to an amiable nonentity, only to perform the President's bidding.

Premadasa's Vision

It was with a cabinet thus clearly moulded in his own image that Premadasa now embarked upon a programme of far-reaching reforms that marked him out as the most innovative leader Sri Lanka had since independence. Crucial to his vision was a dynamic programme of privatization which the Jayewardene government had avoided, despite its rhetoric about a new economic dispensation. Though he had presented himself as the harbinger of an open economy, done away with many import restrictions and allowed entrepreneurship to develop in areas that had suffered from excessive regulation previously, Jayewardene was a firm believer in state control of the economy. In fact, relishing the powers of patronage it gave him, he had actually taken more of the economy into state hands than Mrs. Bandaranaike had done. Areas such as plantations and newspapers, the takeover of which he had objected to in the seventies, were kept firmly under his control, with the actual management of them handed over to personal friends. Indeed he went further and actually took over another newspaper group as well as the first television network set up in Sri Lanka (so that in addition to the later developed government channel Rupavahini, the country had a superbly titled Government Owned Business Undertaking of the Independent Television Network). With earlier statist legislation used to take over other businesses, despite the new enterprises that had begun after 1977 the proportion of the economy in private hands had gone up in 1988 only to 34% from 30% in 1977; the state sector, which the 1970 government had raised from 30% to 70%, was still 66% in 1988.

Premadasa reversed all this radically. After the internal crisis in the party he moved even more swiftly. By the beginning of 1993 the state sector had gone down to 33%. During his tenure of office the state divested itself of a number of holdings accumulated over the years, various 5 star hotels, Ceylon Oxygen, the State Distilleries Corporation, even the National Development Bank. He also relinquished the monopoly in radio and television, and in insurance, and pushed through a plan to hand over the estates in government hands into private sector management. It was during this period therefore that the Colombo Stock Exchange developed into an active, well regulated organization.

Premadasa's principal functionary in all this was Paskaralingam, the most senior Civil Servant, practically the last one who had entered what was still an elite body before the early sixties when it became part of a consolidated Ceylon Administrative Service. The CCS had always seen itself as a superior body. Enjoying Premadasa's absolute confidence Paskaralingam was able to take and implement decisions quickly, and proved efficient in an era in which administrators were often inhibited by their less able political superiors.

In a context of such overwhelming power, and with the marketing of extremely valuable assets, there were allegations of corruption on a massive scale in which Paskaralingam figured prominently. Less was said at this time about Premadasa, in contrast to his earlier years; the assumption was that in his present position he could command officially the sort of contribution that he had to collect more subtly earlier. It was widely held that Premadasa, having achieved the Presidency, was firm in stamping

Reforms and Reactions

out corruption amongst politicians as well as officials who were not part of his inner circle. Indeed one reason for the unpopularity amongst politicians which led to the attempt to impeach him was that the era of bread and circuses which Jayewardene had initiated to maintain his hold on his party members had been brought to a halt. Jayewardene had encouraged corruption on a large scale, because this enabled him to have a hold over his underlings. In addition, though he presented himself as incorruptible, he certainly abused his position to grant favours, in contracts and in kind, to members of his family. Thus it was useful to him to have more flagrant instances of corruption in his administration, so that he could shine by contrast.

A characteristic instance of the way in which the different regimes functioned can be seen in how mobile telephones were introduced to Sri Lanka. Under Mrs. Bandaranaike's socialist dispensation this would have been done by the Telecommunications Department, however inefficiently, with priority given to politicians. Under Jayewardene a single license was issued to a company owned by his private secretary's son, in partnership with the son of the civil servant who was Wijetunge's secretary as Minister of Telecommunications. Under such monopoly conditions phones were sold at about $2000 each, ensuring massive profits. Under Premadasa, on the contrary, two more licences were issued, one to a joint venture in which Sri Lanka Telecom had a share. Prices plummeted. The difference was symptomatic of the shift from crony capitalism, protected by state regulations, to a more open market.

At the same time Premadasa was always aware of wider social goals, and was certainly not satisfied with the simplistic notion that the benefits of an open economy would necessarily trickle down. The Janasaviya programme, implemented by Charitha Ratwatte, previously Permanent Secretary to Wickremesinghe at the Ministry of Youth Affairs and noted for both dynamism and integrity, was an example of Premadasa's social concern. There, instead of simple handouts, the aim was to promote self sufficiency through training and encouraging entrepreneurship.

Such a philosophy guided Premadasa in his dealings at more sophisticated levels too; and he was ready to use state directives for this purpose within the commercial framework he had promoted, as in the scheme he initiated to open 200 garment factories in rural areas. The scheme met with scorn amongst policy makers in Colombo, and howls of protest from industrialists who were quite content with the factories they had set up in the Free Trade Zone and in areas near to their own Colombo residences. Premadasa's point however was that, given the generous quotas his government had been able to negotiate over the last couple of years with the United States government, the benefits of the industry should be extended to areas with greater needs. His claim was that employment should be provided to youngsters in their own environment, so that they were not forced to migrate to urban and semi-urban areas where living conditions were appalling and expensive, and they were subject to various forms of exploitation. The complaint of some factory owners, that to maintain one of the far-flung factories Premadasa had insisted on they had to close one in the Free Trade Zone, would have been music to his ears. He felt that the state had a responsibility to ensure development across the board, and those who benefited from the economic openings he had created had to be directed towards assisting such priorities.

The construction of such factories, not only in distant Tamil and Muslim areas in the North and East but also in long neglected Sinhalese areas, was an advance that no previous government had contemplated on such a scale. Since previously the state had assumed that it could function only through state-owned and state-controlled institutions, the expansion of industrial activity had necessarily been limited. Premadasa's very simple notion of harnessing private enterprise to fulfill social goals, while using state resources to help such ventures to be profitable, through easy loans and infrastructural development, proved far more practicable. The fact that not all 200 ventures got off the ground did not detract from the basic achievement: employment in rural areas. Employment had been provided to more people on a sustainable basis than under any previous programmes.

In other fields too Premadasa proved determined and able to extend opportunities to deprived areas, in line with the new society he was trying to create. Previously universities in Sri Lanka had been confined to major urban areas. He started Affiliated University Colleges in eleven other centres nationwide, at least one in each province, concentrating on subjects that could provide employment rather than academic courses based on outdated British models that dominated the existing universities. The most popular courses set up included Accountancy and Finance, Small Business Management and, at six of the colleges, English. This last was directed at those who had not had access to English previously, and concentrated on language development, unlike English Literature courses based on a great British tradition that other universities offered for the benefit of the urban middle class.

Premadasa also initiated far-reaching administrative reforms. He had always been lukewarm about Provincial Councils. He regretted that Village Councils, responsible for areas of particular concern to small communities, were abolished with Jayewardene's first attempt at devolution through District Development Councils in 1981. As Minister of Local Government in Jayewardene's cabinet Premadasa had prepared proposals for his own programme of devolution, based on manageable sized units rather than ethnic considerations. By 1991 he was ready to implement this programme, which established Pradeshiya Sabhas, small units of local administration that were presented as not incompatible with the Provincial Councils. These units had little power as to policy, but a number of functions that had accrued to the centre in the last decade were taken over by them, making access for the ordinary citizen much easier.

With regard to the wider issues which had roused the demand for devolution, Premadasa established quite clearly that he himself was above racial considerations. Though with the Tamils this took time, his cultivation of minority political parties was by and large successful, and by the time he died he was able to look on them all as potential allies. In addition, by his own regular forays into their areas, through his Presidential Mobile Secretariats as well as by the developmental projects he put into operation, he created a sense that had been lacking since independence, particularly as far as the Eastern Province was concerned, that the centre actually cared about people at the periphery. Thus the UNP did comparatively well at the Pradeshiya Sabha elections held in May 1991 in the East, and in the few areas in the North that were able to poll. Conversely, though the UNP did better than opposition parties in the rest of the country, Premadasa was comparatively disappointed with the results, which may have fuelled his determination to concentrate even more on rural development schemes over the next couple of years.

The 1991 elections were the fairest that had been held in the country since 1977, and their results were accepted as such. After the UNP had come to power in 1977, it had begun a process of ensuring that elections produced the result the government wanted, through violence, supported by the security forces. The process had been first tested at the Jaffna DDC election in 1981, and was brought to a fine art at the 1982 referendum. No one except the government thought the results of elections from 1981 onward a fair reflection of the views of the electorate. Contrary to all this, the 1991 Pradeshiya Sabha elections were widely accepted as fair. Though there were still some instances of manipulation, they marked the beginning of the restoration of democracy in Sri Lanka.

In this regard indeed Premadasa, unlike Jayewardene, actually believed that he was acting on behalf of the people he governed. In other respects too he showed himself a complete contrast to Jayewardene, whose specialty had been the destruction of institutions and the safeguards they offered against arbitrary authority. In appointing the Chief Justice for instance, Jayewardene had shown distinct partiality. He appointed his personal lawyer, then the judge who had presided over the tribunal used to deprive Mrs. Bandaranaike of her civic rights, finally a partisan, instead of the most senior judge; the latter had incurred his displeasure by delivering an unfavourable minority judgment on the Provincial Councils Bill. When this last appointee was about to retire the Attorney General, who had behaved in a shamefully partisan manner over the Richard de Zoysa case, made his own claims known. Though there were precedents for such an appointment, this would have been seen as a clear indication that partisanship was again at a premium. Premadasa however appointed the most senior serving judge, who had maintained a sterling reputation for integrity even in Jayewardene's time. The appointment was a momentous turning point, the opposite of the government sponsored attack eight years earlier, after Jayewardene had won his referendum and seemed securely in power, on the homes of the judges who had found police officers guilty of violating fundamental rights.

The attempted impeachment

Yet if Premadasa initiated and carried through a great many admirable programmes suggesting significant conceptual advances in state policy, and in general showed himself willing to restore some of their lost status to official institutions, he was still most definitely an autocrat. He also showed himself as pettily vindictive at times. Thus, though independent newspapers and magazines began to emerge during his tenure, there were heavy handed measures to try to rein them in, including limitations on newsprint and advertising. It was only after the revolt in his party that journalists began to be as outspoken as they had been before Jayewardene muzzled them.

When Premadasa's controls seemed at their height, following the local elections of 1991, a challenge to his authority occurred within his party. Athulathmudali, feeling sidelined, came together with Gamini Dissanayake, to get together enough UNP rebels to defeat the government on a money bill, which would have necessitated the resignation of the Prime Minister and the cabinet. Since the rebels together with the opposition would then command a majority in parliament, Premadasa would have been compelled to appoint a new cabinet from amongst them.

To achieve this the cooperation of the SLFP was required. This proved relatively easy, since Mrs. Bandaranaike was as anxious as the rebels to have Premadasa removed. Meanwhile Athulathmudali had also met the Speaker, M H Mohammed, who was also known to be opposed to Premadasa. Confident of getting TULF support as well, Mohammed convinced Athulathmudali to begin with a motion to impeach the President. That required a 2/3 majority for referral by parliament to the Supreme Court for investigation but Mohammed believed, once the process began, that many would support them. Meanwhile the Speaker could entertain such a motion if he were satisfied that half the members of parliament had signed it. Once that happened the President was precluded from dissolving parliament. That it was thought Premadasa might do this, and that it had to be guarded against, is an indication of the mindset of the rebels. Though confident they could muster a majority in parliament against him, they were fearful that Premadasa would be able to win a general election.

With their plan of action decided, Athulathmudali and Dissanayake set about getting the required signatures. Though secrecy was observed, towards the end of August news of the plan began to leak and Mohammed and Dissanayake decided they had to act immediately, both of them not quite sure whether Athulathmudali would stay committed. Mohammed accordingly sent an official intimation of the motion he had received to Premadasa while he was in a cabinet meeting. He telephoned the IGP and the service commanders to inform them of his action, so that the President was precluded from dissolving parliament. He ordered them to give full protection to all MPs in view of possible threats to their lives.

The Speaker's letter reached Premadasa while he was in cabinet and was read out there. As the motion itself was not attached, Premadasa had no idea who had signed it and he sought a motion of confidence from his ministers. This was passed unanimously. Athulathmudali, who had no idea that the plan was to be activated so soon, resolutely concealed his own involvement. When on the next day too he concealed his involvement, the other conspirators became suspicious, especially because just after the cabinet meeting he had had a long private meeting with Premadasa. In fact the suspicions were amply justified, for Athulathmudali had put it to Premadasa that the whole thing could be dropped if he were made Prime Minister and some constitutional changes to reduce the power of the presidency were adopted.

Premadasa decided to refuse the offer and fight back. The conspirators went ahead therefore with a press conference on Friday August 30th, at which Athulathmudali declared himself after it had been agreed that he would be recognized as the leader of the struggle. Though he had to be thus dragged into the open, from then on he showed himself the keenest and most dynamic of the conspirators. One other cabinet minister made the break with him on that day, as did seven other MPs; no great effort was made to bring anyone else who had signed out into the open.

By this stage perhaps some who had initially extended support had begun to change their minds. Premadasa certainly acted with speed to ensure this. First he prorogued Parliament for a month; this had not been anticipated. This reduced pressure on MPs who had signed and allowed him to bring arguments and resources to bear on them. In particular he made it clear that he was prepared to forgive and forget, while allowing more privileges to the MPs who had felt neglected earlier.

Given the secrecy that had been maintained, it did not prove too difficult to get the party to close ranks behind him. Athulathmudali continued confident, especially after a rally at which substantial public support for the rebels made itself felt. He was optimistic enough, when a meeting of the chief ministers of the various provinces was being held, to declare that almost all were about to announce their support for the rebels. Yet they unanimously pledged their support to Premadasa. In such a context of distrust and uncertainty, with no big names following Athulathmudali and his single cabinet colleague, it became easier for those who supported Premadasa to claim that the rebels had never had the requisite numbers. All MPs who had not come out into the open were persuaded to sign a motion of confidence in the President, which was handed over to the Speaker.

Meanwhile, having decided not to bargain with Athulathmudali, and finding Dissanayake determined in his opposition, Premadasa set to work on Mohammed. A number of methods were employed, including pressure from various Muslim envoys. Premadasa's relations with the Arab states had always been good, and he could also claim to have closed the Israel interests section, housed for a few years in the American Embassy; it had been opened at Athulathmudali's behest when as National Security Minister he had obtained military aid from Israel.

As time passed without any resolution of the crisis, the rebels became more desperate. A great deal of emphasis was laid on the allegation in the impeachment motion that Premadasa had traitorously provided arms to the Tigers. This formed the substance of a no-confidence motion proposed by the SLFP against the government. The rhetoric used about this in public sounded racist, and Tamil support for the motion began to fade.

In this context Mohammed reported that he had ceased to entertain the motion to impeach the president, since it did not have the required number of valid signatures. Given the vote of confidence in Premadasa conveyed to him by all the other UNP members, his ruling could not be challenged. This fact did not prevent comments about his duplicity or the sum that he was supposed to have been paid. Yet it could be argued that Mohammed had only begun to waver after it became clear to him that Athulathmudali had tried to negotiate his own settlement.

In terms of the other UNP members who came out into the open, only one of whom was held in respect, the move seemed to be that of disgruntled politicians no longer able to take advantage of the system. But in the wider sense the initiative radically changed Sri Lankan politics. It immeasurably weakened the solid hold the UNP had had over the proponents of a modern political outlook and methodology, and propelled some of them who were articulate and able politicians to the forefront of opposition. The impeachment thus restored a balance that had been lacking for years.

It was a significant turning point in the country's history. Athulathmudali, swallowing his disappointment at what he took to be only the temporary failure of his ambitions, entered with relish into his new role as the *de facto* leader of the opposition. The enthusiasm and energy he displayed in this role, without even a seat in parliament, made it clear how much better both he and the country would have been served had he entered politics under an ordinary democratic dispensation, instead of the top heavy authoritarianism introduced by the UNP in 1977.

Chapter 14

Restoring the Balance

The new opposition

Athulathmudali, Dissanayake and the other dissidents who had declared themselves were expelled from the UNP and lost their seats in parliament. The expulsion was challenged in the Supreme Court which ruled it valid in that the rebels had clearly violated party norms. Meanwhile Premadasa made great play of the fact that almost all those who had followed Athulathmudali and Dissanayake had appalling reputations. In fact there were enough unsavoury specimens on the other side for Premadasa to mock the rebels' claim that they had wanted to clean up the party.

With almost all who had signed their motion falling in line behind Premadasa, it was a daunting task that awaited Athulathmudali and Dissanayake as they set about establishing a new party. They called this the Democratic United National Front, and claimed it was the true heir to the UNP which Premadasa had perverted. They had indicated earlier that Jayawardene supported them and, though disappointed that during the crisis he had declared himself a loyal party man, they still kept on good terms with him. They were harsh however in their criticisms of Wickremesinghe, who they had initially hoped would join them. Wickremesinghe was the other prominent representative, apart from Athulathmudali and Dissanayake, of the elite of Colombo, which might have been much more supportive of the new party had Wickremesinghe too joined it. Since however he stayed with Premadasa, the upper classes could, despite their personal distaste for Premadasa, happily stay loyal to the UNP, to the chagrin of the rebels. This led to Dissanayake in particular being critical of Wickremesinghe, whom he characterized as a young fascist. Having earlier been seen as the rising star of the UNP when he was part of its old establishment, he now saw Wickremesinghe slotting into the position almost effortlessly.

Though Dissanayake had been resolute to begin with, over the next eighteen months he found the struggle wearisome. Negotiations were opened with Premadasa, helped by the fact that in private the latter acknowledged that Dissanayake's opposition had been understandable, given that he had been dismissed from the cabinet. It was rather Athulathmudali whom Premadasa saw as the villain of the piece, whom he was determined never to forgive, and who was his principal rival. And it was Athulathmudali who steadily built up the DUNF so that by the time Provincial Council elections were held, in May 1993, it was a force to be reckoned with. He had to work against heavy odds, but he persevered, in isolation sometimes, except for his personal staff who had stuck by him.

Premadasa meanwhile had taken the warning to heart. For the rest of his tenure he made sure that his MPs continued happy and enjoyed the perks that under Jayewardene they had come to expect as their due. However, though he set up advisory committees, to give ordinary MPs a role that could be compensated, he did not change the pattern on which he had governed previously. Real power was concentrated in the same hands as before, for he took over Athulathmudali's Education portfolio and gave Premachandra's Labour Ministry to Wijetunge.

1992 saw the full flowering of Premadasa's innovations. That was the year in which many state ventures were privatized and the plantations given over to private management, nine university colleges were established, and plans drawn up for the development of the harbour at Galle and the establishment of a Free Trade Zone in its vicinity. The Janasaviya programme too seemed to be having an impact; though implemented on a more limited scale than had at first been promised, targets had been carefully chosen, and concentrated on in the allocation of jobs. The thrust to create jobs through the financial allocations under the programme, instead of using them as mere handouts, had borne fruit.

During this period Premadasa also made attempts to establish himself as a national leader. The allegations against him that had the widest coverage concerned his dealings with the Tigers; and it was over the next year that General Kobbekaduwa planned and executed the various sorties that made clear Premadasa's determination to overcome the Tigers. At the same time he took shrewd advantage of the impression the opposition had managed to convey during the impeachment, that it might adopt a racist position to win Sinhalese votes. He fine-tuned his approach to evince his own moderation as compared with the alternatives presented by other politicians.

In the SLFP a realignment was taking place, parallel to the one that had occurred after the deprivation of Mrs. Bandaranaike's civic rights when Mrs. Bandaranaike had turned to the Kumaranatungas. After the 1982 presidential election the balance had shifted the other way and Anura Bandaranaike had once more come into the ascendant. With the 1988 election defeat however he found life less comfortable. Traditionalists in the party argued that Mrs. Bandaranaike had lost the election because of his right-wing influence and that Chandrika Kumaratunga, as she now called herself, was the only hope for the party. Mrs. Bandaranaike seemed in agreement, perhaps seeing this as protection for her own position, as some of Anura's supporters were making clear their belief that it was time she retired.

Chandrika tried to take over the SLMP on her return to Sri Lanka, intending to move it back en masse into the SLFP. Ossie Abeygunasekera, who had taken over the SLMP in her absence and contested the presidential election as its nominee, resisted this, and the party supported him. Chandrika and some of her supporters, most prominently a radical dentist called Rajitha Senaratne, then set up a party called the BNP. But before long Chandrika gravitated back to the SLFP. With her return the forces opposed to her brother in the party were able to formulate a pact with the old left parties. This new umbrella alliance, called the People's Alliance on the lines of the earlier United Socialist Alliance, was registered with the Elections Commissioner in time to contest the 1993 Provincial Councils election. As a counter weight to this Premadasa cultivated Abeygunasekera, and obtained his support, though a majority of the SLMP parted company with him at this stage and ended up in the PA.

Double Jeopardy

By early 1993, despite setbacks suffered due to General Kobbekaduwa's death, Premadasa was quite confident. In March he dissolved seven provincial councils and scheduled elections in May. A sign of his confidence was the decision to hold all the elections together, unlike in 1988 when Jayewardene had staggered them, holding them first in areas where the government was strong and enabling government resources to be concentrated in different places in turn to ensure victory. Despite this confidence, it was clear from the start that the results would be close.

The biggest opposition draw was Athulathmudali, who fulfilled a punishing schedule, addressing four or five meetings every day. Complaints against Premadasa included the allegation that he had initiated a reign of terror and masterminded the deaths of Ranjan Wijerame and General Kobbekaduwa. The former had been getting too powerful for Premadasa's liking. He had also shown determination to overcome the Tigers, whereas Premadasa had wanted to keep the war going since it allowed him to maintain a hold on the rest of the country. The war allowed Premadasa and his friends, including those in the army who had implemented the reign of terror, to make a great deal of money. Similar reasons were adduced for the death of Kobbekaduwa: successes he had achieved indicated that he could conclude the war more quickly than was to Premadasa's convenience.

Reflecting even more adversely on Premadasa was his link with Ronnie Gunasinghe, who was generally known to have murdered de Zoysa and was now in charge of Premadasa's personal security. As though to make clear the absurdity of a simplistic view that Premadasa was the inspiration of all evil, the other police officer renowned for excessive brutality, SSP Udugampola, was firmly in the other camp. Having supplied the DUNF with material pertaining to UNP attacks on opposition politicians during the JVP period, he was said to have gone into hiding to avoid being charged with excesses. The DUNF leaders had been part of the government during that period, while Udugampola's history of aggression dated from before Premadasa's assumption of the presidency; there had been no murmur of dissent from the rebels then, hence their claim to uphold law and order at this stage was somewhat suspect.

In addition to allegations concerning Paskaralingam, and also the Maharaja business organization which had cultivated Premadasa for years with substantial profits to themselves, other arguments used to attack Premadasa involved his close confidante Sirisena Cooray. Cooray had been Minister of Housing since 1989, and had supervised the Gam Udawa programme which had grown over the years. Premadasa's dependence on Cooray was deep, and he had appointed him General Secretary of the party on Wijeratne's death. His critics however alleged that Cooray had associations with the underworld, and was responsible for several deaths. Such allegations were spread most effectively through Dissanayake's brother-in-law, Wickrema Weerasooriya, who had masterminded scurrilous campaigns for Jayewardene in the past, and also for Premadasa during his own presidential campaign. Weerasooriya had since moved to Australia, but he came back to help the DUNF campaign, and inspired a series of posters that denigrated Premadasa.

It was in such a context that on the night of 23 April Athulathmudali was shot dead while addressing an election meeting in Colombo. Suspicion immediately focussed on the government; and the manner in which it reacted to the death served to exacerbate this. Athulathmudali had made several requests for enhanced security over the past few months but, instead of receiving a positive response, he was given even less security. When a body was discovered in the vicinity on the next day, the police were quick to declare that this was the assassin, and that he was Tamil. This was on the strength of an identity card soon discovered to be forged, and without any fingerprints on it, not even those of the policeman who was supposed to have found it on the body.

With Ronnie Gunasinghe given responsibility for the interrogation of witnesses, it seemed clear that the government was not interested in a thorough job. The conclusion seemed inescapable that the forces of law and order believed the assassination had to be shrouded in secrecy to guard Premadasa's interests. What was not clear was whether they thought Premadasa's own circle was responsible, or whether they were only protecting one or other of the Tamil militant groups which were close to Premadasa. Indeed, it was even mooted that, if the Tigers were responsible, they had acted in Premadasa's interest, if not on his instructions.

Over the next few days the extent to which such assumptions were widely accepted became clear, not least through the violent demonstration at the funeral. This was quelled with tear gas, which created an even more forceful impression of a state under siege. Premadasa's pronouncements began to take on a hysterical tone, though there seemed about them a sincerity that indicated anguish at being convicted in the public mind for a crime he had not committed. But it was not possible to dismiss the possibility that he or his associates had known that the murder was being planned and had decided to turn a blind eye. Certainly, a week after Athulathmudali's death, barring a miracle, the hold Premadasa had on a substantial proportion of the population was bound to be loosened.

But the miracle did occur. On 1 May Premadasa himself was killed, blown up by a suicide bomber in the midst of the UNP's May Day match. The assassin was a man named Babu, who it later transpired was known to the President. The explosion killed a large number of people including Ronnie Gunasinghe. There was little doubt that it was a Tiger operation, since the suicide bombing bore the hallmarks of Tiger techniques, on the pattern of the killing of Rajiv Gandhi. The question remained open as to whether Premadasa was aware of Babu's background, whether indeed he was Premadasa's link to the Tigers, and if so how close the relationship was.

Apart from eliminating an effective leader, the Tigers also anticipated chaos in the short term, both sides blaming each other, perhaps attacking each other, with no firm authority to quell the riots. On the other hand, if suspicions fell on Tamils, and there were calls for revenge, that too was all to the good. The LTTE had no illusions that the greatest fillip their movement had received had been provided by the anti-Tamil riots of 1983. Uncertainty and bloodshed could only help them.

That things remained calm was due largely to quick action by Cooray and Wickremesinghe, who between them effectively took control. First a curfew was declared, and the news of Premadasa's death was only made public after it had come into effect; this minimized the possibility of violent reactions. Wijetunge was promptly sworn in to act as President as constitutionally required, and was later nominated to serve for the remaining eighteen months of Premadasa's term. The opposition chose not to contest him, and he was unanimously elected by parliament to fill the vacancy. Cooray, as the older man, having indeed been offered the post once before by Premadasa after the impeachment, was invited to become Prime Minister but refused on the grounds that Wickremesinghe was better suited to the job. He preferred to continue as General Secretary of the party, a post more suited to his talents, which were organizational; he was not an effective performer on political platforms.

Wijetunge indeed was not one either, and he was nervous after recent events to appear in public; it was left to Wickremesinghe to carry through the election campaign when it resumed. Wijetunge got rid of some of the trappings that had made Premadasa vulnerable to criticism, such as the ornate chair resembling a throne that he used on public occasions. Wijetunge also made it clear that the one-man show that had been so resented would not continue. At the same time it was stressed that the policies that had proved so popular, both the economic principles that had encouraged investment, and the social policies that had won support in rural areas, would continue.

But that it was not only the social and economic policies that were to be continued was suggested from the start. When Wijetunge was sworn in as President, it turned out that he intended to hold on to all the portfolios he had before, as well as all those Premadasa had held. Thus while President he was also Minister of Finance, Education and Higher Education, Defence and four other subjects. The impression was that he took very seriously the point he made in one of his election addresses that the spoon was now in his hand. The Sinhala saying he cited made it clear that, when one had the spoon, one used it to serve oneself as well as one's friends. He had used it to suggest that there was no point in voting the opposition into power in the provinces, since he would use his powers to limit the resources available to them; but there was little doubt of the further implications of the remark, as it applied to someone always known to be corrupt. In earlier years admittedly he had been known to be modest in his desires, sticking to the pattern of the corrupt in the 1970 government when opportunities were limited. The expansion that took place under Jayewardene's new economic dispensation had passed him by. But he had moved onto bigger things as Prime Minister and Minister of Finance. Now, as President, he saw the sky as the limit.

Part VII

Using the Spoon

Wijetunge as President (1993–1994)

Chapter 15

The New Dispensation

Corruption compounded

Apart from personal advantage, it is possible that there were other reasons for Wijetunge to cling to so many portfolios. The bureaucrats who had run these ministries previously could be relied upon to maintain continuity more effectively than the politicians. Certainly the UNP as now constituted suffered from a singular lack of talent. He was also keen to woo the DUNF, and needed to have some ministries available for them if the move succeeded.

It was certainly a possibility, since the DUNF rhetoric had been primarily anti-Premadasa, and there were no essential differences of policy. Dissanayake, who had even contemplated the idea of going back while Premadasa was alive, had indicated that he favoured the idea. If he went over, it was likely that the rest would have to follow since, with Athulathmudali dead, there was likelihood of a paucity of resources, and no one with enough electoral appeal to attract votes.

And there were certainly very good personal reasons for Wijetunge to want the DUNF back. He had got where he was because he had been seen as Premadasa's man, but from the time he took over the Presidency he showed determination to distance himself from his predecessor. He argued that the UNP had lost support to the DUNF, and it made political sense to try to get the DUNF back to revive the earlier majority.

But important also was the lesson he had picked up from Jayewardene, of precluding an obvious successor. With Dissanayake back it would be difficult for the party to dump Wijetunge if he proved a liability. Given the community of interests between Cooray and Wickremesinghe, the former with no personal ambitions, it was clear that Wijetunge would be vulnerable to a palace coup. Perhaps he realized that this would be attempted sooner or later, given his own lack of political appeal, in a situation in which the party had to put forward a candidate for the executive presidency. With Dissanayake back in the UNP however, he would have some sort of insurance since no one would dare to show their hand openly, for fear of being superseded by someone with commensurate claims.

Wijetunge then had good reasons for wanting the DUNF back in. Yet even those who could only lose from this seem to have accepted that it was inevitable. Otherwise it is difficult to explain the decision of the government, implemented by the party stalwarts appointed governors of the Northwestern and Southern Provinces, to install the previous incumbents as Chief Ministers of those provinces after the Provincial Council elections, even though they did not have majorities. The UNP was the largest single party; but, given the DUNF had pledged its support to the PA, and that the PA had agreed that in the Northwestern Province the former Cabinet Minister Premachandra would be Chief Minister, it was foolhardy for the UNP to set up minority administrations unless the DUNF came over.

The UNP's action in this regard was particularly unfortunate; it frittered away the goodwill that it had gained because of the recent events. The assassination of Premadasa had created a wave of sympathy in areas where his policies had been popular, while Wijetunge's low key approach had regained for the UNP some support it had lost in urban and semi-urban areas. Thus it won outright majorities in four provinces, while it was only in the Western Province that it was not the largest single party. This distinction had gone to the PA, with Kumaratunga doing extremely well in the Gampaha District in her first electoral test. In Colombo, where Athulathmudali had shone in the past, the DUNF polled over 20% of the vote, more than it got anywhere else. Yet the UNP had expected to lose here, and its performance elsewhere reassured it that in future elections too it could poll enough nationwide to win. The jugglery over the two provincial administrations, where it did not command a majority, however, raised a question mark over its bona fides.

That Wijetunge was now fulfilling his own agenda was suggested by the appointment that accompanied this stratagem. The legal luminary whose advice was taken on this issue was elevated to a new position of Minister of Constitutional Affairs. This was Premadasa's lawyer, K N Choksy, appointed to parliament in 1989 but given no official position. His elevation to a Ministry at a time when the spirit of the Constitution was being flouted signaled that manipulation of the constitution as well as the institutions that should safeguard it was once more on the cards. This was contrary to the legacy of Premadasa who had managed to maintain a distinction between his personal domination and a respect for forms.

It took barely three months for Wijetunge's honeymoon to be over. The suspicions as to political improprieties, roused initially by the attempt to cling to power in the Provincial Councils, proved well founded. What conclusively marked the administration insupportable was the impression of corruption in the public mind. Though corruption had existed before, with Wijetunge it became a major issue. Both Jayewardene and Premadasa had known that corruption had to be discreet. Wijetunge had no such qualms. His statement that the spoon was in his hand absolutely reflected his beliefs.

Counterpoint, the monthly political magazine edited by Waruna Karunatilleke, de Zoysa's former colleague, now back in Sri Lanka, made clear Wjetunge's total lack of propriety. The magazine had begun publication in March 1993 as the English equivalent of a Sinhala journal which had been hard hitting in its criticism of the government. Attempts to muzzle that journal had failed, and in the end Premadasa decided that it would be less trouble to let it continue. The first issue of *Counterpoint*, had included a detailed critique of Premadasa's garment factory scheme. The next issue, also published before Premadasa's death, focused on shady dealings in Air Lanka, the national carrier set up by Jayewardene in the days when he thought Sri Lanka would soon emulate Singapore. Since then it had provided pretty pickings for whichever favourites of the moment ran it.

The account in *Counterpoint*, in common with most criticisms of shady dealings in Premadasa's time, could only point out misjudgments that did not necessarily involve dishonesty. In contrast the August 1993 issue highlighted a number of instances of blatant abuses noted by internal government monitoring procedures. A number of these abuses had occurred in Premadasa's time; but, as the editorial of the next issue put it, what was astonishing was the absence of any reaction. In Premadasa's time what might have been anticipated was anger, attempts to cover up areas in which Premadasa or his associates were involved, corrective action in other areas. Now what seemed apparent was that public accountability was considered of no consequence. The cover of the September 1993 issue was captioned 'One Man - No Show', with a cartoon of Wijetunge flexing his muscles, flanked by anxious figures of Wickremesinghe and Cooray.

That issue contained a number of articles about corruption in a range of government institutions. These instances and others were taken up again in the next four issues of the magazine, which suggested that even greater irregularities were occurring during this period. Finally, in February 1994, *Counterpoint* came to the conclusion that Wijetunge was the moving spirit behind this plundering. The issue contained detailed accounts of how he had interfered with officials to ensure advantages to friends and associates and defrauded the state. The article was accompanied by photographs of actual minutes he had sent in such instances.

The most outrageous instance of Wijetunge's utter disregard of the norms of responsible behaviour occurred when he issued a Presidential pardon to two party thugs who had been convicted of attempted culpable homicide. Such cavalier use by Wijetunge of his powers of office extended to areas where criminality was not involved as when he decided to dismiss the University Grants Commission. No reason was given; it seemed that the refusal of the Chairman to accommodate requests regarding university admissions from Wijetunge's underlings had motivated what stymied any further developments in the field. The new appointees, chosen on purely partisan grounds, had no interest in trying to understand the reforms their predecessors had initiated. The system therefore sank back into the inertia from which it had been stirred under Premadasa.

Alienating minorities

While administrative confusion proliferated, Wijetunge was also alienating many in the political arena whom Premadasa had cultivated. This might

The New Dispensation

have been predicted, for Wijetunge had been amongst Mathew's most prominent supporters in the backbench revolt which put paid to Dudley Senanayake's attempts at devolution in 1968. In the general goodwill extended to Wijetunge as he assumed the Presidency that fact was allowed to lie dormant. It came to mind soon enough however, for very early in his tenure Wijetunge decided to take on the role of a Sinhala nationalist. Thus he claimed that there was no real ethnic problem in Sri Lanka, but rather just a terrorist problem, by which he indicated that the political settlements discussed over the preceding years were beside the point. All that was required was to crush the Tigers. Again, the Sinhala nation was a tree, to which the minorities clung like vines, and he would ensure that they did not destroy it. Wijetunge decided to accept the assurance of his army commander that the Tigers could be defeated militarily. An operation launched in mid-September however proved disastrous, and was followed by an assault by the Tigers which nearly over-ran a vital military outpost. Fortunately that prompted the replacement of an aggressive army commander with one less flamboyant.

The community of interests that Premadasa had created was swiftly disrupted by Wijetunge's approach. It was more important to him to be cheered on by nationalist ideologues and chauvinistic politicians, one of whom declared that Wijetunge was born of true Sinhala parents. Such reactions inclined Wijetunge to flex his muscles more aggressively. He was brusque with Thondaman, to make it clear that the special relationship he had enjoyed with earlier presidents could no longer be taken for granted. Ashraff, understandably, began to despair early on. He suggested to Abeygunasekera and Amaratunga, with whom he had often acted together earlier, that they should revive the Civic Forum, an umbrella group for pluralist policies that they had tried to stitch together with the TULF previously. Meanwhile the Tamil groups, the TULF as well as the militants, had begun to have discussions with the SLFP and with Mrs. Kumaratunga, who was one of the few politicians who had eschewed any form of racism in her pronouncements and policies.

That both the style and the substance of Wiljetunge's government were bound to lead to disaster was discerned early by Sirisena Cooray. Cooray like Premadasa was disdained by the Sri Lankan elite, and even more detailed reasons were adduced as to why he was unsuitable for public office: he had connections with organized crime and had profited from corruption. Yet such things could also be said about just anyone of any standing in the UNP. Close associates of establishment figures such as Athulathmudali, Dissanayake and Wickremesinghe had been involved in criminal activities, extending to gangland killings; allegations with regard to shady dealings were rife against the first two; Jayewardene and his immediate family too had benefited from his position, while the use Jayewardene's government had made of criminal elements to suppress opposition was widely known; yet, given the social background of such figures, their misdemeanours were ignored by the elite. Cooray on the other hand, given his antecedents, was like Premadasa a target for moral outrage.

At the same time it could not be denied that he was an able organizer. Patent too was his personal devotion to Premadasa. Indeed, while there was almost an air of festivity leading up to and at Premadasa's funeral, which reflected the lack of real feeling towards him, Cooray's tears before the burning pyre, after all the other major figures had left the scene, indicated the very real bond between the two men.

Wijetunge, on the contrary, had shown himself from the start as determined to repudiate Premadasa's legacy. What was initially welcomed as statesmanship, as he dismantled some of the more unsavoury features of Premadasa's rule, could be seen as arising from the resentment that had accumulated over the years at the disregard with which he had been treated, even though raised to high office.

In a letter Cooray sent Wijetunge in August 1993 he stressed the need for a clear cut political agenda like Premadasa's. He pointed out that this was lacking and, unless imaginative leadership were provided, the UNP would certainly lose any election that was to be held. Wijetunge did nothing in response. The letter was subsequently leaked to the press but Cooray found no one willing to support him. So the subject was shelved. Wijetunge's own view was that Cooray's analysis was motivated by personal ambition, and in particular by opposition to what Wijetunge wished, that Gamini Dissanayake return to the UNP, if possible with the rest of the DUNF.

The New Dispensation

The rest of the UNP continued to indulge Wijetunge. The Appeals Court delivered a scathing verdict on the decision of the governors of the Southern and Northwestern Provinces to appoint chief ministers in violation of the expressed intentions of a majority of elected members, so that the UNP administrations were accordingly replaced by PA/DUNF coalitions. The UNP, however, declared Wijetunge its unanimously agreed candidate for the presidential election to be held a year later.

Inconsequential manoeuvres

This was enough to keep Wijetunge happy for the moment. Then, forgetting his attempt to bring in the DUNF, he embarked on another initiative that he thought would strengthen his position. This was to split the SLFP.

Anura Bandaranaike, worried about his position in the SLFP, opened discussions with Cooray and Wickremesinghe with whom he had been in school. The latter, vulnerable at this stage to the threat posed by Dissanayake, proved positive. Emboldened by this, Bandaranaike gave an interview in which he was critical of the SLFP alliance with Marxists.

The SLFP suspended Bandaranaike from the party because of his interview. His mother probably expected a reconciliation, but both were too wrought up to make the first move. After a couple of months of suspension, with no sign of resolution, Bandaranaike resigned from the SLFP. Cooray and Wickremesinghe having secured a commitment from Wijetunge, Bandaranaike was enrolled as a member of the UNP, with the promise of a portfolio.

That commitment took some time to be fulfilled, contrary to his expectations and indeed the expectations of those he had negotiated with. First he needed a seat in parliament, for he had lost his SLFP seat on his resignation and a UNP national list vacancy had to be created to put him back into parliament. Cooray achieved this with the compliance of one of Premadasa's followers. Appointment to a Ministry however was delayed for several weeks. Bandaranaike was keen on the Foreign Ministry but Hameed, who had got it back in the last reshuffle, refused to budge. Instead Bandaranaike was offered the Ministry of Finance, but with a budget due shortly he did not think he had anything to gain from the criticism he would have to face.

Soon he realized that he would have to take anything suitable that was offered. Even so his entry into the cabinet was further delayed inexplicably, unless uncertainty on Wijetunge's part were a satisfactory explanation. It was only at the very end of the year that he was finally made Minister of Higher Education. Bandaranaike's entry into the government was celebrated in the government newspapers as a coup on Wijetunge's part. It was also claimed that a great many of his supporters in the SLFP were waiting to join him in the UNP, the moment they had served five years in parliament, to become eligible for pensions. Buoyed by this sort of adulation Wijetunge became even more contemptuous in his treatment of Thondaman. A number of requests Thondaman made for meetings were not granted, which was the more worrying for him since he knew that the Plantations Restructuring Unit was pressing for full privatization.

When Wijetunge seemed determined to ignore him, Thondaman decided to do battle with his customary subtlety and skill. He entered into discussions with Gamini Dissanayake, who announced that the opposition in the Central Provincial Council, to which he himself still officially belonged, intended to propose a motion of no-confidence in the Provincial Ministry. The members of Thondaman's CWC, who had been elected on the UNP ticket, but preserved their separate identity, declared that they would support the motion, which would have been enough to pass it and bring down the Ministry.

The revelation of this strategy caused panic in the UNP. Wijetunge however, instead of entering into talks with Thondaman, continued to cultivate Sellasamy, the General Secretary of the CWC, in line with his earlier plan to reduce Thondman's influence. Sellasamay proved easy to win over, but it turned out that he had hardly any clout in the party and he was dismissed from his post, while the CWC Central Provincial Councillors continued adamant.

The situation seemed worrying; but it was at this stage that Wijetunge evoked a new situation that for a short time suggested that he had been underestimated, and that he was a greater maestro of political survival than his predecessors. The motion of no-confidence was disallowed by the Central Provincial Council Chairman, a member of Abeygunasekera's SLMP, which had contested the election with the UNP. This ruling was not challenged because Dissanayake now proved amenable, having been convinced by Wijetunge that his interests would be looked after if he simply rejoined the UNP, a move that those who feared him could not easily oppose.

Dissanayake accordingly resigned from the DUNF, giving up his seat in the Central Provincial Council, and rejoined the UNP as an ordinary member. There he set about re-establishing contacts he would find useful. In pursuit of this, but as an accomplished master of public relations, he maintained his association with Thondaman and succeeded in effecting a rapprochement between him and Wijetunge. The unfortunate Sellasamy found himself out in the cold, and expelled from his party.

Wijetunge's principal achievement, which may have contributed to Dissanayake's decision, was the toppling of the Southern Provincial Council administration set up after the Appeal Court ruling. The coalition there only had a majority of one. Though the DUNF members seemed to be solidly behind the administration, it transpired that an SLFP member close to Bandaranaike was willing to assist the UNP. Bandaranaike brought him to Wijetunge; subsequently he was to claim that he was not privy to Wijetunge's arrangements.

So the new administration was defeated on a money bill with the member in question not present at the vote. Promptly the governor dissolved the Council and called for fresh elections, avoiding the alternative of allowing the administration to muster a vote of confidence. The missing member meanwhile claimed he had been kidnapped, which was why he had not attended the crucial meeting. What prompted such an excuse was uncertain, since it convinced no one and added to the impression of double-dealing.

At the time however it was argued that Wijetunge had pulled off a great political coup. Even though the Southern Province DUNF councillors seemed to give the lie to this, in that almost all of them contested the election that was subsequently held on the PA ticket, it was claimed that with Dissanayake in the UNP it was only a matter of time before the

DUNF also rejoined it en masse. This assumption seemed the more realistic in that his successor as leader of the DUNF, the former Minister Premachandra, now Chief Minister of the Northwestern Province, supported him. In time therefore even DUNF councilors in the Western Province, who owed allegiance to Athulathmudali and were not in favour of rejoining the UNP, would have to accept the inevitable or be expelled.

On this scenario it was illogical that the Southern Council should have been dissolved, because it meant the disappearance of the DUNF there as an entity that could be won over. Instead, all votes cast against the UNP at the forthcoming election would remain with the opposition. But at this stage logic had nothing to do with it. The President had found himself in a tight spot, and crafty manoeuvring had brought him out on top, with all the cards on his side.

The election was set for the 24th of March. Wijetunge was now so full of confidence that he agreed to lead the campaign himself, albeit with precautions that involved him being taken by helicopter to meetings, and then rushing hurriedly up the steps to the platform. There a bullet proof cage awaited him. He could count upon a wealth of talent. He had the forces Premadasa had won over, Abeygunasekera and Amaratunga, who had provided Wickremesinghe with oratorical support in the previous Provincial Council election campaign ten months earlier. He also had Dissanayake and Bandaranaike, major figures from the two parties that had on the previous occasion managed with their combined strength to get only one more seat than the UNP in the south. He even had Rajitha Senaratne, who had been the secretary of the BNP that Chandrika Kumaratunga had set up on her return to Sri Lanka when she had been unable to take control of the SLMP. This last Wijetunge thought a particular asset, since Mrs. Kumaratunga was now clearly his principal rival with Athulathmudali and Dissanayake as well as her brother absent from the opposition campaign. Her mother's increasing frailty made it almost impossible for her to appear on public platforms, so Mrs. Kumaratunga was the only major national figure in the opposition. With some of her principal former associates who could be relied upon to attack her without quarter now with him, Wijetunge felt that she would not amount to much of a threat.

It was at this stage that he coined the description of the UNP as an 'ambalama', a wayside resting place providing shelter for all who wanted to rest in it. He did not consider the wider implications of his image, or the varying motives of those who used an 'ambalama'. Instead, as he settled in his glass box to the strains of Senaratne, his most fervent supporter now, calling him the new Dutugemunu, the king who had after the first major Tamil invasion repossessed the ancient Sinhalese kingdom that covered the entire country, he must have thought the comparison apt.

Chapter 16

Internal Combustion

The writing on the wall

The UNP lost the Southern Provincial Council election very badly. Though on a higher poll it got more votes in two of the three districts than previously, the PA by itself got many more votes, and a higher percentage, than it and the DUNF together had managed ten months previously. After 16 long years it now seemed capable of forming a future government by itself.

Analysis of the result took many forms. The DUNF vote at the previous election had been claimed as, not just the vote of UNP supporters disgruntled with Premadasa, but rather of those waiting to return to the party once his ascendancy had passed. This had been Dissanayake's claim, but the result showed that his participation in the campaign had brought nothing to it.

Another assumption that the results seemed to disprove was that it was desirable for the UNP to repudiate Premadasa's legacy. Research afterwards confirmed what was apparent in reactions to Wijetunge's performance at meetings, namely deep resentment amongst sections of society that had benefited from Premadasa's policies, at how he had been totally forgotten by his successor. This was particularly apparent in the Hambantota district, where the UNP did much worse than in the previous year. Premadasa's son Sajith resided there, and the fact that he had not been invited to participate in any election meeting made the current neglect of Premadasa obvious.

The result in Hambantota seemed also to reflect on Wickremesinghe's own capacities as an organizer, in that that was the district entrusted to his particular charge. Similarly the fact that Matara, which had been entrusted to Cooray, showed a percentage decrease for the UNP, was used to argue that his reputation as an organizer was inflated. In this respect Bandaranaike, who was in charge of Galle, had emerged better; the UNP marginally improved its performance and held on to the same number of seats as previously. In his case however comparisons with his sister were inevitable: whereas when he had been at the helm the SLFP had won no election victories, Chandrika had triumphed at her very first attempt.

Wijetunge was considered the primary cause of the UNP debacle Leaving aside the excesses he had committed just prior to the election such as his pardoning of convicted criminals, he was clearly not a leader who could inspire either confidence or affection.

Unfortunately, given the overwhelming power of the president, conveying this general perception to Wijetunge would have required great courage and dedication. As it happened, there was still one individual in the UNP who possessed these, who could not understand that no one else would support him. Convinced that there was no future for the UNP if Wijetunge was seen as its long term leader, and sure from his private discussions that he had the support of almost all his senior colleagues, Sirisena Cooray encouraged the main government newspaper to publish a detailed analysis of the election result written by Amaratunga. This appeared under the headline 'Premadasa Betrayed'. The main argument was that the debacle was due mainly to Wijetunge's actions and pronouncements. Amaratunga was particularly scathing about Wijetunge's treatment of the minorities, with whom he himself had always enjoyed close ties. Now he pointed out that what was considered the heartland of Sinhala nationalism, the Southern Province and in particular the Hambantota District, had decisively rejected the racist rhetoric that Wijetunge had assumed would keep him in power.

Cooray hoped that the article would rouse debate and build up confidence in those who shared his views. Wijetunge however realized what was happening and, if slow in other respects, showed himself adept at self-preservation. Without allowing time for opposition to build up he demanded the resignation of the chairman of the newspaper group, a close associate of both Premadasa and Cooray, and then asked Cooray too to resign from the post of General Secretary of the UNP. The request was made decorously, with the argument that he needed his own team in harness for the forthcoming election, but the determination to sideline Cooray was obvious.

Cooray's initial response was that he needed time to consider the request. He did not however canvass support, on the grounds that his colleagues had to support him if they wanted the party to survive in power. If they did not, he would not put himself out further. Indeed he was particularly disappointed that Wickremesinghe, whom he was promoting as the alternative, did not speak up on his behalf, but played safe and said that the question could be left to the other two to sort out between them.

Wijetunge meanwhile canvassed energetically, with assistance from Dissanayake and his supporters. He even had a meeting with Mrs. Premadasa, to apologize for his previous conduct towards her, and make her understand that he would nominate her to Parliament as soon as possible. The impression he gave was that the stumbling block in this regard was Cooray. Meanwhile the media was full of the arrest of an associate of Cooray's in connection with gang warfare. Newspapers, in highlighting the connection, reported too the expressed determination of the President to clean the UNP of its underworld connections, a line Dissanayake too had used when returning to the UNP. Faced with these pressures, and irritated too at not receiving in public any support from those who had expressed the need for change in private, Cooray resigned from the post of General Secretary. He did not resign from his ministry; the pressures on him eased immediately. The parting too was amicable, with Cooray warning Wijetunge, as he had warned Wickremesinghe, that Dissanayake sought not his post but theirs.

Wijetunge had probably been mindful of this from the start. He did not replace Cooray with any of the candidates suggested by Dissanayake; instead he brought in Gamini Wijesekera, the former secretary of Rukman Senanayake's party. He too had rejoined the UNP when that party was dissolved, following Senanayake's return to the fold after Premadasa's victory. Wijesekera had an untarnished reputation for integrity; neither the corrupt nor the violent practices that most UNP politicians engaged in had ever been attributed to him. However, while his appointment was welcomed for that reason, it was also recognized that he had never shown himself effective as an organizer. That he should have been appointed to the main administrative post in the UNP at a time when, after seventeen years in power, it was seen to be vulnerable also seemed evidence that Wijetunge had little idea how elections were won.

An alternative leader

Afrer the Southern Province elections the opposition was now on a winning streak; and, it now had a charismatic leader who could be presented as a credible alternative. In fact Mrs. Kumaratunga was extremely lucky to have achieved this position. Had Athulathmudali not been killed, his status as a long established national figure, and his emergence as Premadasa's main rival, would probably have led him to eclipse her. Again, if Dissanayake had made a concerted effort to take Athulathmudali's place, and indeed to cultivate the SLFP as Athulathmudali had done, he would surely have emerged as the leading figure in the opposition instead of Mrs. Kumaratunga. His decision to head back to the UNP left the SLFP dominant as the alternative to the UNP; and what might then have presented problems to Mrs. Kumaratunga within the SLFP was resolved by Anura Bandaranaike's decision to leave.

It was around this time that it became clear that her mother, who had held on grimly to her leadership of the party all the years when Anura was in a position to succeed her, was in a very feeble state. Having suffered a stroke in the previous year, her speech was slurred though her mind still seemed clear. This made it impossible for her to campaign effectively. At the same time she had shown no inclination to give up, and the party confirmed regularly that she would be its candidate at the presidential election to be held at the end of 1994. However, since Mrs. Kumaratunga was given an opportunity earlier in the year to establish herself as an effective campaigner and a leader in a contest from which Mrs. Bandaranaike could excuse herself because of its relative parochiality, the stage was set for the younger woman to take over as the effective leader of the party.

With superb self-confidence Mrs. Kumaratunga had invited leaders of Colombo's business community to lunch on the day after the southern election. The event had been arranged at a five-star hotel with the assistance of the Maharaja Organization; the latter had grown increasingly irritated by Wijetunge's attempts to distance them. The Maharajas could have begun to move over simply because they were sensitive to changing circumstances. Yet despite this evidence of shifting allegiances on the part of a leading player, a number of the invitees to the lunch had sent in excuses, fearing to be seen in what was still thought of as compromising company. After the results were announced they flocked to attend, and indeed were gratified by the event.

Its aim had been to make it clear that, contrary to the radical reputation that had dogged her for the last two decades, since she had served on the land reform commission set up by her mother's 1970 government, Mrs. Kumaratunga was by no means opposed to big business and would continue with the open economy if she came to power. Her criticism, she wanted to make clear, was of the crony capitalism that had been permitted to flourish and of the government's failure to develop a genuine production base. She did not contest that the principles on which governments since 1977 had claimed to operate were preferable to the statist socialism that had earlier characterized the economy.

Given the realities of the new world order, with regard to politics as well as economics, there was little doubt that someone of Mrs. Kumaratunga's age and academic qualifications would have been sincere in such an approach. The greater fear was whether her own party would allow her to pursue such a line. Her main supporters within it were radicals, and the alliance she and they had helped build up was with Marxist parties. But, as though to allay such fears, Mrs. Kumaratunga made it known that she had her own think tank, with a much more modem outlook, which included international civil servants and leading academics. As though to confirm this a few weeks later G L Pieris, the Vice-Chancellor of the University of Colombo, one of the most respected academics in the country, resigned from that post to involve himself more thoroughly in SLFP politics. The general impression being created was of a potentially very modern leader who would sweep aside the dogma that had made the SLFP suspect for so long in the eyes of the business community.

Over the months that followed Mrs. Kumaratunga put her advantages to good use. The Southern Province election had shown that Wijetunge's racist rhetoric had had no positive impact. Indeed it could be argued that the party had lost the Matara District in part because, with Thondaman sidelined and not participating in the campaign, the few Tamil votes there had gone the other way. This seemed plausible as the biggest slip in UNP votes was in the Deniyaya electorate, the only electorate in that district where there was a substantial Tamil estate vote. As a consequence Wijetunge toned down his comments, and tried hard with Dissanayake's assistance to mend fences with Thondaman. But there was no hiding that he was a racist and, given his previous contortions, any pledges he might make could not be relied upon. Conversely, Mrs. Kumaratunga had from the very start of her public career emphasized her pluralist outlook, and had never swerved from this. Thus she was soon able to come to a very close understanding with Ashraff, who overcame his personal distrust of Mrs. Bandaranaike to once again come to an electoral arrangement; it was even easier to build up contacts with the various Tamil groups that Wijetunge had so quickly and effectively alienated by his tactless pronouncements.

Thus it was clear that the UNP could no longer rely on the votes of the minorities that had made up Premadasa's majority five years earlier. In accordance with this Wijetunge began to think of a new strategy, realizing that without minority support he would be unlikely to win a presidential election. So, at the end of June, without even consulting his Prime Minister, he dissolved parliament so as to have the general election first, on August 15th. This would compel UNP candidates to work their hardest, whereas they might not have done the same for him in a presidential election. In a context in which executive power was still in UNP hands, with 92 ministers continuing to control a range of resources that could be used, it was likely that nationwide the UNP would poll more than the 43% it had obtained at the southern poll. It was possible that it could even form the next government. And then Wijetunge could well hope to win the presidential election.

Internal Rivalries

It is typical of the state the UNP had reached by now that even this strategy, which demanded maximizing all the resources available, should have fallen prey to infighting which destroyed any chance of success. It was Wickremesinghe who turned out to be the most volatile element. Perhaps this was understandable in a context in which he had had to cope with Wijetunge's contortions for over a year. Tense as he was, he may have thought that with the UNP certain to lose, he should cut his losses and concentrate on ensuring that there could be no challenge to his assuming the leadership in succession to Wijetunge.

His main objective was to do well at the poll, and get over the criticism leveled at him from his early days in politics and reinforced by the recent Hambantota result, that he was not a charismatic public figure. His first move was to withdraw from the Gampaha district, and the Biyagama seat that he had represented from 1977, but which had swung heavily the other way in the May 1993 provincial election. However hard he worked, it was likely that the seat would be lost, and that he would poll less than Mrs. Kumaratunga; so he decided to move to Colombo.

Having taken on the leadership of the UNP list for Colombo, Wickremesinghe's next fear was that he would be outshone there by Mrs. Premadasa. Despite renewed exasperation with Wijetunge she had agreed to campaign in support of the UNP provided that she and her son were given nomination. Wijetunge fought off the bid as regards Sajith Premadasa but acknowledged that Mrs. Premadasa was essential; when she resisted his suggestion that she appear on the national list (from which nomination to parliament depended on the whim of party officials), he agreed that she be on the Colombo list. There she had no doubt, given her husband's following in the area, that she would do extremely well.

The same thought had occurred to Gamini Dissanayake, who remarked that it was ironic that his greatest allies should turn out to be the Premadasa family. Mrs. Premadasa was bound to top the list in Colombo and do better than Wickremesinghe; that would destroy the latter's claims to be a national leader. This perhaps roused Wickremesinghe to action. On nomination day she arrived at the place where the list was to be handed

Internal Combustion

in, only to find that her name was not on it. Refusing to appear on the national list, she withdrew from the campaign, along with her son. Dissanayake, with his customary charm, condoled with her publicly at a press conference the following day, and began a process of reconciliation that was helped by the fact that she was convinced Wickremesinghe was responsible for her humiliation.

Abeygunasekera too found himself at one stage left off the Colombo list, and suggested to Amaratunga that, since the UNP was going to let them down, the two of them should contest the election together; perhaps Ashraff too would join them, as he himself had proposed some time earlier when Wijetunge's attitude to him had first become clear. Amaratunga however, having returned from abroad in response to a summons from Wijesekera, in accordance with a written agreement the Liberal Party had received that he would be on the UNP national list, assured Abeygunasekera that there must be some mistake. The latter contacted Cooray and Wickremesinghe withdrew his objections under persuasion from Cooray. In the end Abeygunasekera did come second in preferences on the UNP list, but the gap between him and Wickremesinghe was a large one, so that the latter's supremacy was not affected.

Amaratunga himself was less lucky. He held Wickremesinghe responsible, though since this was in connection with a place on the national list, the motivation must have been different. It probably related to his friendship with Dissanayake, which had survived his support for Premadasa after the impeachment. Having been left out now by the UNP, Amaratunga ended up in alliance with the Muslim Congress. He was placed at the head of its national list, with a pledge from Ashraff that he would be nominated to parliament if the SLMC obtained enough votes overall to be entitled to a national list seat.

There was also confusion in the need to accommodate members of the DUNF, now in formal alliance with the UNP, as well as Thondaman's CWC. By contrast the PA had a much easier time. The mass defections rumoured earlier did not occur, given the incentive to stay with the party provided by the southern election. Again, while the members of the DUNF who had resisted the move to the UNP had to be accommodated, there were relatively few, and they were well-known enough to be assets, as for instance Lalith Athulathmudali's widow Srimani. The SLMC, with whom an alliance was formalized on Mrs. Kumaratunga's personal initiative, also proved accommodating, being content to place its candidates for all provinces except the North and East on the PA lists. Also importantly for the PA, potential rivalry between mother and daughter was obviated because without any loss of face to Mrs. Bandaranaike it could be reiterated that she would be the party's presidential candidate, and Mrs. Kumaratunga was simply its candidate for the post of Prime Minister.

Yet the results of the election were close, and justified the strategy Wijetunge adopted at the end, even though his earlier conduct made it impossible for the UNP to benefit from it. Of the 225 seats in parliament the PA won only 105, and its declared ally the SLMC 7, fewer than the 108 and 12 *Counterpoint* had given them in what it called the best case scenario for the UNP. The UNP won 94 seats. The PA had a bare majority in the house, since it could also count on one seat won in the Nuwara Eliya District by Chandrasekharan, a youthful challenger to Thondaman's previous monopoly of the estate Tamil vote. Of the remaining seats one went to the JVP, through a front organization that had been registered just in time to contest the election, five to the TULF and three to the DPLF, the Tamil militant organization that dominated Vavuniya. In the Jaffna District, where polling took place almost entirely in refugee camps controlled by the EPDP, on a poll of just 2.3% of the registered vote ten members were elected, nine of them from the EPDP with one from the SLMC.

Given the previous pledges of the SLMC and of Chandrasekharan, there was no doubt that the PA would be able to form a government. This was Wickremesinghe's view, and he saw no alternative to giving up office. Wijetunge however was keen for the UNP to continue in power, and he found an ally in Dissanayake who assured him that a coalition could be cobbled together. Taking advantage of the ban on private aircraft, the government sent military aircraft to transport Ashraff and various TULF leaders to Colombo. The latter refused this assistance. Ashraff accepted it, but made clear that he would not negotiate with the UNP.

He later declared that he had no option, given the total lack of sympathy for the government of those who had voted for him. The same view was shared by the members of the TULF, who appreciated the mood of those in the North and East who had voted for them, the bitterness of feelings in those areas, after the collapse of the promise Premadasa had seemed to hold out. Soon afterwards the TULF declared support for the government from the outside, and before long both the DPLF and the EPDP too, which Mrs. Kumaratunga had earlier accused of having taken out a contract on her life, had adopted a similar position.

Wijetunge finally accepted the inevitable, and on 17 August Mrs. Kumaratunga was sworn in as Prime Minister. Her foreign minister was a Tamil, Lakshman Kadirgamar, a former international civil servant, who had been President of the Oxford Union just after Athulathmudali. He had retired a few years earlier, and come back to Sri Lanka, where he had advised the DUNF in its legal battles. After the collapse of the DUNF as an independent entity he had been approached by the PA to stand on its national list, to help assuage anxieties about its lack of rapport with urban Tamils.

Mrs Kumaratunga had earlier pledged to reduce her cabinet to 20, in contrast to the plethora of ministers the UNP had had. When the cabinet was sworn in, it turned out that she could in effect claim to have kept her promise, though this involved not including in the calculation either the President, who continued as Minister of Defence, nor herself, as Prime Minister and Minister of Finance. In addition she had to exclude from the count Mrs. Bandaranaike, who was sworn in as Minister without Portfolio, 24 years after she had become the world's first woman Prime Minister.

Chapter 17

The End of a Long Road

The UNP under Dissanayake

Almost immediately after the election, Gamini Dissanayake announced that he intended to challenge Wickremesinghe for the post of leader of the opposition. The announcement came as a shock. Though throughout the campaign Dissanayake had suggested that he was the more popular candidate and could restore to the UNP the dominance it had squandered, the results did not quite prove his point. Given his strong showing in Colombo, and also the public acclaim he had received for stepping down, Wickremesinghe had not thought himself open to challenge.

It was true that the only Districts the UNP had won were those in the hills, which Dissanayake suggested constituted his own fiefdom. However the UNP did much better percentage wise in Colombo than it had done in the Provincial Council elections, and Wickremesinghe got nearly 300,000 preference votes, 100,000 more than Dissanayake, and slightly more too in percentage terms.

Despite this it seemed as though Dissanayake's challenge had the blessing of the party hierarchy. One reason for this may have been Wickremesinghe's refusing to cling to power after the election, which could well have damaged him in the eyes of a party unable to conceive of losing office. Wickremesinghe's supporters claimed that even Jayewardene was backing Dissanayake, on the grounds that, whereas Wickremesinghe would be content to spend the next few years in the opposition, Dissanayake would do his utmost to topple the government which had a narrow majority. Feelings ran high and some of Wickremesinghe's partisans even tried to involve the SLFP in the battle. They urged the Speaker to rule that a former Prime Minister had to be the leader of the opposition, and could only be deprived of the post if the entire opposition, not merely the principal party in it, voted otherwise. This however was not an acceptable position since it was clearly a matter for the UNP alone to decide who its leader was. The fact that, at Wijetunge's behest, this was to be by secret ballot, was a particular disappointment to Wickremesinghe; he felt this would make it easier for those he had worked with for years to betray him.

The SLFP then stayed aloof. Wickremesinghe lost the ballot narrowly; this could be attributed to the panic that had beset him before the general election about the prospects for such a contest. Dissanayake's strongest supporter turned out to be Mrs. Premadasa, and it is likely that some of the phone calls she placed on his behalf swayed one or two crucial votes. Besides, even those who had no affection for Dissanayake could well have thought him the best bet to pull the party together, and lead it into any future election. This was the view of Premadasa's old associate Mallimaarachchi, who had said as much after the southern election.

Both sides claimed that the other had the support of the thugs and scoundrels who were still represented in good measure. Indeed such persons, willing to use any means at their disposal to win votes, had done relatively well in the election, in a system which allowed voters to cast three preference votes each instead of just one. Those who had achieved notoriety by their behaviour were divided fairly evenly between the two sides. Adhikari, for instance, the Minister from the North Central Province, who had been arrested just before the election for involvement in the murder of a PA supporter, was on Dissanayake's side; Nanda Mathew, Cyril's son, in whose electorate had occurred one of the most bloody and gratuitous massacres during the JVP period, the skeletons of which were dug up over the next few months, supported Wickremesinghe.

With Thondaman and his six party members deciding not to participate in the ballot, Dissanayake won by just a couple of votes and was duly recognized as the leader of the opposition. He was also shortly afterwards acclaimed the UNP candidate for the presidency, the election for which had been fixed for 9 November.

Wijetunge as Executive President still continued as head of the government in theory, and he declared that he would not participate in the campaign. Dissanayake's suggestion that he should step down as leader of the party before the election did not find favour. But it was generally accepted that Dissanayake would take over as leader after the election, and that Wijesekera too would step down to allow Dissanayake to appoint his own General Secretary. Meanwhile Wijetunge made it clear to the government that he saw no real role for himself, and left almost all decisions to Mrs. Kumaratunga and her cabinet. This was most obvious with regard to the most decisive step the new government took as soon as it assumed office – a ceasefire with the Tigers which was reciprocated. Though Wijetunge was still ostensibly Minister of Defence, preliminary negotiations began immediately.

Kumaratunga as Prime Minister

Policy wise, there were few other changes except for the fulfillment of the election pledge to lower the price of bread. More important, from the point of view of parties that had been out of power for so long, were the opportunities for patronage. Sweeping changes were made with regard to posts considered political ones, directorates of state corporations for instance, or statutory bodies such as the University Grants Commission. The UNP had politicized the diplomatic service, or rather personalized it, for many of its appointees had no political credentials but were simply friends of those in high places. It was announced that all heads of mission abroad were to be recalled.

As regards the administrative service, the new government made relatively few changes. This was understandable, given the problem it faced, of having to carry through and develop a modern economic programme. Mrs. Kumaratunga's cabinet included members of the former Marxist parties, as well as some of her early supporters from what had been the left-wing of the SLFP. Since she also had to cope with several politicians who saw the chance to exercise patronage as one of the main rewards of political office, there was bound to be tremendous pressure on her to strengthen and even expand the areas under the control of the centralized state. She had hardly any politicians of significance on her side to combat such pressures. Though some of her younger favourites had a more modern approach to government, they did not have the clout or the experience to move the revised agenda of the party forward. Mrs. Kumaratunga was left as having to depend for policy matters on G L Pieris, with the risk that, given his recent accession to the party, he was especially vulnerable to criticism from perspectives different from his or her own.

It was scarcely surprising that most senior civil servants remained in place despite objections from extreme elements in the party. An exception to this was Paskaralingam, who had been abroad at the time of the election, and stayed abroad. His deputy however kept his position, as did the Governor of the Central Bank and secretaries to most significant ministries.

In other respects too Mrs. Kumaratunga showed a balance that seemed heartening. In her very first public speech after taking office she declared that the security forces had orders to deal firmly with anyone, whether they were PA supporters or otherwise, who attempted to disrupt the peace. This statement, which might have seemed an obvious one, was in marked contrast to the attitudes expressed by UNP leaders in the past, and it had its effect. Whereas UNP election victories, beginning from 1977, had seen the unleashing of violence, unrestrained and indeed often encouraged by the forces of law and order, this did not happen on this occasion; some unfortunate incidents did occur in November, after the presidential election was won, but in general peace was preserved.

In fact the principle criticism of the government was that Mrs. Kumaratunga was unable or unwilling to get over her habit of turning up late for appointments, sometimes by hours. The argument that this was due to security considerations was in the end untenable.

Meanwhile Mrs Bandaranaike made it clear too that she would not contest the presidential election herself. It might have been conceivable that, despite her age, she could have stood against a feeble candidate like Wijetunge. Against Dissanayake this was impossible so she withdrew and the party was able unanimously to adopt Mrs Kumaratunga as its candidate. She could therefore launch her campaign without the uncertainties that might have plagued the party had Mrs Bandaranaike actively sought the nomination which, only a few months earlier, it had been declared would be hers.

The presidential election of 1994

This was necessary, for Dissanayake had decided to start his campaign as soon as possible, and by the end of September it was in full swing. From the start he made it clear that he was totally different from Wijetunge; there were some areas in which he seemed at odds with Premadasa, for instance in his continuing claim that he intended to clear the party of elements that had brought it into disrepute, but in other respects he seemed to hark back to his former enemy.

He was at pains to stress his determination to rebuild the broad coalition that Premadasa had set up, and he seemed by and large to succeed. Mrs. Premadasa and her son became his ardent supporters. Abeygunasekera had stipulated that he would not campaign unless it was on the understanding that he would lay stress on Premadasa's achievements; Dissanayake promptly declared that he had no objection to this, and agreed that Premadasa had done a great deal for the country and that programmes such as Janasaviya and Gam Udawa deserved to be highlighted. Abeygunasekera then took up a major role in the campaign, while Anura Bandarnaike too participated actively.

In addition, Dissanayake went out of his way to get Amaratunga's support, which might have seemed odd given the latter's lack of an electoral base. However, apart from their personal relationship, it transpired that Dissanayake wanted Amaratunga to write up his manifesto, since he had decided that radical change from previous UNP ideas was essential. Amaratunga had not been appointed to parliament by the SLMC, mainly because Kumaratunga, perhaps uncomfortable about Amaratunga's ties to Dissanayake, had been unhappy about it. This left Amaratunga free, with the consent of his party, to respond to Dissanayake's overtures.

The manifesto he wrote up was to a great extent adopted by Dissanayake; unlike the DPA manifesto, under which Mrs. Bandaranaike had contested the presidency six years previously, which had also been Amaratunga's work, Dissanayake monitored the document carefully and stamped his own distinctive mark upon it. On the previous occasion Mrs. Bandaranaike had accepted the draft without examining it closely, which perhaps supported the view that she had not intended to take it seriously.

Dissanayake on the contrary studied the initial draft carefully, and added sections, such as the preamble on education, that summarized the thrust of the original proposals. He also demanded amendments in areas on which he had very definite views, as when he refused to accept Amaratunga's commitment to abolish the Executive Presidency. He suggested a modification and wanted this included as an alternative to abolition, with the pledge that he would offer the nation a choice between the two at a referendum. The modifications that he outlined indicated careful thought about the whole system and included adjustments that subjected the Presidency to other controls.

With regard to devolution, the proposals in the manifesto went far beyond anything that had been offered by any major political party before, and could have proved a means of winning back the minority vote. Dissanayake's principal target was the Tamil voter who had traditionally supported the UNP but been alienated by Wijetunge's rhetoric. In addition he hoped to woo back at least some of the Tamil parties which Mrs. Kumaratunga had won over. Though they had been enthusiastic about the ceasefire, and acclaimed the decision of the government to talk to the LTTE, they had no illusions about the animosity that lay between them and the Tigers. Dissanayake, while objecting to the talks, made it clear that this was not because he was opposed to a negotiated settlement, but because he believed the record of the Tigers belied their sincerity. In putting forward comparatively generous proposals, while referring to his previous record as the principal dove in the cabinet at the time of the Indo-Lankan Accord, he was able to get the endorsement of one militant group; the EPDP too began to move towards him. In addition he made much of his close relationship with India. Since it was unlikely that the North would poll, given the determination of the Tigers to establish that the area they controlled had no stake in the rest of the country, this was not likely to damage him much. In the East it was more likely to go down well, and in fact the meetings he held in that area were very successful.

He was also careful to keep Thondaman in line. After the election Thondaman, whose influence amongst the estate workers depended on his position in the cabinet, and the resultant ability to extract concessions for his flock from the government, found himself in a quandary. To meet the challenge of his youthful adversary, a deputy minister able to present himself as the man in power now, he embarked with characteristic swiftness on negotiations with the government, with a view even to joining it. Dissanayake moved equally swiftly and prevailed upon Thondaman to sign a memorandum of understanding that confirmed the alliance between the UNP and the CWC. While Thondaman was unwilling to commit the CWC to official support of Dissanayake, he agreed it would remain neutral and individuals could work for him if they wished. Given his excellent relations with most of the party leaders, and in particular the Provincial Council members of the Central Province, Dissanayake was confident of holding the Tamil vote there.

Dissanayake seemed sincere in his pledge to clean up the party. He made rapid changes with regard to organizers of constituencies and wasn't partisan in his decisions. Thus both Adhikari and Mathew were removed. In general Dissanayake did not suffer unduly from adverse reactions to this, perhaps because of the perception that, whatever happened at the election, he would continue in control of the party, and there was no future in opposing him openly. At the same time he was not unduly worried about a few defections; he was concerned not with the immediate future, but with the aftermath, when he hoped to develop a new style of political party such as he thought essential for a developing society. Though he had succeeded in restoring confidence to a party shattered by its first electoral defeat in years, and though he exuded confidence in public, and most notably in a series of television interviews in which he took on a quality of balanced statesmanship never seen before on the Sri Lankan political scene, he himself did not expect to win. He hoped only to put on a good show after which he planned to build up the party in opposition so that it would be irresistible at the next election. He believed that he could force such an election in a couple of years.

It was possible that this, and the prospect of a dynamic opposition, unsettled the Tigers. Whether they hoped to achieve peace or simply a breathing space to regroup their strength by the talks, Gamini Dissanayake as leader of the opposition would have stepped up pressure on the government with regard to such talks. Such fears on the part of the Tigers were exacerbated by a brief trip Dissanayake made to India in the midst of his campaign, which led to the belief that he would agitate for the extradition of Prabhakaran, who was wanted for the murder of Rajiv Gandhi. Perhaps too even the very remote possibility that Dissanayake would win could not be discounted. Whatever the reason, at a rally in Colombo, just after midnight on October 23rd, eighteen months after Athulathmudali had been killed, a bomb exploded a few seconds after Dissanayake had finished his speech. It was detonated by a suicide bomber, whose severed head was found later on the roof of a nearby building; she had attended several of Dissanayake's meetings in the preceding weeks, as photographs later revealed.

Over 50 people died in the explosion. Dissanayake succumbed to his injuries shortly after being admitted to hospital. Other leading figures who died included Premachandra, his former colleague in the DUNF; Mallimaarachchi, Premadasa's close confidante who had nevertheless fervently backed Dissanayake; and Gamini Wijesekera, who had left Jayewardene's UNP but returned under Premadasa and then become Wijetunge's General Secretary. Ossie Abeygunasekera, Premadasa's rival for the presidency but now an ally, who had voted against Dissanayake for the leadership of the opposition but then campaigned for him enthusiastically, lingered in hospital and died on November 9th, the day of the presidential election,.

The country was stunned. There was no doubt in anyone's mind that the Tigers were responsible. Mrs. Kumaratunga was uncertain about whether to go on with the negotiations, but Mrs. Bandaranaike was firm in insisting that the talks, begun a few weeks earlier and to be continued on the following day, be suspended. The reminder of the possible reach of Tiger activity was awe-inspiring, in that it suggested the efforts of Sri Lankan politicians were of little account compared with the capacity of the Tigers to remove them at will.

Shattered though the UNP was, it had to take some quick decisions. Election provisions permitted a party to substitute a name within three days, if its candidate for the presidency died after nominations but before the election was held. This had to be done by the General Secretary of the party, which again required that someone had to be appointed urgently to that post.

It was assumed that Wickremesinghe would have to step in to fill the breach and, despite the danger, he expressed himself willing when Wijetunge asked him. When he turned up at the meeting that had been called, he assumed to ratify his candidature, he had a rude shock. Wijetunge had been persuaded to permit a committee of senior party members to decide the issue, and it transpired that with just a couple of exceptions they were all against him. The final decision was that Dissanayake's widow Srima should be the alternative candidate.

It was a bizarre decision. From those who had opposed Wickremesinghe aggressively, and feared they would lose all influence when he took over the party, it was understandable. But while there were a few such, as for instance Dissanayake's brother-in-law Weerasooriya, that was hardly the position of those who had constituted the selection committee. Though many of them had rallied behind Dissanayake after he became leader of the opposition, they could hardly be faulted for that.

The most that could be said for those who were determined to deprive Wickremesinghe of the nomination was that they genuinely believed, in spite of his recent electoral success, that he would do disastrously in the poll. One very senior colleague told him that he was bound to lose by over a million votes, whereas Mrs. Dissanayake would be sure to get a sympathy vote and the margin of defeat would be more respectable. The consensus with which he was greeted moved the normally emotionless Wickremesinghe to tears. It was an appalling way for him to have been treated by a party which he had himself stood by so conscientiously.

Yet it was probably the best thing that could have happened to him. Given that he could not have won, his performance would have been subject to criticism, which would have spawned challenges to his leadership. As it was, perhaps through shame, the UNP decided that he would assume the leadership of the opposition immediately, and take over the leadership of the party from Wijetunge the moment the latter's term as President was over the day after the election. Equally importantly, the General Secretary appointed temporarily, Dissanayake's original choice to take over the post from Wijesekera after the presidential election, made it clear that he did not wish to continue. It was agreed that he should be replaced even before the election by Wickremesinghe's choice, which was Gamini Athukorale, Dissanayake's bitter enemy, appointed to the Mahaweli Ministry when Premadasa's intention to victimize Dissanayake crystallized.

In fact the real victim of the UNP decision was Mrs. Dissanayake. Persuaded in her first grief to accept nomination, she made it clear that she would not campaign in public. Given the danger of her position this was accepted and she confined herself to television appearances. These might have proved acceptable had she acquitted herself well but no one trained her, or even insisted on careful recording that might have conveyed the impression of statesmanship. All that came across was a grief-stricken widow, aspiring to a job for which she was unsuited. The contrast with Mrs. Kumaratunga was startling.

Another factor that proved disastrous to the campaign was the decision to run it on what amounted to racist lines. Grief and fury with regard to the Tigers was understandable, but this spilled over into blame of the government for negotiating with the Tigers and even into the suggestion that the government was in some way responsible for the murder as Tigers in custody had been released shortly after the general election. The rhetoric suggested that there was nothing wrong in treating Tamils in general as suspects, conveying an impression Dissanayake himself had studiously avoided, that terrorists and Tamils were not two distinct categories.

Such rhetoric had clearly been rejected in the recent general election; whatever the anger about Dissanayake's death, a clearsighted appraisal would have suggested that all it would achieve was the alienation of the minority vote. In fact it did more than this. It led to Thondaman joining the government. He may of course have been looking for an excuse anyway, in that with Dissanayake dead opposition politics did not seem very promising in the short term. Whereas Wickremesinghe, at the age of 45, could wait for the long term, Thondaman who was 86 could not. As speakers on UNP platforms moved from anti-Tiger to anti-Tamil pronouncements, he took his chance. Declaring that he could not be identified with such a stance, he joined the cabinet a few days before the election. That he sat in parliament as a nominee of the UNP from its national list did not deter him, and in fact the UNP was powerless to protest.

By then it was clear that the campaign was a disaster. While Dissanayake had been alive, there had been as many green posters visible throughout the country as blue ones. By the beginning of November there were hardly any of the former. His tremendous organizational capacity was lacking and the confidence that he had been able to instill. In addition the central party organization, now under the control of Wickremesinghe and Athukorale, saw little reason to exert itself.

The UNP then had given up well before the election. The government panicked, and its own campaign went into overkill, with flagrant abuse of the media which, if not quite as bad as that of the UNP in its heyday, served as a reminder of the fallibility of ideals under pressure.

The result made it clear that the panic of the PA had been quite unnecessary. Mrs Kumaratunga got a massive 60% of the vote, Mrs Dissanayake trailing her by nearly two million votes. It was in fact in only one constituency in the whole country that she got more votes that Mrs Kumaratunga. That was Mahiyangana where the main Mahaweli settlement schemes were situated. As that was the area where Dissanayake had first made his mark the vote could be seen as a touching tribute to the man himself. In the rest of the country whatever benefits had been derived from UNP rule now weighed less than other factors.

On November 10th Mrs. Kumaratunga took her oath as the country's fourth Executive President, at the same time as Wickremesinghe took over at UNP headquarters as leader of that party. A couple of days later Mrs. Bandaranaike was sworn in as Prime Minister for the third time. Apart from the fact that she wanted the post, the appointment also made sense in view of the PA's commitment to abolish the Executive Presidency, which Mrs. Kumaratunga had pledged during her campaign would happen by 15 July 1995. The scenario envisaged by the government was that then Mrs. Bandaranaike would become a ceremonial president, while Mrs. Kumaratunga would revert to the post of Prime Minister, endowed now with full executive authority.

It was also noticeable that there was no acceptable alternative. Mrs. Kumaratunga's own preferred candidate would probably have been Ratnasiri Wickramanayake, whom she had made leader of the house. He was the most senior member of her cabinet since he had also been a minister in Mrs. Bandaranaike's 1970 government. However, he had been an adherent of Mrs. Kumaratunga throughout the last few years, and like her had moved through the SLMP and the BNP before reverting to the SLFP. What was acceptable in a daughter and heir would not have seemed so in the case of someone else, and other senior figures in the SLFP would not have been very happy about accepting him as Prime Minister.

When the question of a deputy leader came up in the UNP there was no obvious candidate. Hameed, who had remained loyal to Wickremesinghe, had been named party chairman, largely a ceremonial post. The other person who had been a minister at the very start of Jayewardene's government, before Wickremesinghe was promoted to the cabinet, and who had succeeded Wickremesinghe as Leader of the House after Premadasa's death, wanted the post but had no real following. In such a situation Wickremesinghe decided to put off the decision. He also announced that the vacancies on the national list, created by the deaths of Premachandra and of Wijesekera, would not be filled immediately. He felt no obligation to fulfill the commitment Dissanayake had made, which Mrs. Dissanayake had confirmed, that Mrs. Premadasa would be nominated to parliament as soon as possible.

The absence of a second rank of leaders was particularly grave in a context in which so many politicians had been eliminated so suddenly. The manner in which the leaders of the two main parties so thoroughly overshadowed everyone else was a sad change from the plethora of talent that both those parties had had in the past. The situation in 1994 was perhaps a salutary reminder of the havoc that had been created by the presidential system, which not only raised a single individual to dizzy heights, but led to bitter and destructive rivalries.

Part VIII

The Procrastination of a Princess

Kumaratunga in Charge (1994–2001)

Chapter 18

Wasted Years

A domestic dispensation

Chandrika Kumaratunga served eleven years as Executive President. For the first five years she had a secure parliamentary majority and was in undisputed control of the country. During this period she kept the economy on a course of steady if limited growth, and continued to open it up, albeit on foundations laid by Premadasa. Thus plantations, handed over previously to private sector management, were privatized during her tenure. Again, the rapid opening up of the telecommunications sector followed the initial enforcement of competition during Premadasa's regime.

The credit she received for this achievement, all the more remarkable in that the more senior ministers of her cabinet still had a predilection for old fashioned socialism, was limited. One reason for this is that, even during her first tenure in office, the ethnic problem became more complex, and the separatist Tigers far more powerful. In addition, her managerial skills were weak, and her dependence on cronies, many of them selected with little regard for ability, increased over the years.

This was a problem endemic to the SLFP. Ever since Bandaranaike was abandoned, shortly before the 1956 election, by the most able of his allies, the SLFP had been lacking in talent at the top, and had generally had to bring in capable administrators from elsewhere. Bandaranaike himself had presided over a coalition which included former Marxists, a situation that led to dissension even before his death. Mrs Bandaranaike, with a cabinet that at least had some experience, still brought in Felix Dias Bandaranaike, and later the Trotskyists and Communists, who went on into her second administration.

When Mrs Kumaratunga came to power hardly any of her party stalwarts had administrative experience. Though some of the younger members of her cabinet showed talent, and an outlook that matched modern needs, she relied initially at the highest levels only on two recent recruits to her cause, Foreign Minister Lakshman Kadrigamar and her Minister for Constitutional Affairs, G L Pieris.

The former proved her greatest asset during the eleven years of her Presidency. It was largely due to him that Sri Lanka, having been a pariah on the international stage, was able to persuade the world that the Tigers were not innocents fighting for freedom against an oppressive majority. As a Tamil himself, he was able to argue first for the pluralist credentials of the new government, and later, when she seemed to have been overtaken in this respect by the UNP, for her enduring commitment to a negotiated solution.

Pieris however, who should have promoted a solution at the time when the government had international sympathy and the support of the majority of Tamils, proved a broken reed. After the resumption of hostilities, a desultory attempt at constitutional reform was swiftly abandoned, to be trotted out again only in 2000. Pieris, instead, seemed more concerned with promoting his own political career and authority. His manoeuvres led to the dismissal of two Ministry Secretaries, the Secretary to the Treasury and later the Secretary to the Ministry of Justice, a senior administrator who insisted on written instructions for orders she considered improper.

The President's way of dealing with such problems was symptomatic of her whole approach. At the very beginning of her tenure, when Kadirgamar, believing in doctrines of cabinet responsibility, raised an issue of corruption, she made it clear that Ministers were expected to concentrate only on their own portfolios. Having initially resisted Pieris's demand that the Secretary to the Treasury be changed, she then accommodated him as Governor of the Central Bank. Over the change in the Ministry of Justice she gave in, but by then she was hostile to Pieris, and included him in her broad swipes at her colleagues in general.

But she did nothing in practice to curb either inefficiency or dishonesty. It would have been absurd to expect this, for in her own private office she tolerated both. Her approach to politics was essentially cronyist, based on the belief that loyalty had to be rewarded, which did not however preclude her belabouring those by whom she was surrounded. Their incompetence could always be blamed for shortcomings, while it never occurred to her that ultimately she was responsible for her choice of her colleagues.

Perhaps because of her lack of previous administrative experience, or the bitter suspicions of her early years, she was incapable of looking for independent talent. Occasionally, as with Kadirgamar, or Tara de Mel, whom she used for her educational work, she found people able to work out her idealism. But more often than not she rested content with mediocrities. This led to the suspicion that she found them convenient for her own inability to follow things through, while some went further, in claiming that she too benefited from the irregularities amongst her confidantes.

For instance she kept on as Secretary to the President, a position of enormous power and influence, someone who had served her loyally in the past, but who was lacking in the vision required by the post, and obsessed by the obligation to perform favours for any acquaintance who demanded them. In a sense this was exactly what Jayewardene had done, and both Secretaries indeed shared another feature, in that their sons got involved in arms deals, which were amongst the most lucrative government contracts.

The powers of the Presidency proved as fatal for the country under Mrs Kumaratunga as they had done under Jayewardene and Wijetunga. Though an infinitely warmer person than either of them, and certainly not single-minded in seeking power or profit as they had been, she proved incapable of thorough planning or implementation, whilst holding the reins tight in her own hand. This was accompanied by the desire not to rock the boat, provided those in it were nice to her.

Thus, in key areas where reform was essential, such as education or public administration, she put up with old-fashioned ministers who were incapable of implementing her vision. Again, with regard to power for instance, where it was clear that with increased consumption new schemes, hydro-electric or thermal, were needed, she dithered in the face of protests from stakeholders. Thus, though there was substantial economic progress in the country, at least during the first five years, the development of infrastructure and of human resources lagged behind.

Military Debacles

Ethnic conflict was the area in which Mrs Kumaratunga's approach proved most disastrous. Having come into power with the goodwill of most Tamils, including the Tigers, she believed perhaps that her commitment to pluralism would suffice for a solution. While later the Tigers were to argue that the lack of status of the negotiators she sent to them initially was proof of her lack of seriousness, it was symptomatic of her whole approach. She preferred to trust personal friends rather than politicians whose motives she suspected. In addition, there is no doubt that she believed that the Tiger demand for self-determination, understandable when faced with an oppressive government, would swiftly be modified in the light of her own pluralist credentials.

Thus she did not take seriously the Tiger demand that army camps be reduced. She also cultivated the Tamil groups represented in parliament, not appreciating how bitterly the Tigers resented them as having connived with the Indians when they turned their guns on the Tigers. Neelan Tiruchelvam, known to be close to the Indians, was her principal adviser on constitutional reform. Even Douglas Devananda of the EPDP, which held nine of the ten seats for the Jaffna District, had allied himself firmly with her after Gamini Dissanayake's death.

Indeed, the Tigers, by assassinating Gamini Dissanayake, had removed the greatest threat to them, given his international credentials; their action had forced the other Tamil groups into Mrs Kumaratunga's orbit, and practically bestowed absolute power upon her. Dissanayake would have kept her on her toes, whereas Wickremesinghe seemed content to wait, having achieved total control of the UNP, with all potential rivals dead. Her incentive for a settlement with the Tigers then might have been reduced. Conversely, her position later was that the Tigers had simply talked while they built up their strength, and had intended to resume war all along.

The resumption of hostilities was sudden. Though 72 hours notice was formally required before termination of the truce, the President received at 10.30 pm on 19 April 1994 a fax to the effect that the agreement would terminate at midnight. It is argued that a deadline had been given earlier, but that was only on the lines of the Tigers declaring that they felt compelled to "consider whether to withdraw from the peace process". Shortly after the fax was received, the Tigers blew up two gun boats in Trincomalee to commence what became known as Eelam War III.

This time the Tigers seemed to have even better weapons than before, and the war was marked by the destruction of several planes. It became apparent that, apart from deploying anti-aircraft guns and missiles, the Tigers were also in the process of developing flying power. Their capacity at sea had increased and they had also built up a merchant fleet. This fleet, it seems, was on one occasion employed by the Sri Lankan Ministry of Defence to procure arms, with the result that the whole shipment was hijacked.

While in this, and in the success of several attacks on military bases, fortune seemed to favour the LTTE, the period from 1995 to 2000 revealed the corruption and incompetence in the Sri Lankan defence establishment. One problem was that Mrs Kumaratunga appointed as her Deputy Minister of Defence her uncle, Anuruddha Ratwatte, who had virtual control of strategy in this period. His credentials included having been a volunteer officer, but more important was the relationship, and her belief that she could trust him absolutely.

Initially, after the debacles of the Wijetunge period, the armed forces welcomed Ratwatte's appointment. It is arguable that his principal decision, to concentrate on retaking Jaffna and establishing a line of communication to the peninsula, made sense at first, in a context in which the Tigers had established themselves firmly in Jaffna after the Indian army withdrew. When Jaffna came under government control towards the end of 1995 Ratwatte was treated as a hero. The danger that the Tigers would declare a separate state, which would be recognized *de facto* by at least a few countries, had been overcome.

But the army had not fully subscribed to this strategy, on the grounds that it would involve withdrawing troops from crucial bases. Finally, it was only an officer on the verge of retirement who undertook the task, and thus continued as army commander for four years. After the success in retaking Jaffna there was nothing but failure. The Premadasa strategy of concentrating initially on the East, not only militarily, but in terms of economic development and psychological operations, was wholly forgotten. It was argued that since the North was the nerve center of the Tigers, the East could be dealt with quickly after the North was taken. The whole strategy should have been rethought when it proved impossible to take full control of the North.

But rethinking was not Ratwatte's strong point and he persisted in increasingly unsuccessful attempts to open up the road to Jaffna over the next four years. Meanwhile the base at Mullaitivu was over-run in the middle of 1996, with a loss of over 1000 men and vast quantities of weapons. Though Kilinochchi, just south of the Jaffna Lagoon, was taken by the army soon after, it was lost again in 1998. Then, in 1999, shortly before the Presidential election, the Tigers retook, in a blitz in which the army was routed, all the territory north of Vavuniya that had been so painstakingly won by Ratwatte. In April 2000, the Tigers conquered the camp at Elephant Pass, on the neck of the peninsula. This almost led to the fall of Jaffna. It was only with massive assistance from other countries that this was averted.

Meanwhile rivalries and suspicions were rife. It was widely known that vast sums were being made on procurement contracts in which officers and influential civilians were involved. One of the most distinguished officers in the army, taken to Elephant Pass when the situation was worsening, advised immediate retreat, only to be told that his advice could not be communicated to the Minister. He was transferred and when the camp was taken many lives, that could have been saved by an early evacuation, were lost. The officer who led the rescue of Jaffna, a man, widely acknowledged as inspiring confidence, was retired instead of going on to become Army Commander. And, most worrying of all, when the Tigers swept through Kilinochchi there were rumours that some senior officers had anticipated and contributed to the rout. And, though treachery need not be assumed when incompetence provides an acceptable explanation, palpable instances of treachery did emerge with the change of government. There seemed greater justification then for the state of insecurity the forces suffered towards the end of the decade.

Terrorist successes

In addition to their military successes, the Tigers also pulled off some remarkable terrorist operations. Following the assassination of Gamini Dissanayake, no leading Sinhala politician was killed during Mrs Kumaratunga's first term of office, but Tamils suffered badly. Jaffna's inhabitants practically evacuated it when it was taken by government forces. The assumption that evacuation had been enforced by the LTTE was strengthened when the citizenry returned shortly afterwards. A couple of years later local elections were held and, despite Tiger opposition, Sarojini Yogeswaran, widow of the Jaffna Member of Parliament, who had been killed by the Tigers in 1988 along with Appapillai Amirthalingam, the leader of the Tamil United Liberation Front, was elected Mayor. Four months later, in May 1998, she was shot.

Her successor Ponnathurai Sivapalan was also blown up four months later, along with several senior security personnel who were attending a meeting in his office. A couple of months earlier Douglas Devananda, the leader of the EPDP who had emerged as the most forceful Tamil opponent of the Tigers, narrowly escaped being bludgeoned to death while visiting Tamil prisoners in the south. And some time the next year Prabhakaran ordered the execution of his former deputy Mahattaya, who had been incarcerated since 1994 on suspicion of negotiating with the enemy.

In July 1999 the Tigers eliminated Neelan Tiruchelvam, who had been in the forefront of negotiations since the TULF emerged as a strong political force after the 1977 elections. Tiruchelvam, who was widely respected internationally, had ensured that the TULF maintained its identity as an independent political movement. One of the saddest aspects of the control the Tigers exercised over Tamils, who accepted that they were their only hope, was the glee with which Tiruchelvam's death was greeted. S Sivanayagam, former editor of the Jaffna based *Saturday Review*, which had bravely combated Jayewardene's authoritarianism in the early eighties, gloated over the murder in *Hot Spring*, the pro-Tiger journal he later edited in Paris. In support of his stance he cited approval for the deed from A J Wilson, who had been Tiruchelvam's senior partner in the negotiations that led to the District Development Councils of 1981. Wilson had continued close to Jayewardene despite that debacle, and the burning of the Jaffna Public Library, and had accepted a safe conduct out of the country from him in July 1983 when Tamils were being attacked in Colombo. Tiruchelvam had stayed and struggled on. Wilson justified his murder by describing Tiruchelvam's attitude to Mrs Kumaratunga as one of 'abject genuflection'.

Apart from these murders, Tiger successes included a suicide bomb outside the office of the Chief Minister of the Western Province in the heart of Colombo. Intended for Ratwatte, it killed twenty two people and injured over fifty. Two months later, in October 1996, Colombo's main oil depot was attacked and several storage tanks blown up. Suicide cadres killed over twenty people outside army headquarters a few weeks later, and in January the entrance to the Central Bank in the heart of Colombo's business district was blasted, with nearly a hundred killed and 1500 injured.

In October of that year a truck packed with explosives blew up near the World Trade Centre, Colombo's most prestigious office space. The attack may have been aimed at the Galadari Hotel, which suffered substantial damage, since it was reported that American Green Berets, brought in to assist the security forces, were staying there. Three months later another truck driven by suicide bombers blew up near the Temple of the Tooth in Kandy. This was because Prince Charles had been due there on 4 February to celebrate the 50th anniversary of the country's independence from Britain. Though the damage was minor, and swiftly repaired, the celebrations had to be moved to Colombo.

All this was justified on the grounds that the operations of the security forces brought untold suffering to civilians in Tamil areas, and that the forces were involved in several incidents of brutality and murder. These latter were highlighted, while through extremely efficient propaganda the Tiger diaspora institutionalized the perception of the Tigers as freedom fighters who concentrated on military targets and attacked civilians only in situations of grave provocation. Meanwhile the Sri Lankan government,

Wasted Years

which was quite hopeless at publicizing its own position, did what it could to rein in extremists in its forces. A sensational rape case was thoroughly investigated in a well publicized trial in which the convicted soldiers implicated their officers. Though a representative of the Physicians for Human Rights lauded Sri Lanka as "the only country to allow such a probe at a time when government forces were still locked in combat with rebels", such perceptions were rare. Despite its campaign of terror, directed very often at Tamils who stepped out of line, the Tigers easily won the propaganda war.

The Presidential Election of 1999

The Sri Lankan army marked its 50th anniversary in October 1999, with the first indigenous army commander, a Tamil now settled in Australia, gracing the occasion despite his 90 odd years. Shortly afterwards, confident of her other achievements, though there was little to show on the ethnic question, President Kumaratunga decided to go for an early Presidential election. Having initially prescribed fixed terms of six years, Jayewardene had through the third amendment to his constitution permitted an incumbent President to seek re-election any time after completing four years. Kumaratunga, who completed five years on 10 November, decided to have an early election on 22 December.

It was after she had announced the election that the government suffered a debacle; the Tigers retook about 1,200 square kilometers of the area north of Vavuniya. The attack was led by Prabhakaran's most accomplished military commander, Karuna, who hailed from the Eastern Province. He had succeeded, during the preceding five years, in bringing the government control of the East into question, despite all that Premadasa had done to integrate it with the rest of the country. After Karuna's successful operation in 1999 even Vavuniya, which Premadasa had converted into a prosperous town that attracted Tamils from the less developed areas to the North, seemed under threat. But with the Tigers deciding to hold back, conditions became more settled, and the Presidential election went ahead as scheduled. Mrs Kumaratunga seemed the favourite, in spite of the military setbacks, and the Tigers sent a suicide bomber to assassinate her at her last rally.

The bomb went off just as she was about to get into her car. This saved her life since the bullet-proof vehicle took the bulk of the blast, though shrapnel struck her in the face and the right eye, which was badly injured. The driver was killed, along with twenty others.

There were those in the UNP who claimed that the Tigers had intended to evoke sympathy for the President, and that was how she won, by a far narrower majority than in 1994. The story was similar to the ridiculous one spread by Premadasa's opponents after his assassination in 1993, that it was a manoeuvre to attract sympathy that failed. Interestingly, despite this clear mark of Tiger hostility, she obtained more votes than Wickremesinghe in the Jaffna District as well.

With the results announced on 23 December 1999, Mrs Kumaratunga took her oath immediately. This was not necessary since constitutionally, under a bizarre provision Jayewardene had introduced in his Third Amendment, while a challenger took office immediately if successful, incumbent Presidents continued under previous steam, so to speak, and only commenced their second term on the next date following that corresponded to the one on which they first took office. Mrs Kumaratunga's second term therefore was, according to the constitution, to begin only on 10 November 2000. However, even though Sri Lanka's most erudite constitutional expert pointed this out, Mrs Kumaratunga did not clarify the point. This failure was typical of the carelessness that was to mark a Presidency that began, not once but twice, with so much goodwill.

Chapter 19

Hurried Elections

The Parliamentary Election of 2000

It was only after the Presidential election that Mrs Kumaratunga and Pieris sought again to pass legislation designed to alleviate the ethnic problem by providing greater self government for the Tamils. A package had been prepared early in her tenure, which was also supposed to solve other problems created by Jayewardene, particularly with regard to the overweening powers of the President. The package however proposed to abolish these only after Mrs Kumaratunga's term; and now in 2000 it was to happen only at the end of her second term.

This enabled Wickremesinghe, as previously, to oppose the package, since it could be argued that it was more concerned with the interests of the incumbent President than with resolving problems. Nevertheless, fresh from her electoral victory, the President was able to attract several crossovers from the UNP. Many of them believed, as she seemed to do, that Wickremesinghe had initially promised to support her proposals regarding devolution, so his later criticism of these seemed cynical. When he sat impassive whilst members of his party burned the proposals on the floor of the house, he seemed to concur with the view that Mrs Kumaratunga was conceding too much to the Tamils. However, with the TULF declaring that the package was inadequate, it became clear that the required two thirds majority would not be obtained, and the attempt lapsed.

By this stage, following Tiruchelvam's assassination, the TULF was firmly under Tiger control. But, apart from fear of Tiger reprisals, there was also another reason for Tamil politicians not totally committed to the President (as was for instance Douglas Devananda) to oppose her. This was the murder, in January of that year, shortly after the Presidential election, of Kumar Ponnambalam, Tiruchelvam's long-standing rival. Ponnambalam, son of the first leader of the Tamil Congress, had remained aloof from the TULF after his father's death. Though the Tamil Congress, his father's original party which he continued to maintain as an independent entity, was not represented in Parliament, he had stood in the Presidential election of 1982. The TULF had not participated in that, and Ponnambalam had come fourth, after Jayewardene and the SLFP and JVP candidates. Subsequently he had been a member of the Democratic People's Alliance under which Mrs Bandaranaike had contested the 1988 Presidential election, and had, together with Chanaka Amaratunga, helped draft a manifesto committed to minority rights and substantial devolution.

Following Mrs. Bandaranaike's defeat, and her retreat into a more chauvinistic posture for the General Election that followed, Ponnambalam had in turn grown more hardline. With the alliance between Mrs Kumaratunga and the TULF as guided by Tiruchelvam, he had drifted towards the Tigers. Though convinced that they would use him and, as he put it, thereafter squeeze him dry like a used towel, he felt there was no alternative for Tamils. When therefore he was murdered six months after Tiruchelvam's death, elements in the government, albeit not acting officially, were suspected. Ironically the TULF, now following the Tiger line, mourned him more than they had done Tiruchelvam.

Kumaratunga, in her first term of office, took no measures in Parliament to resolve the ethnic problem, or to remedy the absurdities of Jayewardene's constitution. After her early re-election she dissolved Parliament when its term was up and asked for a fresh mandate to deal with these issues. Before that she had finally accepted Mrs Bandaranaike's resignation as Prime Minister. She appointed her old confidante Ratnasiri Wickramanayake to the post. Wickramanayake had been a Minister in Mrs Bandaranaike's 1970 government, but had followed her daughter out of the SLFP during the internal struggles of the eighties.

Mrs Bandaranaike was 84 by then. She voted at the General Election on October 10th and died later that day of a heart attack. Before that, during the campaign, another loyal supporter of the President, the leader of the Sri Lanka Muslim Congress, M H M Ashraff, had been killed when his helicopter crashed, possibly as a result of a Tiger bomb. Ashraff was the greatest barrier to Tiger domination of the East, because he commanded the support of the Muslims there, who constituted as high a percentage of the population in that Province as Tamils. After his death the leadership of the party passed to his General Secretary Rauff Hakeem, who was a Colombo product, as previous leading Muslim politicians had been.

The SLFP, or rather the People's Alliance, since the party was allied with the old left parties as in 1994, won the election, though they needed the support of the SLMC to form a government. Douglas Devananda's EPDP, reduced in strength with the now Tiger supported TULF in the Jaffna District, was also part of the government, and he entered the cabinet for the first time. Kadirgamar continued as Foreign Minister.

Anura Bandaranaike was elected Speaker. His elder sister, Sunethra, had ensured not only reconciliation between the President and her brother after their mother's death, but also sympathy towards his political claims. The UNP, as a member of which Bandaranaike had got into Parliament this time too, was quite happy to nominate him for the position, and he was elected unopposed.

Developments in the UNP

Wickremesinghe, who had now lost a string of elections in succession, had to face some criticism in his party, led by its General Secretary Gamini Athukorale, who had earlier been his strong supporter against Gamini Dissanayake. By now he believed that unless Wickremesinghe was more aggressive, a different leader was necessary, and he began to promote the Deputy Leader, Karu Jayasuriya.

Jayasuriya was a technocrat, used prominently by Premadasa, and brought into active party politics by Wickremesinghe when he needed a new Chairman. The position had been occupied in 1994 by the elder statesman and former Foreign Minister ACS Hameed, but they had fallen out over Wickremesinghe's insistence on appointing one of his young friends to a parliamentary vacancy caused by the mass deaths at the time of Dissanayake's assassination. Hameed, worried at the takeover by

Ashraff's SLMC of what had earlier been an area of support for the UNP, had wanted an Eastern Province Muslim. The widespread rumour, scurrilously carried by *Counterpoint,* that the reasons for the appointment were sexual, had caused some embarrassment to the party. Though Wickremesinghe married in 1995 and rode out that particular storm, Hameed resigned from his position.

Karu Jayasuriya however proved a popular replacement, whose mass appeal was confirmed when he was elected Mayor of Colombo and did an excellent job. Unfortunately he was plucked out of that position to contest the Western Provincial Council in 1998. The PA had won all Provincial Council elections, so Jayasuriya was merely leader of the opposition until the 2000 election. In that year he was assigned to the Gampaha District, since it would not do for him to contest from Colombo and do better than his leader.

However he did very well electorally in Gampaha too, and early in 2001 Athukorale began to collect signatures from members of the parliamentary group urging that he become leader of the opposition. Wickremesinghe was away in Norway at the time, but alerted by Anura Bandaranaike, he rushed back. Fortunately for him Jayasuriya was both loyal and diffident, and he and Athukorale assured Wickremesinghe that if he changed his style and sought to topple the government they would serve him loyally.

Precipitating an election

This was the spur that Wickremesinghe needed to take advantage of the problems Kumaratunga was creating for herself. Perhaps unsettled by the bomb attack, which had necessitated frequent trips abroad for medical attention, she was alienating several of her party members, including S B Dissanayake, her most ardent supporter earlier, whom she had appointed Secretary of the SLFP.

More seriously, she failed to deal firmly with one of her MPs whose supporters had attacked Muslims in his electorate. The reasons were financial rather than racial, but resentment grew amongst Muslims. Hakeem, during a visit to the East, realized that his leadership might be in question if he continued to acquiesce in what might happen. His response was to move closer to the Colombo businessmen who preferred the UNP, and who now saw their opportunity to move the SLMC to the other side.

By now problems were mounting for all businessmen. Even the gods seemed opposed to the President, for there was a severe drought that led to power cuts which drastically curtailed production. And then, in July, the Tigers scored their most spectacular success to date, as far as both Colombo and international perceptions were concerned, when they infiltrated the country's only major airport and destroyed a number of planes. Panic-stricken firing by security personnel, resulting in several deaths, increased the impact of the operation so that tourism dropped to zero, and increased insurance and transport costs damaged the economy further. Given economic problems elsewhere, exacerbated by the attack on the Twin Towers in New York on 11 September, there was negative growth in the Sri Lankan economy in 2001.

With the writing on the wall by the middle of the year, the business community was prepared to do anything, including offering financial incentives, to precipitate a change. Wickremesinghe, pushed by his colleagues, was up and running for the first time in seven years, and negotiations opened on several fronts. Mrs Kumaratunga realized what was happening, but she was not prepared to make concessions to those she saw as traitors. She did have discussions with Wickremesinghe, which proved unsatisfactory to both, and then she decided to negotiate with the JVP, which saw an opportunity to make full use of the ten seats it had obtained in 2000, as opposed to its single seat in 1994.

The result, after a prorogation of parliament, was what was termed a probationary government, with the JVP pledging support without accepting any portfolios. Their conditions included a limit of 20 on portfolios, though they failed to have this entrenched in the constitution. What they did introduce into the constitution, supported also by the UNP so that it obtained the required two thirds majority, was an amendment to limit the absolute power of the President with regard to major appointments, such as to the Public Service Commission and the Chief Justice.

The 17th amendment to the Constitution instead instituted a Constitutional Council, on the recommendation of which alone the

President could make such appointments, as also to an Elections Commission (to replace the Elections Commissioner), a Police Commission and a Media Commission. Unfortunately the legislation was hastily drafted, and the Council itself was composed in a confusing manner. Worse, there was no provision as to what would happen if it failed to meet or make recommendations, or if the President failed to accept its recommendations.

In a sense the legislation was typical of a legislature that, following Jayewardene's lead, did not understand the distinction between a Presidential system and Westminster practice. The amendment sprang from the Westminster concept that a nominal Head of State makes appointments in terms of recommendations from the real decision maker. Under Westminster that decision maker is the Prime Minister. Contrariwise, in an Executive Presidential system, it is the prerogative of the President to select those to be appointed to vital positions. However, his discretion should not be unfettered, i.e. his selections should be ratified by another body.

Handing over the actual selection to another body, with the Executive President reduced to a rubber stamp, did not make sense given the existing constitution. At the same time the acceptance of the principle that the overweening powers of the President should be curtailed was an advance on the previous situation.

But that was practically all that was achieved in that session of parliament. With more crossovers, that now included S B Dissanayake, G L Pieris and the SLMC, the government no longer commanded a majority. The President would not call on Wickremesinghe to form a government, but dissolved Parliament and fixed an election in December.

The result was a victory for the UNP, or rather UNF as it now called itself, to accommodate the SLFP rebels. Together with the SLMC they just had a majority, but once the government was in power they were secure, with the support not only of the Tamil parties other than the EPDP, but also the CWC. The TULF had been replaced for this election by what was termed a Tamil National Alliance, which included old TULF members but was intended to be the mouthpiece of the Tigers. Meanwhile, in the CWC, though the elder Thondaman was dead, he had passed the mantle onto his grandson. So once again there was a Thondaman in the cabinet, as there had been in every cabinet since the elder Thondaman and the CWC had abandoned the TULF in 1977 and joined Jayewardene.

Kumaratunga had to accept defeat, and appoint Wickremesinghe as Prime Minister and allow him to select his own cabinet. She did try to retain the Defence portfolio, alleging that it was a constitutional requirement; so Wijetunge had done in 1994 when she became Prime Minister and formed a cabinet, but Wickremesinghe was adamant.

Surprisingly, he did not appoint Athukorale to Defence as expected. He chose instead Tilak Marapana, who had been Wijetunge's principal adviser as Attorney General. Marapana was on the National List, as was K N Choksy, Wijetunge's former Minister of Constitutional Affairs, who was appointed Minister of Finance. Jayasuriya, who might have expected this post, was given Energy and Athukorale Transport, both tough portfolios.

That this was punishment of sorts was apparent from a confidante of the Wickremesinghe family, who claimed that the duo could not be trusted. She cited in particular Jayasuriya's claim that he had dreamed one of the Senanayakes had appeared to ask him to save the country. Jayasuriya, who had reported this dream to Wickremesinghe, interpreted it as a call for action, not for himself to lead the party.

However, such a dream, in the eyes of a superstitious clan, and the cabal that surrounded Wickremesinghe, indicated that Jayasuriya could not be relied upon. He however was a gentle sort. Athukorale might have been less easy to control, but within a month of the election he was dead. He had driven home after a party on New Year's Eve, and gone to bed and never woke up. He was not yet 50, but since he had a mild heart condition, given the stress of the preceding period, foul play was not suspected at the time. Later suggestions that Wickremesinghe was involved seemed ridiculous, on par with the suggestions that tied Premadasa to the deaths of potential rivals in the UNP, but on hindsight it is possible that the Tigers saw in him the one obstacle to achieving what they wanted through the UNP.

The Tigers and the Ceasefire

The Tigers announced a ceasefire from 24 December, which the new government reciprocated. In fact the previous December also the Tigers had announced a unilateral ceasefire, which had not been reciprocated by Mrs Kumaratunga's government. At that stage, despite the territorial losses of the previous year, the government still thought it could proceed with the war.

Though the attack on the airport, after the Tigers had abandoned their long ceasefire, seemed to suggest that they had the advantage, there were reasons to think otherwise. In the first place, following 9/11, the climate for international terrorism was less favourable. There was some evidence that the Tigers were amongst the leaders in international terrorism, that techniques similar to those developed by them were being used by Al-Qaeda, and that they were central in narco-terrorist networks. Further acts of aggression, terrorist or conventional military ones, which they had carried off successfully in the preceding years, could have led to forceful international reactions; the United States had in any case been less tolerant than Europe of the Tiger claim to be freedom fighters.

The brilliant offensives of 1999 and 2000 had taken their toll; the increasing numbers of child combatants involved made clear the Tigers had difficulties with recruitment. Military offensives would have been less easy than hit and run terrorist activity, but the latter would have more readily attracted hostile international attention.

In addition, the army had developed a technique of Long Range Patrols which had scored considerable successes. Using a closely guarded set of Tamil informants and agents, the government had been able to infiltrate into Tiger territory for targeted attacks. In May Thamilselvam, the leader of the LTTE's political wing, had a narrow escape when a claymore bomb exploded under a vehicle that was accompanying his, while in September the experienced commander Shankar was killed. The Tigers were deeply worried about these, and needed to find a way to stop the LRPs.

This happened on 2 January, the day after Athukorale's death, when a police team led by one of the Udugampolas, a family fanatically loyal to the UNP, raided an army safe house in Athurugiriya. The excuse was that it had been involved in a plot to assassinate members of the UNP in the run up to the election. However, apart from the fact that it was operated by the Directorate of Military Intelligence, which Udugampola knew, the raid was widely publicized to suggest that was its purpose rather than an attempt to deal with dangerous activities.

That the LTTE had been relying on Wickremesinghe for this performance seems obvious now. Sivanayagam, the editor of the Tiger mouthpiece *Hot Spring*, puts the TNA squarely within Wickremesinghe's UNF in his account of the 2001 election. This suggests that from the start it was assumed that they would help Wickremesinghe set up a government. He also makes no bones about the fact that, following Udugampola's raid, "An army officer and five men, including a Tamil were taken for questioning and detained under the Prevention of Terrorism Act. The men were members of a deep penetration unit that used to infiltrate Tiger-controlled areas and carry out attacks on LTTE leaders, as in the case of Tiger leader Col. Shankar."

The names of many involved in the operation, not just these six, were made public, and over the next couple of years the Tigers, while the ceasefire was still ostensibly being observed, picked off many of the Tamil informers. Sivanayagam and the Tigers would have appreciated the irony of members of a unit dedicated to the prevention of terrorism being detained under the Prevention of Terrorism Act.

Apart from what they thought they could secure from Wickremesinghe, the ease with which a ceasefire agreement was negotiated with Norwegian assistance also raised questions about the motivations and varying commitments of the Norwegians. Though it was in Mrs Kumaratunga's time that the Norwegians had originally got involved, Wickremesinghe too had maintained close contact with them. He was indeed in Oslo at the time when Bandaranaike had to call him back to deal with Athukorale's challenge to his leadership.

Though there can be no certainty which of the three parties took the initiative, Wickremesinghe or the Tigers or the Norwegians, some sort of understanding seems to have developed even before Wickremesinghe took office. By February a Ceasfire Agreement had been signed, by Wickremesinghe and Prabhakaran, ignoring the constitutional prerogatives of the Executive President. The agreement gave the Tigers full political rights in government controlled areas; this was bound to facilitate their control of the administration if the government continued passive. Conversely, Tiger controlled areas continued effectively outside the ambit of the government.

Kumaratunga objected to the agreement and some of its asymmetrical provisions, but was unable to do anything more. The election results had indicated that peace was wanted and, with Wickremesinghe acting on the assumption that the Prime Minister was the effective Head of Government, she was not in a position to resist.

Part IX

The Baby without the Bathwater

Wickremesinghe as Prime Minister (2001–2004)

Chapter 20

Jayewardene's Heir

Cronyism and Corruption

Ranil Wickremesinghe was Prime Minister from December 2001, for a little over two years. He came into power on a wave of good will which seemed to increase after the Ceasefire Agreement he signed with the Tigers – the UNF triumphed in the local government elections that were held shortly afterwards.

Two years later however he lost conclusively in the General Election that the President called in April 2004. To a large extent this was due to what was perceived as his singleminded appeasement of the Tigers. As the constitutional expert Rohan Edrisinha, at first a fervent supporter of Wickremesinghe's peace move, was to put it later, Wickremesinghe's approach made clear that an excess of pragmatism was bound to be disastrous.

Yet it was apparent that Wickremesinghe's lack of principle extended to all areas of government. He had appointed his close friend and confidante, Charitha Ratwatte, Secretary to the first Ministry he had presided over in the late seventies, to the position of Secretary of the Treasury. His brief was to cut government spending and exercise tight discipline. Ratwatte was sincere and determined about his task, but found himself undermined by Wickremesinghe's selective indulgences. Loyal as he was, Ratwatte complained about everyone else, but failed to register that the rot started at the top.

He was scathing about the Secretary to the Foreign Ministry when totally unqualified young men were sent as drivers to various embassies. The papers had blamed the Minister of Foreign Affairs for giving jobs to youths in his electorate, but in fact Wickremesinghe too had got into the act, sending one of his young security officers to New York as a driver, from which post he was later promoted to Public Relations Officer. Ratwatte insisted that the Foreign Secretary should have stopped all this. He ignored the fact that the new Representative at the United Nations, a former diplomat turned UNP politician, was indebted to Wickremesinghe and could make appointments the Foreign Secretary could not prevent.

Less innocent was Wickremesinghe's elevation to influential positions of persons he himself had reasons to worry about. Premadasa's former confidante, the experienced Civil Servant Paskaralingam, also thought to be an accomplished fund-raiser, was brought back to an advisory position in the Treasury, where he presided over various deals that Ratwatte on his own could not have made. Paskaralingam however could have been considered a loyal supporter of the section of the UNP to which Wickremesinghe himself had belonged. More surprisingly, Wickremesinghe appointed to advisory positions at the Central Bank as well as the Ministry of Higher Education, where a well funded World Bank Project was on line, Wickrama Weerasooriya, who was Gamini Dissanayake's brother-in-law. A brilliant propagandist and the brains behind some of the more vicious assaults on the Bandaranaikes at the 1977 General Election, he was thought to have been responsible for assaults on Wickremesinghe's sexuality at the time the DUNF was created. At that time Wickremesinghe alone amongst elite politicians had stuck with Premadasa.

Wickremesinghe's reliance on people who raised hackles amongst his more high-principled supporters was understandable in a context in which his repudiation by the UNP in 1994 in favour of Dissanayake had shattered him. Unable to accept that Dissanayake was the more accomplished politician, he put it down to the money that Dissanayake had at his disposal. Scrupulous as he had been not to profit personally from the offices he held, as leader of the UNP he had no qualms about raising money for the party, which he could then dispose of as he wished. In such a situation, the solidity of Charitha Ratwatte was insufficient, and he needed the worldly experience of Paskaralingam and Weerasooriya and their ilk. Given such needs, Wickremesinghe could not afford to keep in mind the danger he should have recalled from Wijetunge's time, that funds intended for party coffers could also be diverted to private uses when transparency and accountability were considered impractical.

It was interesting that, half way through the Wickremesinghe regime, a newspaper editor who supported him but had no illusions claimed that there were only three senior ministers untainted by credible allegations of corruption. These were Wickremesinghe himself, Jayasuriya and the Minister of Education, Karunasena Kodituwakku. Of these three, Kodituwakku lost the election that followed, largely because he did not have the funds to publicize himself through lavish posters as did his colleagues on the UNP list for the Colombo District. With regard to Jayasuriya, he had eschewed posters as a matter of principle, and it is a tribute to his ability that he nevertheless triumphed. He had maintained good electoral performances in the Gampaha District to which he had been dispatched since Wickremesinghe had to be allowed to shine alone in Colombo.

Wickremesinghe, unlike others in the UNP, did not have to use his own money to publicize himself, since the party spent lavishly for him. Indeed, it decided to concentrate on him personally, and the city and the country were covered with glossy posters that capitalized on his good looks and his reputation for integrity and determination which were considered important assets. But following the verdict of the electorate in 2004 the party commissioned a report from a committee headed by a Chairman from Jayewardene's first days in power, N G P Panditharatne, which delivered a harsh verdict on the strategy of concentrating on Wickremesinghe personally. Typically, the report was suppressed, and Wickremesinghe continued to lead the party as his personal fiefdom, buoyed by the prospect of winning the next Presidential election against a candidate less attractive than Kumaratunga. What was not even studied was how the money that had been spent had been obtained, and whether that had contributed to the view that the UNP was irredeemably tainted.

Wickremesinghe's own handpicked lieutenants contributed to the general impression. When Athukorale died, Marapana was given the Transport and Highways portfolio, in addition to Defence; within a few months it was widely accepted that he and his family were taking full advantage of the opportunities these two portfolios presented. Even Wickremesinghe's pet paper, *The Sunday Leader*, was full of allegations of corruption, in a strategy of emphasizing Wickremesinghe's integrity as compared with that of everyone else in politics. Jayasuriya too came under attack, even while he was being prevented from taking the necessary measures to solve the country's energy crisis. In that regard Wickremesinghe, like Kumaratunga, gave ear to the protests of the CWC over a long planned new hydro-electric power scheme and to elements in the Catholic Church over a long planned coal power plant.

With regard to Choksy, it was his wife who came under suspicion rather than he. Officially however it was he who made clear the commitment of his party to its sources of funding when he pushed through parliament an amnesty for tax evaders. He and Marapana were proof that the excuse proferred by some of Wickremesinghe's more honest supporters, that he could not afford to alienate corrupt politicians who brought him votes, was untenable. These two favourites from the National List – and also those he elevated to high positions in the bureaucracy – had no electoral strength, but were tolerated and encouraged purely because of the other support they gave Wickremesinghe.

Regression in education

Symptomatic of Wickremesinghe's idiosyncractic and highly personalized style of management was his virtual destruction of the Ministry of Education. That had been an area of deep concern to President Kumaratunga, but with her usual lack of concentration she had allowed things to slide during her first years in office. In 2000 however, realizing that concerted action was essential to promote the reforms that had been proposed, she appointed as Secretary to the Ministry her close confidante Tara de Mel, who immediately began to move things forward. She was assisted in this by her senior Additional Secretary, Lalith Weeratunge, one of the brightest members of the Administrative Service. Having worked initially for Mrs Bandaranaike when she was Prime Minister, he had gone on to the Ministry of Youth Affairs under Wickremesinghe and Ratwatte, to whom he paid tribute for encouraging efficiency and initiative.

Unfortunately he had upset Wickremesinghe, who was not one to forgive lightly. When the government changed Tara de Mel was not reappointed Secretary, since she was seen as a personal friend of the President. Ratwatte however thought Weeratunge would be a good choice as Secretary, and a number of senior Civil Servants, who were advising Wickremesinghe on such appointments, recommended him.

Personal grudges took precedence, and instead Wickremesinghe appointed a retired Civil Servant who, as Premadasa's former Secretary K H J Wijeyadasa put it, spent hours looking up Administrative and Financial Regulations so he could explain why he could not do what he had been asked to. Weeratunge, knowing that whatever he recommended would not be followed through unless there were several other signatures in support, took leave of absence to pursue a doctorate. With neither leadership nor commitment, the bureaucracy at the Ministry took a downward dive from which it never recovered. Wickremesinghe's response, when told that the Ministry was in a mess, was that he knew this, but had no time to attend to it. With a pompousness fuelled by his sycophants, he announced that during the first couple of years he had to concentrate on the economy, and it was only after he had settled that that he could turn his attention to matters such as education.

Underlying this was also a dislike of Kodituwakku, explained by his suspicion that Kodituwakku had been thinking of crossing over to Kumaratunga's side when constitutional changes had been proposed in the middle of 2000. Wickremesinghe was always slow to forgive, which perhaps explained why, in forming his cabinet in 2001, he had left Kodituwakku out, though he was Minister of 'Human Resources Development, Education and Cultural Affairs'. He had also appointed, as Ministers of Education and of Tertiary and Vocational Education, two loyalists, who had promptly taken advantage of theoretical parity of status to establish their own empires.

Wickremesinghe cavalierly claimed, a couple of weeks later, that the omission had been a mistake, and that it would be shortly corrected. However it was only in March 2002 that Kodituwakku became a Cabinet Minister, and by then his position had been totally undermined. The job descriptions in the gazette were unclear, since it seemed he had no responsibility for higher education even though the youthful Kabir Hashim's brief noted that he would assist the Minister of Human Resources Development etc. Given the close connection between Wickremesinghe and Hashim on the one hand, and on the other the Minister of School Education, one of Wickremesinghe's henchmen in his youth, and also the allegiance of the Secretary to the Prime Minister rather than the Minister, Kodituwakku felt himself powerless. He was in a totally unenviable position though he could be faulted for not asserting himself.

The denial of English

Wickremesinghe's almost frivolous approach to government was also apparent in his criticism of the English medium, which had finally been reintroduced by Mrs Kumaratunga in 2001. Contrary to popular opinion, it was not the Bandaranaikes who had abolished the English medium. That had originally been proposed in the 1940s by Jayewardene, who had claimed then that Ceylon, as it then was, consisted of two nations, those who spoke Sinhala or Tamil, and those who spoke English. To integrate the nation, and remove the unfair advantages enjoyed by the latter, it was necessary to prohibit the use of English as a medium of education. The consequence of this measure, two nations speaking Sinhala and Tamil, and unable to communicate with each other, would not have occurred to a man to whom English came naturally.

The proposal was not accepted fully, but in time it was implemented and by 1980 there was no English medium in the Sri Lankan school system, since the private schools also had to follow state regulations. It was then that there sprang up so-called International Schools, which offered English medium education at a massive cost. For a couple of decades there were very few of these following foreign curricula, but gradually there also sprang up international schools which taught the Sri Lankan curriculum in English. Technically however these were illegal; the majority of Sri Lankans had no access to English medium education.

In 2001 a Cabinet Paper presented by the Ministries of Education and of National Integration proposed that ordinary schools which wished to start English medium at the secondary level be permitted to do so.

These schools were to be known as Amity Schools, since in time students of more than one race would be able to study together in English. Though difficulties were envisaged in producing textbooks and training teachers, it was decided that the project had to be started immediately to take advantage of the rapidly declining existing capacity.

The government changed before the school year commenced in January 2002, but teacher training had begun, and Kodituwakku proved enthusiastic. With attractive books distributed on time over the year several more schools joined the 100 or so that had started the programme in January.

Wickremesinghe had been opposed to the idea, but given Kodituwakku's keenness, and given too the enthusiasm for the programme amongst his supporters in Colombo, he did not impose his will. However he, and the Permanent Secretary he had appointed, kept imposing obstacles so that training slowed down, as did book production. Fortunately a World Bank funded project started by Tara de Mel ensured that books were couriered to schools in time for the first couple of years.

Wickremesinghe, when difficulties were pointed out to him, said that he had told Kodituwakku not to start the programme, and now it would have to stop. He was obviously not concerned about the effect this would have upon the 4000 and more students who had already begun studying in English, including in several schools in rural areas that had enthusiastic and committed principals and staff.

Wickremesinghe's opposition to the programme seemed inexplicable unless, as Tara de Mel suspected, resentment that it had been commenced by Mrs Kumaratunga affected him. Perhaps since his own English was perfect though he had studied in the Sinhala medium, he assumed that this could be achieved by anyone. Whatever the reason, it typified an approach that combined arrogance with a vindictiveness that suggested deep insecurity.

Constitutional and Media Manipulation

Unfortunately these idiosyncrasies went together with an assumption that the excesses of Jayewardene's government could be repeated. So it was that Wickremesinghe introduced a constitutional amendment that replicated Jayewardene's second amendment, which permitted opposition members of parliament to cross over to the government side while preventing the opposite.

The provision that members who resigned or were dismissed from the party through which they had contested an election should also lose their seats in parliament was based on the assumption that voters exercised their choice for a party. This would happen with the introduction of proportional representation but Jayewardene had ensured that the provision applied also to the 1977 parliament in which members had been elected individually. However, to facilitate crossovers from the opposition, in particular the TULF, he introduced a constitutional amendment which permitted parliament (ie, the government, since it would have a majority in parliament) to decide on such cases for the 1977 parliament. The effect of the amendment lapsed when that parliament was dissolved at the end of 1988.

It was argued that the existing constitutional prohibition inhibited the freedom of conscience of members of parliament. This seemed the more improper because members of parliament were now selected by a scheme that allowed voters to cast preferences amongst those on the list of the party they chose. Amidst talk of restoring this purported freedom of conscience, the Wickremesinghe government, in a package designed to reduce the powers of the President, introduced, not a provision that permitted crossovers in general, but one that allowed such cases to be decided by a majority in parliament. Clearly Wickremesinghe was hoping to win over enough support from the opposition to carry his full package.

However the Supreme Court, now less malleable than it had been in Jayewardene's time, found the provision unconstitutional. Wickremesinghe realized that he could not take over without another poll, either a referendum to pass the amendment or the Presidential election that he believed was due in 2005, six years after Kumaratunga had been elected for a second term. Since at this stage Kumaratunga was, despite her constitutional status as President, allowing him to make all the decisions, he bided his time. Instead the papers aligned with him suggested that

Wickremesinghe had been misled as to the provisions of the bill to amend the constitution by the former Attorney General Marapana, the former Professor of Law and current Minister of Justice Pieris and the Attorney General Kamalasabeysan. All happened to have gone to S. Thomas's, the rival school to Wickremesinghe's Royal College, and archaic schoolboy humour was invoked to suggest that Wickremesinghe had been deceived by a team that had a different ethos from his own commitment to democracy.

The media coverage of this manoeuvre, very much in the Jayewardene tradition of which Wickremesinghe was the last surviving serious politician, involved that a cabal reporting direct to the Prime Minister pay close attention to all headlines. With two independent newspaper groups and all three independent television channels committed to him, and with control also of the state media, Wickremesinghe and his associates had a free hand in projecting the image they wanted, of a clean and decent man, struggling with corrupt and devious people in his own party and coping with a hostile and volatile President.

In a sense the strategy was similar to that adopted by Jayewardene, who used to encourage newspaper columns critical of members of his cabinet, provided he was not affected. What Wickremesinghe, harking back to that distant past, did not realize was that he did not have the stature Jayewardene had commanded, when he achieved supreme power at the age of 70; the constitution he had helped to introduce in 1978 still gave considerable powers to the elected President, despite his own majority in Parliament; the electorate was more sophisticated, and the development over the years of an independent media had made impossible the propagandist excesses that Jayewardene had engaged in.

And he did not realize that, unlike in Jayewardene's time, when the President was doing all the running, he had to deal with an ally he was incapable of controlling. The appeasement of the Tigers that was the foundation of his strategy was not to the liking of the country at large. As the extent of his subjugation became clear, the goodwill he had enjoyed at the beginning of 2002 gradually declined.

Chapter 21

The Tiger's Tail

Abusing the Ceasefire

Within three months of Wickremesinghe's assuming office as Prime Minister a Ceasefire Agreement had been signed with the Tigers. For this purpose the Norwegian government had acted as facilitators, and they were now responsible for a Sri Lanka Monitoring Mission to ensure that the Ceasefire was observed. Over the next couple of years the SLMM had its work cut out, with their records indicating that the Tigers had violated the Agreement on over a thousand occasions. The record of the government was substantially better.

This precision in recording suggests that the Norwegians aimed at objectivity. This was not the perception of most Sri Lankans who felt that the CFA had been designed in the interests of the Tigers. Thus they saw the LTTE taking control of the mechanisms of government in what had previously been government controlled territory, while the government had no role in the North and East in which the Tigers had held sway.

Such perceptions may not have been fair to the Norwegians. Certainly many of those involved started from an assumption that the two parties to the agreement were equal in stature; there was a tendency to assume that morally the Tigers were superior, given perceptions fuelled by Tamil refugees in Norway (politically influential) that Sri Lankan governments were majoritarian and racist. More importantly, Ranil Wickremesinghe's government expected such an approach. Wickremesinghe was determined not to rock the boat to ensure Tiger support during the interim period before he could assume Presidential powers. If this meant giving in to Tiger demands he saw no alternative; it seemed government policy which the Norwegians, their own predilections leading them in that direction, followed.

Thus what seemed to be the officially sanctioned raid on the Athurugiriya safe house led to the decimation of the most successful strategy developed by the security forces, the Long Range Reconnaissance Patrols that the LTTE feared following the elimination of Commander Shankar. Apart from the large scale elimination of Tamils, who had cooperated with the forces, was the systematic killing of members of other Tamil political groupings.

According to the CFA, the government was committed to disarm paramilitary forces. Though the Tigers were supposed to function without arms in government controlled areas, they continued to function as a military force, which meant they had access to weapons. They were able thus to eliminate members of the disarmed EPDP and PLOTE and other groups whom they charged with having abetted both the Kumaratunga government and the armed forces. The Norwegians dutifully recorded such murders but, with their role restricted to monitoring rather than enforcing the agreement, they could do nothing about such one-sided violence.

Gathering Arms and Equipment

Another feature of the Wickremesinghe years was the impunity with which the Tigers brought in equipment. The most blatant example of this was the import of sophisticated communications equipment for a broadcasting station, which was actually conveyed through the Norwegian Embassy. Whilst the Norwegians may well have believed that, to develop a balance between the two forces, they had every reason to provide the Tigers with the wherewithal to engage in high tech propaganda, the formal initiative came from the government. The Tigers wanted the equipment, they did not want to pay duty, so the government thought it less contentious than authorizing a waiver for the LTTE to arrange for the consignment to come through the Norwegian Embassy. This provided a better excuse for waiving duty, and it was delivered with unusual promptitude. A few months later it was reported that the government had helped the LTTE obtain underwater scooters, transported to Kilinochchi in an Air Force helicopter.

Even more alarming was the complacence with which the government viewed the Tigers' amassing of more dangerous armaments. Though the armed forces were aware of this, they had to deal with a Minister of Defence and a Prime Minister who wanted the matter ignored. They turned in desperation to the President who was bypassed with regard to all decisions, though in theory Commander in Chief of the Forces.

Matters came to a head in February 2003 when the navy refused to let a trawler pass, and requested the President to ensure that the SLMM inspect it. Not receiving any satisfactory response from the Prime Minister or the Minister of Defence, the President asserted her authority and insisted that the SLMM fulfill its function, demanding a further inspection when the trawler was given a clean bill. This second inspection, more carefully targeted on the President's advice, found an anti-aircraft gun, whereupon the Tigers on board ordered the Norwegian monitors to jump into the sea, and then committed suicide by blowing up the trawler. Though the SLMM, in collaboration with the government, tried to mitigate the significance of the incident, it was clear that the CFA had resulted in *carte blanche* for the Tigers to build up their military strength, with the connivance of the government along with those supposed to monitor the Agreement.

Political Repositioning

More upsettingly, this attitude of the government seemed to have influenced other countries too, in particular Japan, which also now seemed to have adopted the view that the government and the LTTE were equal partners in the peace process. Japan hosted the sixth and last round of talks in March, with a vital role played by its Special Envoy Yasushi Akashi, who had a decade previously presided over the peace agreement in Cambodia. By this stage Sri Lankan commentators had begun to assume that Norwegian interest in the issue was fuelled by their desire to access the deep sea resources that an LTTE ruled North-East would possess. Thus the increased Japanese involvement in the process, and with the LTTE, was seen as the staking of a separate claim. When India indicated it preferred a more restricted role for Japan, while the LTTE blew up a Chinese fishing trawler, there were even greater suspicions that the involvement of the international community was potentially dangerous.

It was in such a situation that the Americans also got involved, with profuse support of the peace process; nevertheless they did not revoke the ban they had imposed earlier on the LTTE. More tellingly, the Americans did not invite the Tigers to a meeting in Washington designed to achieve a consensus on financial support for the process. It was suggested that this was due to Indian refusal to sit together with the Tigers, and increasing American interest in improved relations with India may have contributed to the decision. However, given the intensity of the American critique of terrorists, and the absence of any particular reason to treat the Tigers as a special case, the United States may have seen no reason to indulge the Tigers until they renounced violence.

The Tigers, determined to be an equal partner in the peace process, a determination that Europe led by the Norwegians and Japan seemed to have acquiesced in, were angry at the American stance; this may have contributed to the next Tiger initiative. This was to announce withdrawal from talks until what they claimed were the immediate needs of the Tamil people were met. However they continued to abide by the CFA given the advantages bestowed upon them; the armed forces were hamstrung while they themselves could violate its provisions with impunity.

The Tiger withdrawal was announced in a letter from their Chief Negotiator, Anton Balasingham, who had been resident in Britain for several years. He made two major points, one that the government did not seem interested in interim institutional adjustments and the other that the benefits of peace had not flowed to the majority of people in the North and East. It was clear that the Tigers would not resume talks until they had been given control of the North-East through an Interim Administration; they had anticipated this from the commencement of their talks with the Wickremesinghe government. Similarly, a decade and a half earlier, they had wanted an interim administration they could dominate, before elections were held to Provincial Councils under the Indo-Lankan Accord.

Balasingham's letter made sense; from the beginning Wickremesinghe had avoided detailed discussion of constitutional arrangements. He was aware that, having connived in the tearing up of Kumaratunga's proposed constitution in 2000, he could not credibly offer a much greater degree of autonomy; the Tigers obviously would not settle for much less than an independent state. At the talks in November 2002, in Oslo, Balasingham appeared to accept the principle of a federal arrangement but, whilst that still raised hackles amongst some Sinhalese, it had upset Prabhakaran even more. It was suggested that Balasingham had exceeded his brief. Long term constitutional arrangements were simply not a matter for discussion, the Tigers in any case having made it clear even earlier that they wanted an interim arrangement without the difficulties entailed by democratic structures. On Wickremesinghe's side, the charitable assumption was that he believed the peace dividend of economic development would weaken the appeal of the Tigers and hence the impetus for separatism. On that argument, the longer he could protract the process the more favourable would be the outcome to the Sri Lankan government.

Failures in rehabilitation

More plausibly, he had from the beginning assumed that an interim administration dominated by the LTTE was the price he would have to pay for their continuing support. Certainly his failure with regard to the other aspect Balasingham stressed is explicable only on the assumption that he did not think any other serious arrangements worth exploring. For from the very start his approach to the whole question of rehabilitation and reconstruction had been cavalier, designed to make clear that this was beyond the capacity of the Sri Lankan government.

At first he had appointed as head of the reconstruction authority, not a dynamic administrator such as Ratwatte, but his Secretary Bradman Weerakoon, who had been Secretary to the Prime Minister forty years before. That had been in Mrs Bandaranaike's first term, after which he had given evidence against her brother in what proved to be a trumped up bribery case; thereupon he had had to align himself with the UNP. Over 70 years old now, he found himself at sea with regard to rehabilitation, and anxious donors found him asking for suggestions as to what he could do.

Given the lack of planning, and indeed perhaps capacity, on the part of the Wickremesinghe government, and given the unwillingness of the government as a whole, and even of most donors at that stage, to fund the Tigers direct, what would have made sense was to have entrusted the business to the private sector. This was what the main Chamber of

Commerce assumed would happen. Unfortunately Wickremesinghe did not like its Chairman at the time, and he preferred to keep things in government hands, albeit knowing that Weerakoon was not up to the task.

Accordingly, Tiger complaints grew more vociferous; towards the end of 2003 Weerakoon was replaced by a Sub-Committee on Immediate Humanitarian and Rehabilitation Needs. Astonishingly, this had more Tigers than government representatives. There were four Tigers, two representatives of the government, and also two Muslims, which seemed to confirm the Tiger view that the government represented only the Sinhalese.

Astonishing as was the composition of this committee, Wickremesinghe assured his supporters that it had little power since all funds would have to be approved by the Treasury. Whether this was deliberate or not, SIHRAN as it was known proved ineffective; within a few months the Tigers were demanding what they called an Interim Self-Governing Administration.

This was essential for access to the foreign aid that so many countries were anxious to contribute, but the Tigers might have thought of it simply a formal acknowledgment of what was already in operation. Given the acquiescence of the government, they had a great deal of influence already with administrators in the North and East, and their courts and police already commanded allegiance over the conjoined provinces.

Authoritarian Dispensations

Typical of the authoritarian approach they had enshrined in government was a document they issued entitled "Judicial Administration of Tamil Eelam". Its first section, on the "Structure of Tamil Eelam Judicial Administration", began – "It functions on the basis of the direct approval of His Excellency Mr. V Prabakaran, the National Leader," and adds "Only he has the authority to reduce or increase the sentences of the Courts wherever the need arises. All laws are made with his approval."

For review of legislation there was a committee which "after having discussed and reviewed the Legal drafts drawn by the legislation submits the final form of draft to the National Leader for approval. This Committee will meet as and when needed."

The head of the judiciary seemed to be someone called "Official in Charge (all)" whose first duty is "Implementing the views of National Leader in respect of Judicial Administration informing him."

Because it was clear which way the Tiger wind would blow, there had been concern from the beginning of negotiations that mechanisms should be in place to enforce human rights. At the fifth set of talks in Berlin, at the time the trawler smuggling arms was blown up, it was agreed that a representative of Amnesty International would draw up a road map on human rights issues. However his draft did not prove acceptable to the Tigers, particularly as regards international monitoring. In addition to the issue of child soldiers raised by international organizations, though the Wickremesinghe government did not seem to think it important, the Tigers were worried about the concept of pluralism, which went against their systematic destruction of other political forces in the region they intended to dominate.

Indeed their determination to dominate had also affected relations with the leader of the Tamil National Alliance. Though this was controlled by the LTTE, it also included members of the old TULF, and the veteran politician Veerasingham Anandasagarai was its leader. His independent approach did not suit the LTTE, which tried to sideline him. This led to a clash with the Jaffna Municipal Council, which had invited him as Chief Guest at the opening of the Jaffna Public Library.

The Library, burnt in 1981 by the section of the UNP which had included Wickremesinghe at that time, had been rebuilt by the Kumaratunga government; the Tigers perhaps feared that the opening would draw attention to the pluralism of that government. Though their threats led to the postponement of the opening, the Municipal Council resigned *en masse*, recalling that the Tigers had killed two former Mayors.

Though there had been talk of local government elections, and Balasingham seemed to accept the need for these at the final round of talks, almost immediately it was reported that he had said that such elections should be conducted under Tiger supervision, and that only parties approved by them should contest. Later the Secretary to the Ministry of Defence claimed that even G L Pieris, as principal government negotiator, was sincere in his belief that local government elections could be held under normal conditions, but that Wickremesinghe had countermanded this proposal.

Wickremesinghe, who had begun to make speeches in which he suggested that democracy had to be put off for the sake of development, clearly had no problems with the authoritarianism of the Tigers. When, responding to their abandonment of talks, he finally put forward proposals for an ISGA, it was to be totally dominated by the Tigers. Not only would they nominate a majority to the apex body, they were also given the right to nominate the head of each component of local administration within the NorthEast; this meant Muslim and Sinhala areas as well as those with a majority Tamil population.

Typically, Wickremesinghe's proposals were advanced in two different drafts, one sent to the Tigers, the other to the President. The latter gave even greater powers to the Tigers inasmuch as it gave them control also of the coast and territorial waters. Though later Wickremesinghe claimed that the discrepancy was accidental, a more credible explanation was provided by the political commentator of the *Sunday Times*, a journalist close to Wickremesinghe. His claimed that Wickremesinghe had intended Kumaratunga to react angrily, whereupon he could release the other less worrying draft and claim that she had been unnecessarily hysterical.

Kumaratunga had found the draft sent to her so worrying that she had checked back to find the discrepancy. Her objections therefore were to the draft that had Wickremesinghe's seal of approval. Later, when the Tigers demanded even more, there was an attempt to portray her as extreme in her opposition. It was argued that what was presented was simply a draft; Kumaratunga was obviously right in assuming that, with Wickremesinghe's draft a starting point on one side, and the extreme Tiger claim for total authority for a ten year period on the other, the result would be the total abdication of Sri Lankan sovereignty over Prabhakaran's virtual state.

Kumaratunga reacts

By this stage Kumaratunga had reached the limits of her endurance. She had on several occasions proposed to Wickremesinghe that he set up a Security Committee; while never rejecting the suggestion, he had continued to run everything himself, with only occasional information to her. In this isolated condition she spoke to Milinda Moragoda, one of Wickremesinghe's closest allies whom she thought she could trust to convey her concerns; though she believed Moragoda had done his best, there was no change in Wickremesinghe's approach. Indeed Moragoda seemed to have been sidelined; at first he had seemed the chief negotiator on the government side, but gradually his colleague G L Pieris had become more prominent.

This may have been because Moragoda was seen as close to the United States, whereas the Tigers had increasingly felt that, of all the Western powers who dominated the international responses to the negotiations, the Americans were the least indulgent towards them. Whatever the reason, with Wickremesinghe's apparently greater reliance on Pieris, who was one of those who had crossed over and brought down Kumaratunga's government, she felt even more out of things, in spite of the role conferred on her by the constitution.

Matters came to a head when the Minister of Defence came to her for approval for regulations which would allow for personnel changes in the armed forces. Kumaratunga, as Commander in Chief, had kept on officers she thought she could rely on. They had followed the policies laid down by the Wickremesinghe government, but anger had increased in the armed forces at what seemed betrayal of all they had fought for. The leadership of the armed forces looked to her to take a stand against what was happening.

Kumaratunga claimed that Marapana had tried to obtain her signature for what he termed minor changes that would take away the little control she still exercised. Having refused, she was incensed to see the regulations issued under his authority as Minister of Defence. She then applied to the Supreme Court for a ruling as to whether this was permissible, given her constitutional obligations with regard to the defence of the country. When a verdict in her favour was given, the UNP began to collect signatures to impeach the Chief Justice. Wickremesinghe was abroad when this happened but it was clear, given the institutional structure of the UNP, that such an exercise would not have commenced without his approval. At the end of October 2003 then, Kumaratunga dismissed Marapana, and also the Media and Interior Ministers, and took control of these Ministries herself. She also dismissed the Secretaries to the first two of these, who were considered Wickremesinghe loyalists, and appointed Secretaries she thought she could rely on.

International reactions were not favourable, and even India, which Kumaratunga had assumed would welcome her move, given Wickremesinghe's indulgence of the Tigers and his dependence on Japan as well as the West, seemed to think she had erred. But, unable to retract, she awaited Wickremesinghe's return to Sri Lanka and what she hoped would be a mutually acceptable compromise.

Part X

Guarding the Change

Rajapakse's Emergence (2004–2007)

Chapter 22

The General Election of 2004

The failure to compromise

Wickremesinghe was in America when Kumaratunga dismissed three of his Ministers; he continued with his visit instead of returning to Sri Lanka which was in a severe constitutional crisis. The reason for his decision became clear when he did return. Having been met by masses of the party faithful at the airport, he made much of the fact that he had met George Bush and been assured of his support.

As Kumaratunga seemed to have no international backing, Wickremesinghe may have assumed that, if he stayed firm, she would be forced to back down. If she did not, he claimed, he was ready to face another election. This was a threat he had used previously, confident after his victory in 2001 that the electorate was behind him. When he introduced the abortive 19th amendment to the Constitution, he had claimed that it was essential to prevent Kumaratunga dissolving Parliament. This, according to the Constitution, she was entitled to do any time after a year had elapsed following an election. But meanwhile Wickremesinghe also said that, if his proposed amendment were rejected, he would precipitate another election.

This he had not done in 2002, and now at the end of 2003 it was clear that his bravado would not extend to such an action. To do this he would have had to resign, and ensure that Parliament did not extend its confidence to any other Prime Minister Kumaratunga appointed. But he could not take the risk of resigning, since she could then appoint a Prime Minister and take the reins of government entirely into her hands, while proroguing Parliament so that the day of reckoning would be postponed. Besides, there were members of his party who were urging compromise, and he could not be sure that, were he to resign, they would not support Kumaratunga to set up a new government.

So he remained in office and ran the business of the country in general, while Kumaratunga kept charge of Defence, the Interior and the Media. Nothing untoward happened, and it became clear that under Jayewardene's constitution, nothing could prevent the President arrogating such power to herself. In time there might have been a parliamentary censure, or a stoppage of funding, but since that might precipitate dismissal of the whole cabinet and prorogation, and perhaps an election, Wickremesinghe could not precipitate a crisis. At the same time, though discussions took place with a view to compromise, and Kumaratunga expressed herself willing to restore the other two Ministries while keeping Defence, which she claimed she was obliged to following the Supreme Court ruling, Wickremesinghe remained adamant.

Though he continued to rely on international pressure as well as what he assumed was his trump card, another General Election, several of his associates, in particular those dubious about his approach to the Tigers, were not so sanguine. They would have preferred a compromise; but Wickremesinghe was supported by those who had abandoned Kumaratunga to join him, not only members of her cabinets but also Rajitha Senaratne from Wijetunge's time and Ravi Karunanayake from the DUNF. Typical of their approach was the response of this last to the danger of Kumaratunga calling a General Election, in which her party together with the JVP would defeat the UNP. His view was that the UNP would not fall below 90 seats, which, together with the 25 the TNA was sure to win, would ensure a majority. This meant that a class that shuddered at the thought of coalescing with Marxists were quite happy to have a government subject to Tiger influence.

While there was talk of punitive action against Kumaratunga through the budget, an incident occurred that suggested the depth of feeling that had developed in the country against Wickremesinghe's policies. A Buddhist priest who had emerged as a telegenic preacher with a mission to restore the purity of the faith, and who had shown himself an emotive critic of what he saw as incursions by other religions, died in Moscow where he had gone for an operation. Posters sprang up suggesting that there had been foul play. When the body was brought back for the funeral there were outpourings of grief and recrimination that suggested the resentment that had been building up amongst at least some Buddhists. The view that Wickremesinghe would triumph again in a General Election seemed open to doubt.

When his more moderate colleagues were urging Wickremesinghe to compromise, the JVP realized it had to commit itself. Earlier, though lauding Kumaratunga's action, given its hardline attitude to negotiations with the Tigers, it had stayed aloof from an alliance, especially as Kumaratunga had refused to compromise on her commitment to an open economy and showed willingness to abide by the Ceasefire Agreement. But finally in January, the JVP accepted her terms and entered into an electoral agreement, whereby they would contest together with the SLFP, or rather the People's Alliance.

New Alliances

The new alliance was called the United People's Freedom Alliance; once it was sealed Kumaratunga dissolved Parliament and fixed an election for early April. This was constitutionally quite acceptable, and even the claim that morally she had no right to dissolve an elected Parliament rang hollow. After all the mandate she herself had received in 2000 had been lost in less than a year because of crossovers from her party to the UNP, and no one had complained then about the country having to go to the polls early for a fresh mandate.

Meanwhile, given the likelihood of a nationalist, or rather religious, reaction, the Sihala Urumaya decided to revitalize itself to take advantage of the tide. This was an extreme nationalist party that had received a lot of hype but failed to win any seats at the District level in the 2000 election. It had won one seat on the National List, but there had been an unseemly wrangle over who was to take this. The controversy led to the resignation of the Party President, S L Gunasekera, its most charismatic figure, a distinguished lawyer who was also a Christian. Outmanoeuvering him was part of a strategy to emphasize the supremacy of Buddhists rather than just Sinhalese, but this seemed to have backfired when, in the 2001 election, the party did much worse and won no seats at all – thus perhaps justifying the symbol it had chosen, which was a bow and arrow in which the arrow was pointing backward.

Now, in 2004, the party was reconstituted as the Jathika Hela Urumaya (National Sinhala Heritage), and decided to nominate only Buddhist monks. Since there was little love lost between Kumaratunga and the JHU, which had been instrumental in ensuring the failure of her reform package in 2000, some UNP supporters decided that advancing the JHU would deprive the UPFA of its nationalist support. The monks therefore received inordinate coverage in the UNP oriented media, and in particular in the television network run by Wickremesinghe's brother. Kumaratunga made ruthless use of the state media, and also of the Independent Television Network which that brother had founded in the seventies, only to have it taken over by Jayewardene soon after and kept in government hands since.

The UPFA in its campaign highlighted Wickremesinghe's appeasement of the Tigers, with its record of murdered service personnel and independent Tamil politicians. It also critiqued the corruption and double standards that had characterized the regime. The policy document Wickremesinghe put out during his tenure in office, entitled 'Regaining Sri Lanka', had emphasized fiscal discipline. Ratwatte had been ruthless about this, with moratoria on public sector recruitment, while budgets in areas such as education had been slashed. However this had been accompanied by an increase in the number of ministries, some of which had hardly any operational expenses while establishment costs were massive. Symptomatic of the cavalier attitude of Wickremesinghe's associates was the claim of the Foreign Minister that he had saved the country millions by not spending half his travel budget. It turned out that the budgeted amount had been about twice that allocated to the far more effective Kadirgamar during Kumaratunga's government.

The result of the election amply justified the risk Kumaratunga had taken. The UNP won only 82 seats, including its quota on the national list, whereas the UPFA got 107, 15 more than the PA and the JVP had obtained as two separate parties in 2001. The JHU obtained 9 seats, most of them it seemed from former UNP voters, since they only won representation in the Western Province and in Kandy, with very little support in rural electorates. Technically the opposition to Kumaratunga had a majority, but since this would entail the JHU working with the TNA, which had obtained 21 seats, it was obvious that the government would have to be formed by the UPFA.

A new Prime Minister

Initially there had been some speculation as to whom Kumaratunga would nominate as Prime Minister. Ratnasiri Wickramanayake had stepped down as Leader of the Opposition after the 2001 election, and had not contested the 2004 election, though Kumaratunga brought him into parliament shortly afterwards through the national list.

His place as Opposition Leader had been taken in 2002 by Mahinda Rajapakse, who, though comparatively young, was one of the most senior SLFP parliamentarians. His father had been the only other Member of Parliament to cross over to the opposition along with SWRD Bandaranaike when he left the UNP in 1951 to establish the SLFP. The younger Rajapakse had entered parliament as its youngest member in 1970; he had lost in 1977 when the SLFP was decimated, but he emerged as the leader of the party in the south where the resurgence of the SLFP began. He had made a forceful impact in taking up human rights issues during the darkest days of the Jayewardene and Premadasa regimes, in particular after he got back to parliament in 1989. Though he had been particularly prominent then, having organized the Mothers' Front which was a forceful reminder of UNP abuses, he was associated with Anura Bandaranaike, and had dropped out of favour when Kumaratunga came back. He had remained with the party however when Bandaranaike went over to the UNP in Wijetunga's time, and had served in Kumaratunga's cabinet as an efficient if not very influential Minister.

When he declared his intention of standing for the post of Leader of the Opposition in 2002 he was unstoppable, and now his claim for the Prime Minister's post could not be ignored. There was some talk of appointing Lakshman Kadirgamar; this seemed the preference of the JVP, which saw Rajapakse as a threat to their own popularity in the south.

Kumaratunga may in fact have preferred Kadirgamar but, in view of the impressive performance of the JHU, she recognized the need to ensure the confidence of hardline Buddhists too. Soon after the final election results were announced she appointed Rajapakse to the post. It was a measure of Rajapakse's skill as a politician that before long he was on extremely good terms with both Kadirgamar and the JVP.

More contentious was the position of Speaker in Parliament, with the UPFA and what might be termed the UNP group, which included the TNA, the SLMC and Thondaman's CWC, evenly balanced. The UPFA nominated the veteran Communist DEW Gunasekera, while the UNP proposed its former Leader of the House, VJM Lokubandara, who had been a Cabinet Minister since the last days of Jayewardene. After the votes proved even in the first ballot, with the JHU abstaining, rumours spread that one of the monks had been won over by the UPFA. On the view apparently that this had to be balanced, a couple of monks voted the other way, and Lokubandara was elected by one vote.

Despite its lack of a parliamentary majority Kumaratunga's government was there to stay. No one wanted another election and the JHU, having won so many seats, could not risk losing them by appearing irresponsible, and allow the the Tigers once again to dominate an alternative government. Wickremesinghe, though the target of some criticism in his own party for having sacrificed their majority, was able to stay on as leader. He was helped by Jayasuriya's passivity or his principles, which would not permit him to challenge his leader. Besides, it was felt that with a Presidential election due soon, Wickremesinghe should have the chance to stand against a candidate who, with Kumaratunga's enforced retirement, might have to battle to be nominated and then face disgruntled elements in his own party.

Kumaratunga's restored authority

Kumaratunga found herself once more in power, her authority enhanced by her courage in having taken Wickremesinghe on when he seemed at the height of his power and international prestige. She kept the portfolio of Defence, while appointing a separate Minister of Finance, which she had not done since she first took office as President. This was Sarath

Amunugama, formerly of the DUNF and then the UNP, who had crossed over to her in 2000 in support of her proposed constitution.

The other Ministry Kumaratunga kept was Education, with Tara de Mel back as Secretary. This was the area in which, apart from settlement of the ethnic conflict, she most wished to leave her mark. With the Tigers doubtless going to prove intransigent, and a negotiated settlement seeming impossible, it seemed worthwhile concentrating even more then on her other priority of education. Earlier, the policies she had advanced through a Presidential Task Force had not been implemented satisfactorily under various Ministers with their own priorities, so this time she thought it best to allow Dr. de Mel a free hand. But it was typical of Kumaratunga that she simultaneously appointed to statutory posts, with powers that would have to be actively exercised for satisfactory reforms to be successfully pursued, aged party supporters who did not share her vision.

With regard to the peace process, she expressed herself happy to continue with Norwegian facilitation, despite some rumblings from the JVP. After all it was she who had invited them, and they were willing to cooperate with her, given how conclusively Wickremesinghe had been rejected by the country. However they were not able to persuade the Tigers to return to the negotiating table. Amongst votaries of the UNP it was claimed that Kumaratunga had destroyed the peace process, but in reality the Tigers had withdrawn from the talks in April 2003 in anticipation of receiving full authority through the ISGA as constituted by Wickremesinghe. They saw no reason now to return to the negotiating table. Besides they had another problem that was to take center stage in their actions and strategies.

The split in Tiger ranks

In March 2004 the Tigers had suffered their first serious split when their Eastern Province leader Karuna announced that he was breaking away. Though personality clashes and distrust contributed, as previously when Prabhakaran arrested his deputy, Mahattaya, who was subsequently killed, the present split sprang from a fundamental division.

The Tigers, and indeed the TULF before them, had represented the entirety of what were termed Ceylon Tamils, those in the North and East whose ancestors had settled in the country a thousand and more years ago. The term was used to distinguish them from the Indian Tamils, who had been brought over by the British from the nineteenth century onward as indentured labour for the tea plantations in the central hills. However there were also deep social and cultural differences between the Tamils of the North, and those of the East, who had always been considered lower down on the social scale.

Thus, when Jayewardene had tried to win over members of the TULF, he had been relatively more successful in the East, with one of the members for Batticaloa joining his cabinet from 1978 on. Though in reaction to government attacks on Tamils in general, as in 1983, the Tamils had stuck together, the position of Tamils in the East was always sensitive in the Tamil political hierarchy. The Tigers, in particular, had been wary ever since Premadasa's successes in winning territory and sympathy in the East. They had reason therefore to be thankful for Kumaratunga's strategy of concentrating military forces on the North, which saved them from possibly losing the East completely.

However, the retaking of Jaffna had meant that the principal Tiger recruiting ground, where the Tamil population was heavily concentrated, was lost to them. So, during the previous eight years, it was the East that provided recruits, particularly children who were often forcibly taken away from parents. This was graphically recorded by the Jaffna University Teachers for Human Rights, an organization that had had to operate clandestinely since the Tigers had killed its most prominent member, Rajini Tiranagama.

It was largely the East then that provided the man (and woman) power that had allowed the Tigers to take Mullaitivu and Kilinochchi and the Vanni areas up to Omanthai and Elephant Pass. It was Karuna who had planned and led many of these offensives. But after the Ceasefire he found himself sidelined as what became known as the Vanni leadership, Prabhakaran and his confidantes, and their overseas based adherents, almost all of whom were from the North, took charge of strategy and negotiations.

The Tigers suspected outside influences such as the Sri Lankan military and the Indian intelligence of having precipitated the split. Later, Milinda Moragoda, who had been Wickremesinghe's chief negotiator before being superseded by Pieris, was to claim that the UNP was responsible for the split. As in Premadasa's time, the very fact of peace had brought dividends to Tamils in the East that would have made clear to them that their interests, in an obviously multi-ethnic environment, were different from those of the Northern Tamils.

In March 2004, when the split occurred, the Tigers did not highlight the UNP in their recriminations; their anger was reserved for Kumaratunga and the forces she now commanded. Underlying this was suspicion of India. In the run up to the election campaign therefore, they concentrated on this particular threat, quite understandably, given the result of the election and what Kumaratunga's return to power meant for the dominance they had built up under Wickremesinghe.

Through what foreign observers identified as malpractice, the Tigers won almost all the seats in the North. Anandasagaree, whom they had dismissed from the TNA, had an independent slate, which was widely expected to win at least one if not two seats, but he got nothing. Devananda's EPDP was reduced to one seat. In the East the Tigers won less than 40% of the vote, which was not surprising, given the demographic composition of the province. More worryingly, most of the Tamils elected on preference votes were supporters of Karuna.

During the election itself the Tigers struck, crossing over from the North to the East, and managed to take over most areas that Karuna seemed to control militarily. However, from the limited area that remained to him he was able to continue to exert influence, with the Tigers increasingly angry about what they perceived as support from the Sri Lankan armed forces. In urban areas the Tigers held sway again, and they ensured the immediate resignation of all Karuna supporters from Parliament, so that it was their own rubber stamps who took over these vacated seats.

Such blatant flouting of democratic practice did not deter the Tigers from claiming that the election results proved that they were the sole representatives of the Tamils. V K Sambandan, who had first entered Parliament for Trincomalee as a TULF member in 1977, declared that over 90% of the people in the North and East had voted for the TNA. When the falsity of this claim was pointed out, he claimed that the demography of the Provinces had been changed by colonization, and that he had referred to the legitimate inhabitants of the area. Such chicanery was typical of the man who had survived, through acquiescence with the Tigers, to be the senior member of the TULF, as housed now within the TNA. He outlived and outlasted Amirthalingam and Yoheswaran and Tiruchelvam and Thangathurai and Thambimuttu, all killed by the Tigers; also Sivasithamparam, who had been shot by them in 1989 but lingered on for nearly fifteen years more, and most recently Anandasagaree. He showed disregard for the Indian Tamils, since such arguments could have been used by racists amongst the Sinhalese to disenfranchise them, as having been brought over by the British.

Chapter 23

Kumaratunga under Siege

Kumaratunga's dilemma

Though she had won the election, Kumaratunga was not inclined to take on the Tigers. On the one hand, she was anxious for international support for her government. With the Tigers endorsed internationally as the representatives of the Tamils, through Norwegian leadership which the Europeans in particular tended to follow, she was determined not to rock the boat. With her narrow control of parliament she also hoped in time to rebuild her pluralistic support base of the nineties that had included all the Tamil parties.

She was the more anxious to do this, in that the election results had significantly increased the parliamentary strength of the JVP. When nominations for the election had been decided on, the JVP, apparently magnanimously, asked for at most three nominees in each District, the SLFP and its less important allies of the old Marxist parties having the rest. In fact this benefited the JVP, since its supporters concentrated their three preferences on JVP members, whereas the SLFP vote was divided amongst several candidates. Thus in almost all Districts the JVP candidates topped the lists of preferences and were duly elected to Parliament. The JVP thus had nearly 40 of the UPFA's 107 seats, which was a massive increase from the 16 seats they had had earlier.

The JVP had accepted four ministries, but these were not taken by their most senior parliamentarians, amongst them the charismatic Propaganda Secretary, Wimal Weerawansa. The hierarchy could thus concentrate on policies and general propaganda, while younger members could work at ministerial functions and raise issues in cabinet from a more individualistic standpoint. Immediately after the election, given the significant contribution of the JVP to the victory, their supporters in almost all ministries had a field day with posters that asserted their influence.

Faced also with a situation in which her own party seemed to be enamoured of the JVP, Kumaratunga thought she had an obligation to reassert her pluralistic credentials. She continued to work with the Norwegians, to the irritation of the JVP which thought the Norwegians too indulgent towards the Tigers. And increasingly she relied on her personal advisers, who were not attached to any of the line ministries, except for Tara de Mel at the Education Ministry which Kumaratunga herself held.

Rajapakse meanwhile, as Prime Minister, was making a concerted effort to woo all elements in the governing coalition, since he realized he would need their support for the Presidential election at which he assumed he would be the candidate. His only possible rival was Anura Bandaranaike, who had been instrumental in cementing the coalition between the PA and the JVP, and whom the JVP seemed at that stage to consider their preferred candidate, whom it would be easier to influence.

Rajapakse therefore concentrated on winning over the JVP, and made common cause with them in cabinet on various issues. Some of these led Kumaratunga to back down, on what seemed minor issues but were significant in terms of prestige. Rajapakse also worked hard at winning over Kadirgamar who, Kumaratunga was later to claim, had been disappointed with her at being passed over for the Premiership. In addition, while Kadirgamar concentrated on developing very close relations with India, he was suspicious of the Norwegians, as well as the Tigers, and felt in time that Kumaratunga was too indulgent towards them.

Rajapakse had selected as Secretary to the Prime Minister Lalith Weeratunge, whom Wickremesinghe had earlier passed over for personal reasons despite his outstanding record. Weeratunge was overwhelmed by evidence he found in the Prime Minister's office of wanton overspending that seemed a strong indication of corruption. Though Wickremesinghe had been careful to obtain the required approvals for his actions, for instance with regard to computerization of the office, the massive sums expended under the aegis of Paskaralingam showed at least double standards in someone who had been so sanctimonious about fiscal discipline elsewhere in government.

The evidence that emerged too about Wickremesinghe's indulgence of the Tigers, in supplying them with military and communications equipment, upset a regime that had won the election with a mandate to reverse such policies. Given that Kumaratunga was anxious to pursue friendly relations with Tigers as well as Norwegians, gradually there emerged an impression that she was out on a limb in her party, which, led by Rajapakse, was more in tune with the voter base that had restored them to office.

The beginning of the end

The crisis that removed Kumaratunga from office a year earlier than she had expected, and from power and influence in a manner that could not have been anticipated, given her control of her party for the preceding decade, began with the Tsunami of 26 December 2004. She was abroad at the time, as had been her custom during university holidays in Britain over the last five or more years, given her attachment to her children.

The Tsunami devastated Sri Lanka more than any other country save for Indonesia, with the death toll exceeding 30,000. Nevertheless Rajapakse had taken prompt charge, with Weeratunge being in charge of rehabilitation operations, and after the initial shock it seemed that swift action was being taken. Unfortunately Kumaratunga, on returning to Sri Lanka, felt obliged to assert herself. This seemed due to the rivalry she felt had developed between her and Rajapakse, for he and Weeratunge found themselves sidelined, while Kumaratunga set up three agencies to take care of different aspects of relief work.

Both the paucity of talent that she now had to contend with, and her relative isolation, became clear from the personnel she appointed. The forces were headed by officials who already had important full-time jobs, including Tara de Mel who had perforce to be absent from the Education Ministry for much of January. This in turn had a severe impact on the reforms she had initiated, because the next layer of administrators at the Ministry were incapable of taking things forward. Meanwhile her committee consisted largely of personal friends of the President. Though they were by and large competent people, including her sister, the inclusion for instance of one of Colombo's leading fashion designers did nothing to enhance Kumaratunga's image, in comparison with Rajapakse's more down to earth approach.

Typical of the confusion Kumaratunga's intervention at this stage engendered was the decision to ban future constructions within a fair distance from the shore. Environmentally this may have made sense, but it would have caused great problems for householders who had no other land. Conversely, when hotels that enjoyed beach frontages protested, exceptions were swiftly made.

The UNP made hay of this confusion, while the Tigers were drawing attention to the failure to reconstruct the areas under their control with the same commitment as had been shown in the south. To some extent this was due to the secrecy with which the Tigers had treated the Tsunami and its impact on their forces, since they had obviously lost men and materials to significant extents, including at least one very senior commander. However, they soon made capital internationally of the contrast between rehabilitation of Tamil and other areas, which was potentially embarrassing to the government. At the same time they made it clear that they wanted recognition of their own authority if rehabilitation were to proceed, which was a way of trying to claw back, as a result of the Tsunami, at least some powers of the ISGA that they had nearly obtained from Wickremesinghe.

Kumaratunga and her personal advisers negotiated, through the Norwegians, what was termed P-TOMS, a Post Tsunami Operational Management Structure, which gave the Tigers similar authority to what Wickremesinghe had proposed in his ISGA suggestions. This did not stop the UNP from claiming that Kumaratunga was handing over sovereignty to the LTTE. More seriously, the JVP declared that it could not accept such an Authority and would withdraw from the government were it established.

Typical of Kumaratunga's highly individualistic style of government was her failure to consult stakeholders during this process. The Europeans, guided by the Norwegians, knew what was happening, and insisted on such an Authority for the disbursement of aid; but the American Under-Secretary of State for the region, Christina Rocca, seemed to have no idea of the plan when she visited Sri Lanka a few months after the Tsunami. Kumaratunga also refused the JVP a meeting to discuss the document, which led to speculation that it conceded much more than it did. Significantly, Anandasagaree was also opposed to the P-TOMS. Kadirgamar, officially supportive of what was a government initiative, wrote articles expressing suspicioun of the LTTE and saying it was essential to make "it clear to the LTTE and the Government of Norway, that the restoration of democracy including the creation of space for dissent and the promotion of human rights in areas presently controlled by the LTTE, is a priority of the highest order... if the government of Norway is unable to plead the cause with the conviction and determination that it deserves it should stand aside and yield to other parties who could carry the flag of democracy into areas where darkness presently prevails".

In fact the Authority was never constituted because the Supreme Court, before which it was challenged, ruled on 15 July 2005 that it detracted from the sovereignty of the state. Before that the JVP had withdrawn from the government, though they still continued to support it in principle in Parliament. Since their opposition had been primarily to the P-TOMS attempts might have been made to bring them back into cabinet, but personal relations between them and Kumaratunga were so strained that initiatives in this regard seemed pointless.

The early Presidential election

They were also pointless for another reason; there was a far more serious undermining of the Kumaratunga Presidency, which made all other political manoeuverings insignificant. This was the increasing insistence on holding a Presidential election before December 2005, which would be six years after Kumaratunga's re-election on 22 December 1999.

The controversy had first arisen shortly after Kumaratunga, declared elected on 23 December 1999, took oaths on that day. The constitutional expert Rohan Edrisinha wrote an article in which he wondered whether she had thus given up a year of the Presidency to which she was entitled, inasmuch as the relevant clause in the Third Constitutional Amendment (which enabled an incumbent President to hold an early election) read as follows:

31 (3a) (d) 'The person declared elected as President at an election held under this paragraph shall, if such person –
  (i) is the President in office, hold office for a term of six years commencing on such date in the year in which that election is held (being a date after such election) or in the succeeding year, as corresponds to the date on which his first term of office commenced, whichever date is earlier; or
  (ii) is not the President in office, hold office for a term of six years commencing on the date on which the result of such election is declared'

As Edrisinha pointed out, the first paragraph makes it clear that, however unjustly, the term of office of a re-elected President begins on a date corresponding to the date on which the first term of office began. In Kumaratunga's case this was 10th November 1994, and she should therefore have taken her oaths within a couple of weeks of the next November 10th after the next election, viz November 10th 2000.

Kumaratunga and her legal advisors seem to have ignored this article, though it was later claimed that she had taken oaths again, before the Chief Justice, though that was not made public, in November 2000. Given that she had nearly been killed in December 1999, given too that her mother had died in October 2000, her own emotional difficulties may have precluded attention to constitutional niceties. Her advisors however cannot be excused for failing to take prompt action, and at least to have sought a determination from the Court while there was time for an objective view, i.e. in 2004 at the latest. Edrisinha was later to argue that, according to the Constitution, the extent of the term did not depend on the taking or not of an oath.

Wickremesinghe thought he had an issue which would allow for populist agitation, and early in 2005 he announced that the UNP would begin a mass campaign to insist that the Presidential election be held in 2005. Wickremesinghe's hypocrisy was blatant, in that he had been a member of the Cabinet that introduced the 3rd amendment, and he knew well that Jayewardene, having taken advantage of it, and been re-elected in October 1982, began his second term on February 4th 1983 and continued in office well after October 1988.

Pieris however, Wickremesinghe's constitutional expert, ignoring the precedent, insisted that no President could go on for more than six years, and the whole party geared itself to a strenuous campaign. This commenced in July, just before the Supreme Court ruling on the P-TOMS, with a 'People's March' from the south, the stronghold of Rajapakse as well as of the JVP. Initially the march seemed successful, though it is conceivable that government supporters also anxious for a change of leadership contributed their share. Certainly Rajapakse was able to take advantage of the movement to request that the SLFP select its own Presidential candidate.

His argument could not be gainsaid, that the UNP was agitating for a Presidential election in which it was able to project the image of its candidate, and therefore it was essential for the government too to announce its own standard-bearer. Kumaratunga may earlier have hoped that her brother, Anura Bandaranaike, would get the nomination, but over the preceding year, in part because of the controversy over the P-TOMS, preceded by her retreat into what seemed an inner circle of confidantes rather than politicians, she had lost much of her influence over the party. Both Kadirgamar and Mangala Samaraweera, who had emerged as her closest confidante politically during the period of cohabitation with Wickremesinghe, and who had been crucial in persuading her to ally herself with the JVP, understood that Rajapakse was the more popular candidate.

In the end there was no contest, and the party decided that Rajapakse would be the Presidential candidate, with Bandaranaike agreed upon as candidate for Prime Minister. After that was decided it was inevitable that, not only the leadership of the SLFP, but also the other constituent members of the PA, the old Marxist parties, should also rally to Rajapakse's banner.

Meanwhile the JHU had asked the Supreme Court to determine the date of the Presidential election. Kumaratunga's request for a non-binding advisory opinion, that she should have sought the moment the question was raised, had to yield to the JHU application which raised questions of Fundamental Rights. And then, towards the end of July it struck Kumaratunga that she could no longer rely on the Court. The Chief Justice, Sarath Silva, who had been a bugbear to the Wickremesinghe government, ruling very convincingly on the proposed 19th amendment as well as the President's application regarding defence functions, had ruled against her proposed P-TOMS. Now it was likely that he would rule in favour of what Wickremesinghe wanted, which also happened to be what Rajapakse desired.

Kumaratunga's supporters were of the view that the Chief Justice was influenced by his personal friendship with Rajapakse but, given the controversy that had arisen, it would have been difficult in terms of public interest for the verdict to have been different. Though a clear reading of the Constitution would have favoured Kumaratunga, Wickremesinghe's agitation had established that there was ambiguity which even Kumaratunga's lawyers were unable to clarify. With the likelihood of continuing civil disturbances over the next year if the election were scheduled for 2006, disturbances in which both the UNP and the bulk of the government parties would have expressed their displeasure, public interest seemed to demand an early election.

That this was not in Wickremesinghe's interests was the view of some of his supporters, who had imagined that the issue had been raised only to rouse resentment. In that respect Wickremesinghe was still suffering from his adulation of his uncle Jayewardene, who had successfully agitated against Mrs. Bandaranaike's extension of Parliament to 1977 when it had initially been elected for five years in 1970. In that case however the Parliament had continued for two extra years during mounting economic difficulties, which had lent strength to Jayewardene's agitation.

Wickremesinghe may have anticipated a repeat of this situation, and in fact Rajapakse would certainly have done worse in 2006, with economic problems as well as continuing dissension within the government. Wickremesinghe's contention however, which even members of his own party realized was flawed, allowed Rajapakse to be appointed as the candidate before any alternative could be advanced. With the application of the JHU for a Fundamental Rights determination the Courts could decree an early election, which gave him at least an even chance. Though Colombo was convinced that Wickremesinghe was bound to win, the results of the 2004 election showed that Rajapakse would be difficult to defeat if he held his coalition together.

The assassination of Foreign Minister Lakshman Kadirgamar

The determination of the Court was given on 26 August. Two weeks before that Lakshman Kadirgamar had been assassinated, in an extraordinary operation that made clear not only the continuing operational skills of the LTTE but also the shortcomings of government security.

Kadirgamar had long known that he was the prime target of the LTTE, and in April he had observed a directive that kept him gated in his well protected official residence. Tiring of this however, he had ignored a similar security warning in August. He had recently acquired a private residence with a swimming pool in which he was relaxing after the launch at the Bandaranaike Centre for International Studies, the Board of which he chaired, of the inaugural issue of its journal.

The house was in a very wealthy residential area, and it was reported that he had not permitted his security to investigate all his neighbours to circumvent threats. Next door was a house occupied by a Tamil couple of impeccable social credentials, who did not however use the upper floor. A part-time gardener had obtained a key, and it was from a bathroom at the top that a sniper shot Kadirgamar, as he emerged from the pool.

Given Kadirgamar's international reputation it is surprising that the Tigers should have dared to eliminate him; initial reactions were critical, and even the European Union seemed to suggest miscalculation. But all this was soon forgotten. Before long, with the Norwegians pleading indulgence for the sake of the peace process, the Tigers went back to enjoying much of their former status and privileges.

More importantly, they had eliminated Rajapakse's principal Tamil ally, whom it is almost certain he would have appointed Prime Minister. Since international perceptions, assiduously cultivated by the LTTE, are that the Sri Lankan government is a Sinhala one in which Tamils have no position, a high profile Tamil Prime Minister would have enabled Rajapakse to illustrate the very different ground situation. The position of Foreign Minister, whilst admirably filled by Kadirgamar, could not command the same recognition. Furthermore, the determination that Tamils should not vote for Rajapakse would have been less easy to fulfill were his principal intellectual supporter a Tamil.

The outpouring of grief at Kadirgamar's death, from the country in general as well as the JVP and even the JHU, made clear how forcefully he had advocated what were perceived as national interests. Yet it became much easier for the UNP thereafter, aided by the international media, to project Rajapakse as a chauvinist.

Though he won the support of the JHU, he made no commitments except with regard to the Tigers, but nevertheless he was presented as supportive of some of their more extreme policies such as a bill to restrict conversions. Similarly, in his agreement with the JVP, his opposition to the peace process was stressed, though his commitment was to negotiate, but without the secrecy and preconditions that had vitiated the attempts of Wickremesinghe and Kumaratunga.

More serious was a clause in his agreement with the JVP that stressed opposition to the 'so-called' liberal open economy. However, he was able immediately to get the General Secretary of the JVP to clarify the position, and say that the alliance favoured a mixed economy, with a greater commitment to local production. A libertarian economic system, as in operation under Wickremesinghe, with its massive cuts in services such as education, was opposed.

The main architect of Rajapakse's manifesto was Nivard Cabraal, who had been a member of the UNP before being sidelined by Wickremesinghe. Cabraal had, unlike his peers in the UNP, written books to illustrate a private sector dominated approach to economic development that yet stressed pro-active social welfare measures; but that type of thinking was not to the taste of the UNP leadership which preferred an approach dependent on personal loyalties. Rajapakse however snapped up Cabraal, who was able to discuss matters in detail with the JVP and the JHU, and the older Marxist parties, and produce a manifesto that was more modern in its outlook than previous SLFP efforts. As he put it, in dealing with the claim that Rajapakse would not be able to take the country forward if allied with Marxists, it was better to discuss matters with them and reach a compromise than embark on a confrontation that would create further problems.

Rajapakse was being markedly moderate despite his need to ensure JVP and JHU support, but Kumaratunga saw him as betraying some of the principles she had espoused. She spent much of her time abroad during this period, and did not make any public pronouncements that might have damaged his prospects. Anura Bandaranaike however had no such qualms and, though formally he supported Rajapakse, some of his pronouncements seemed designed to undermine him. Meanwhile the UNP press had a field day suggesting that Wickremesinghe, when he won, would set up a national government that included the Bandaranaikes. Wickremesinghe himself made much of Kumaratunga's achievements and his desire to use her in an advisory capacity were he elected.

Meanwhile his more fervent supporters tried to insinuate that a Rajapakse victory would lead to mayhem. What were characterized as Rajapakse's Marxist and chauvinist leanings were targeted, in particular by a wealthy businessman who was also a born again Christian. Just before the election he took out several full page advertisements, one showing a picture of a naked youth being killed on the street, which he suggested was a scene that would be repeated if Rajapakse and his allies came to power. In fact the picture had been taken during the July 1983 riots, by a photographer from the Communist Party newspaper. The paper had accurately reported the government involvement in the riots but was banned when the Jayewardene regime sought to blame the Marxists for what had happened.

Another advertisement included a pastoral letter from the Catholic archbishop that was designed to encourage the faithful to vote for Wickremesinghe. Since the businessman's message was 'Christians Awake', it raised the spectre of polarization on religious grounds. This was not the intention of the Archbishop, but seemed to be the agenda of some of his priests who sought to portray Rajapakse as a Sinhala Buddhist chauvinist. The tactic did not work, and Rajapakse did relatively well in Catholic areas which had in 2001, though not in 2004, voted fairly solidly for the UNP.

Wickremesinghe meanwhile had not doubted that he had the Tamil vote secure. Towards the end of the campaign, it became clear to the UNP, despite the conviction amongst its urban supporters that he was bound to win, that he had lost much of the Sinhala vote. Moragoda declared that the UNP regime had been able to enclose the Tigers in a security net that would prevent them from achieving their aim of a separate state. This did nothing to encourage Sinhala voters who, though Wickremesinghe's manifesto also included a shamelessly populist commitment to build the largest dagaba in the world, ended up voting for Rajapakse. But it did nothing to hold the Tigers either.

It is possible that they had already made up their minds, but Moragoda's pronouncement was also used as a reason for the directive they finally gave Tamil voters in the area under their control, that they should not vote. Their control over voters was limited, since in 1999 for instance, when they had tried to kill Kumaratunga, Jaffna had given her a majority over Wickremesinghe. They may also have thought that, given the overwhelming southern support for Rajapakse, the numbers they controlled might not have been enough to make a difference – and, even if they did manage to push Wickremesinghe over the top, he would have difficulty governing when the majority of the areas he ruled had voted against him.

The Tigers may also have believed the propaganda coming out of Colombo, that Rajapakse would be pushed into war by his allies. The LTTE would be able to present him as a racist and win back the international support that had eroded over the previous decade, with the end of the racist regime established by Jayawardene.

Whatever the reason for what amounted to an LTTE boycott of the election, when the results were announced Rajapakse had won with a majority of 180, 000 votes over the required 50%. With Wickremesinghe having obtained a majority over him of 150,000 in the Nuwara Eliya

District alone, due to Thondaman's solid support, it was clear that in the rest of the country Rajapakse had a more than solid majority.

Though the UNP claimed that the LTTE had stolen the election from them, given their previous reliance on winning the election through the LTTE, their contention did not win them much sympathy. Ironically, the situation was similar to what had happened in 1988 when, because of a JVP boycott that the government had taken advantage of, polling was lowest where Mrs Bandaranaike's support was strongest, and Premadasa had won by an even narrower majority. Wickremesinghe, characteristically, failed to turn up to the declaration of results but a period of uncertainty had ended, and the country now had a President with the authority to govern.

Chapter 24

The New Regime

Trying to conciliate

From the start Rajapakse seemed to want to be conciliatory. In his speech of acceptance, he made mention of not only Mr. and Mrs. Bandaranaike, but also of Kumaratunga, in terms of their contribution to the party he represented. Kumaratunga however was not in a conciliatory mood, and Rajapakse's refusal to appoint Anura Bandaranaike as Prime Minister added to her exasperation.

Given Bandaranaike's performance during the election campaign, Rajapakse could scarcely have been expected to make him Prime Minister. He would have had an easier time had Kadirgamar been alive, for appointing him Prime Minister would have met with universal approbation. It was also a pity that there was no other representative of the minorities who seemed senior and popular enough to have been made Prime Minister, since that would have affirmed the pluralistic outlook Rajapakse was anxious, and indeed needed to, present.

As it was, he avoided a tough choice within his party, and at the same time ensured that Bandaranaike did not feel superseded by someone less senior. He decided to recall Ratnasiri Wickramanayake to serve as Prime Minister. He indicated however that he was willing to keep Bandaranaike in the Cabinet. The latter, who had been appointed Foreign Minister on Kadirgamar's death, would have liked to have kept that position, but in the delicate position in which Rajapakse was internationally, he could not afford such indulgence. He appointed Bandaranaike as Minister of Tourism, and finally selected Samaraweera to be Foreign Minister, in addition to his already heavy responsibilities of Shipping and Aviation.

The New Regime

It proved a fortunate choice, for Samaraweera immediately moved to convince both the Indians and the Americans that the new government was committed to pluralism and the prevailing economic policies. This was vital since the Tigers began to attack servicemen in an obvious attempt to provoke hardline reactions from the government. Combined with the impression promoted internationally, by the Tigers as well as international correspondents who had relied on UNP conversational networks in Colombo, it would have taken very little to establish the government as racist and militaristic.

Rajapakse appointed as Secretary of Defence his brother, who had served in the army as a regular officer. This helped maintain the confidence of the services. However there was a very clear directive that retaliatory measures were not in order and, though these could not be avoided entirely, by and large the services maintained discipline. The government's approach satisfied the international community and, with pressure on the Tigers not to breach the ceasefire quite so obviously, the crisis passed. Indeed the new government was able to ensure that the Tigers were obliged to resume negotiations, which they had broken off in 2003, when Wickremesinghe was still in office.

Rajapakse stuck to his view that Norway was not a suitable venue for negotiations, but gave up his insistence that the talks should take place at an Asian venue, and agreed on Geneva. The Tigers, who had been adamant on Oslo, also compromised, and the two sides finally met in February 2006. Unlike both his predecessors in power, Rajapakse kept the nation informed of progress, and engaged in a consultative process that served to mollify the JVP and JHU, who had hoped that the Norwegians would be removed as monitors and mediators.

This would have been impossible, given the solidarity of the Europeans, though some of them realized that the Norwegians had been compromised, either of their own volition or through excessive adherence to Wickremesinghe's agenda. The only real concession Rajapakse received was that the Norwegian head of the Monitoring Mission was replaced by a Swede. In addition, the chief Norwegian envoy, Erik Solheim, who was a bugbear to some of Rajapakse's colleagues, withdrew from direct involvement, following his elevation to ministerial office after the Norwegian elections. It was clear, though, that his replacement would follow his advice.

Nothing much was achieved at the talks, though the Tigers claimed that the government had agreed to disarm the Karuna group. The government had in fact committed itself to abiding by the Ceasefire Agreement, whereby paramilitaries were to be disarmed. That had been in reference to the other militant groups which, having previously received patronage from the Kumaratunga government, became easy victims for the Tigers under the Wickremesinghe regime.

It was a moot point whether that section of the Ceasefire Agreement applied to the Karuna group which had been part of the Tiger force, and was still in the field. It was unlikely that they would allow themselves to be disarmed by government forces, even had the latter been willing to risk the attempt. This they had no intention of doing.

For the rest, Rajapakse showed himself more decisive than both his predecessors in developing the infrastructure the country needed. Aided by the fact that he owed nothing to Thondaman's CWC, which had been in the forefront of the protests against the Upper Kotmale Hydroelectric Project, nor to the Catholic Church, which had led opposition to the Norochcholai Coal Power Plant, he signed agreements to proceed with these. Given the uncertainties caused by the initial Tiger offensives however, as well as continuing criticism by the UNP oriented media, tourism was slow to pick up and investor confidence still remained low.

Difficulties in the UNP

Though Wickremesinghe continued to try to rouse international feeling against him. Rajapakse had some relief in that several senior members of the UNP finally decided to try to remove him from the leadership. Despite his umpteenth defeat, and the failure of his strategy of relying entirely on the Tigers to put him in power, Wickremesinghe refused to resign. Given the UNP constitution, it was almost impossible to remove an incumbent leader though had Jayasuriya proved determined this might have been achieved after the election. Almost all public figures in the UNP wanted

Wickremesinghe to go and it was only the outsiders and novices he had cultivated who defended him. But with Jayasuriya proving diffident Wickremesinghe was able to survive.

He was also helped when Rajapakse pardoned SB Dissanayake, who had been jailed in 2004 for contempt of court. When he was released, there were suggestions that, given his speaking skills, he should take over the UNP. This happened at a particularly embarrassing time for the party; when nominations were received for the local government elections scheduled for March the UNP list for Colombo was rejected.

This had happened because of internal rivalries, springing from an initial decision once again to field as the UNP Mayoral candidate Sirisena Cooray, Premadasa's chief lieutenant. He had long before been Mayor of Colombo, before going into national politics and becoming General Secretary of the UNP, from which position Wijetunge had removed him. Even though his criticism of Wijetunge had been in Wickremesinghe's interest, Wickremesinghe had avoided him until now. With UNP fortunes at a low however, he had been forced to yield to pressure and accept him to lead the list for Colombo.

The list had been tampered with by one or two leaders close to Wickremesinghe, including Moragoda; this raised questions about Wickremesinghe's bona fides. The damage was probably due to personal reasons; anxiety to omit a particular politician led to his name being tippexed and replaced by that of an under-age boy. Still, this provided further evidence of a party without a sense of direction.

In this context Dissanayake's emergence proved helpful for Wickremesinghe since it prompted some of the senior members who had earlier been critical to rally behind him. Dissanayake decided to take himself out of the country during the election campaign. When the results were announced – Colombo and some other areas where there had been disputes about nominations were being canvassed before the courts and were to poll later – it turned out that the PA had won thumping victories in most areas.

The CWC, possibly under pressure from the Indian government, which was better able to work with citizens of Indian origin when their political representatives were not in active opposition, had joined the PA for the local election. It was understood that Thondaman was working towards crossing over to the government. Hakeem, unused to being out of office for so long, was also believed to be seeking an arrangement, though Rajapakse, secure of the support of Mrs Ashraff and her breakaway group of the Muslim Congress, was in no hurry to strike a deal.

Apart from the UNP, the main losers of the local elections were the JVP and the JHU. Though Rajapakse had been willing to contest the election along with the JVP, they had asked for control of more local bodies than he had wanted to concede; so the two parties decided to part amicably and contest separately. The JVP was also hoping to test its strength but the decision proved unwise, as it ended up only retaining the one local body it had won previously; the PA on its own was able to win several bodies, with just a few in the Colombo district going to the UNP because of the split vote. The JVP percentage of the vote was very respectable but their failure to live up to the expectations raised by the large number of members of Parliament they had secured through their alliance with Kumaratunga made the PA performance seem more successful.

The JHU won hardly anything, as had been expected. This confirmed that Rajapakse, in accepting them into his alliance for the Presidential election, had in no way given them any control over his actions. Though he continued to be conciliatory, it was obvious, after the local election, that he was in full charge. This also helped his quest to take over the leadership of the SLFP, which had remained with Kumaratunga despite her giving up public office. He was confident enough not to insist at party sessions while Kumaratunga was abroad in April, and accepted only the position of Acting Chairman, with the understanding that a final decision could be made after her return to the country in May.

Continuing tensions

The latter part of April saw another spurt of Tiger killings of servicemen, designed it seemed to provoke a reaction that would give them an excuse to miss the next session of talks. Despite Tiger websites claiming prematurely that there had been massacres of Tamil civilians by raging

Sinhalese, the only reaction that might have got out of hand was promptly quelled by the military. In this respect, while the Tigers were anxious for a repetition of the killings of July 1983, the prompt response of authorities made clear that those incidents had occurred because of government instigation.

Meanwhile the younger Rajapakse, while also strengthening the armed forces, voiced his suspicions of the Norwegians. Though this was resented by the outgoing head of the Monitoring Mission, his successor, the Swede, was less diffident about critically registering Tiger violations of the ceasefire. The government was also strengthened when the new Canadian government finally proscribed the Tigers, and raided some of their offices in what seemed a commitment to clamp down on illegal funding.

With pressures on them mounting, the Tigers, having refused to go to Geneva for the second round of talks, exploded a bomb in the heart of Army Headquarters. The target was the Army Commander, who was narrowly saved when his outrider kicked aside a pregnant woman he realized was a suicide bomber about to throw herself on the Commander's vehicle. The outrider and several others died in the explosion, and the Commander was lucky to escape. A couple of months later the Tigers did succeed in killing the Deputy Chief of Staff, the army third in command, who was considered one of the more competent generals still in service – a motorcyclist rammed into his car and blew it up.

Apart from international pressure the Tigers were feeling the continuing impact of attacks by Karuna's forces, which they were convinced were supported by the army. In what seemed to them a war of attrition that was likely to wear them down, with fewer areas in which they could forcibly conscript new recruits, their best hope seemed to be to provoke backlashes that would renew their claims on international sympathy.

Hence, perhaps, an attempt to attack a ship carrying servicemen home for the New Year festival. Some quick action by a naval vessel which sacrificed itself allowed the ship to get away to Indian territorial waters which the Tigers dared not venture into. The Tigers had demonstrated the naval power they had developed recently. It was noteworthy that the attack took place while Scandinavian truce monitors were on the transport ship. This led, for what seemed to the Sri Lankan forces the first time, to a categorical condemnation by the SLMM of the Tiger action. According to the Ceasefire Agreement the Tigers were not supposed to deploy a navy, but the Tiger response was an assertion that such restrictions on their sovereignty were no longer acceptable.

Such defiance made it easier for the European Parliament to condemn the Tigers, which led in turn to them being banned by the European Union. The Americans had pressed for this and, though the Norwegians tried to avert it, by now even the other Scandinavians were less committed to the Tigers. The Tigers demanded that the Sri Lankan Monitoring Mission should no longer include Scandinavians belonging to countries that were members of the EU.

This was their main thrust when they went to Oslo after the Norwegians had finally persuaded them to attend a second round of talks with the Rajapakse government. Even more dramatically, on the morning of the talks they refused to appear, one reason being that the government had not sent any Ministers. Since they saw themselves as equal partners in discussions, they argued that Thamilselvam could not be expected to negotiate with merely the head of the Sri Lankan Peace Secretariat.

Though the international community was beginning to understand that the Tigers were not innocent victims of a racist government, the Tigers continued to believe that with sufficient provocation they would create the backlash they urgently required. In June then they blew up a bus and killed over 60 civilians, including several children. At the same time they organized demonstrations all over Europe to protest against what they claimed was genocide by the Sri Lankan state, with particular reference to the activities of the Karuna faction. Wickremesinghe, commenting on the killings while on a tour of America, could only criticize the government for not taking action to disarm Karuna. This statement was promptly highlighted in Tiger websites.

In July, perhaps because of the constant pressure they were suffering in the East from both Karuna and the army, the Tigers decided to put on a display of strength that would restore the prestige they seemed to be

The New Regime

losing. They stopped the supply of water from an irrigation project in an area they controlled, the victims being Sinhala and Muslim farmers in areas controlled by the government. Their argument was that this simply paralleled the sufferings because of government action of the civilians in the areas they controlled, but it was clearly a grave violation of the CFA.

The monitors accepted this but seemed disinclined to ensure that the Tigers reversed their decision. In such a context the armed forces launched an attack to take over the affected area, and proved successful there, as well as in repulsing Tiger offensives elsewhere, in the North as well as in the Muslim area of Mutur close to Trincomalee.

Cohabitation and the disintegration of the UNP

Though, typically, these successes were followed soon after by an army offensive in the North that failed badly, in general the armed forces seemed to have established their ability to resist any Tiger offensives, and also to continue to make incremental gains, at least in the East.

In such a context, Wickremesinghe seemed out on a limb, and Rajapakse was able to establish lines of communication with what was termed a reformist group within the UNP. His hand was strengthened by the fact that, though the independent list Cooray had supported had handsomely won the Colombo Municipal Council elections, continuing infighting within the UNP about how to control this had prompted the Mayor whom Cooray had selected, and most of his adherents, to join the SLFP.

Rajapakse was able then to invite the UNP as a body to support his government, and with the international community promoting this (in part to reduce the influence of the JVP, as also to promote a negotiated solution to the ethnic problem), Wickremesinghe felt obliged to accept. A Memorandum of Understanding was signed, according to which the two parties were to work together on issues of national interest. Wickremesinghe however was firm about refusing to enter a National Government, though some of the reformists urged this. Conversely some of his personal adherents in the party, including the youthful Tissa Attanayake whom he was promoting to be Secretary General of the Party, were suggesting, in private as well as in public, that the MOU was intended mainly to divide Rajapakse from the JVP, and thus precipitate an election which the UNP could win.

Unfortunately for Wickremesinghe, both he and his more devoted supporters thought that his position had been strengthened sufficiently by the MOU to allow him to reduce the influence of the reformers in the party. Soon after the Presidential Election, when Wickremesinghe was seen as a total liability, it had been indicated that Jayasuriya would be given either the leadership of the party, or the leadership of the opposition, or at least the position of Chairman of the Party, which he had once held, but which he had handed over to Charitha Ratwatte at an earlier period when Wickremesinghe's leadership was being challenged.

None of these changes had been made in the year that followed. Ratwatte had previously been replaced as Chairman by yet another old school friend of Wickremesinghe, who recognized that almost no one of consequence in the party thought him suitable. Instead of appointing Jayasuriya however, Wickremesinghe thought of resurrecting Rukman Senanayake, Dudley Senanayake's nephew, who had been driven away from the UNP under Jayewardene but had rejoined under Premadasa. Jayasuriya, who was almost painfully diffident about putting himself forward, acquiesced in this.

When then the Reformists also agreed to Attanayake's appointment as General Secretary, the Wickremesinghe faction thought that their domination of the party was complete, and they could ignore the other part of the agreement, namely swift reform of Party structures. The Constitution Wickremesinghe had introduced after he took over in 1994 had virtually enthroned him as Leader for life, while allowing him to nominate at will the entire Working Committee.

Instead of prioritizing the suggested Reforms at the forthcoming Party Convention, it was instead given out that Jayasuriya would not be reappointed Deputy Leader. It was argued that there was no such position in the Constitution, and the fact that Wickremesinghe had created this when he wanted Jayasuriya to give up the Chairmanship, and had kept him in that position for more than half a decade, was conveniently forgotten.

Perhaps Jayasuriya was expected to beg for the position, or seek it actively at the Convention in a show of strength, which he was bound to lose given the composition of the Working Committee. Instead, he simply did not appear, and finally gave ear to those who had long urged that Wickremesinghe was determined to keep him at bay. He therefore led a group that negotiated entry into Rajapakse's government.

When Wickremesinghe finally realized that his intransigence had provoked a corresponding response, he tried desperately to reach a compromise with Jayasuriya, or with Rajapakse, by reviving the idea of a National Government which he himself would join. Rajapakse however had by now had enough, and in his response to Rukman Senanayake, who had typically been sent as Wickremesinghe's emissary, he highlighted Wickremesinghe's untrustworthiness, and in particular his undermining of the Sri Lankan government to the international community.

On 28 January 2007 therefore 18 members of the UNP joined Rajapakse, with ten of them being inducted into the Cabinet. Apart from Jayasuriya, they included G L Pieris and Milinda Moragoda who had been Wickremesinghe's negotiators with the Tigers, and M H Mohammed and P Dayaratne who had been Cabinet Ministers in Jayawardene's time. Gamini Dissanayake's son Navin also went over, as did the SLMC, with Rauff Hakeem once more joining the cabinet.

Rajapakse however was careful not to alienate his erstwhile allies, the JVP and the JHU, and invited them too to join his government. Though the former were extremely critical, and seemed ready to move into aggressive opposition, the latter also agreed to enter the government formally and accept a portfolio, for which one of the monks resigned to make way for the layman who had represented the Sihala Urumaya in Parliament in 2001.

Dealing with terror

Meanwhile the government had achieved an important military success in the Eastern Province, when the armed forces retook the Vakarai area, which had been a Tiger stronghold for many years. Though this did not mean total government control of the East, since some areas especially difficult of access continued in Tiger hands, it certainly made crystal clear the hollowness of the Tiger demand, on the grounds that they were the sole representatives of the people therein, for absolute control of a conjoined NorthEast Province.

A few months earlier, following a JVP application to the Supreme Court, the merger effected by Jayewardene had been ruled unconstitutional. Though the JVP and JHU criticized Rajapakse for not acting at once, he sensibly took his time so as to make clear that he was weighing his options rather than responding to chauvinist demands. It was only at the beginning of 2007 that the Provinces, joined up so cynically by Jayewardene two decades earlier, were formally separated.

Just before that high drama had arisen when the committee of experts he had appointed to recommend constitutional changes to solve the prevailing ethnic problem handed in not one but four reports. The majority report recommended the type of devolution that was desirable in a context in which provinces at the periphery had been neglected by the central government, but it also proposed institutional changes that seemed potentially divisive. This had prompted a minority report that seemed in comparison to offer nothing positive to the minorities.

Careful reading of the two reports suggested that much could have been agreed on, but the manner in which the committee had been set up, with no clear terms of reference, seemed to have precluded active progress towards consensus. Despair about this had doubtless prompted two independent reports from the two senior Civil Servants on the committee, but in the furore that arose there was no concerted attempt at synthesis.

Instead, when the Chairman of the Parliamentary Committee, to which the experts had submitted their report, issued his own recommendations, they roused more criticism.

In such a context, the determination Rajapakse had shown from the start, to steer a moderate course while not alienating the extremists who had supported him, seemed even more difficult to pursue. However the accession to his government of so many relatively moderate members of the UNP was likely to help him work out a generally acceptable solution, while the inclusion of the JHU would serve to mediate other points of view.

At the same time he had to be careful since it seemed that some elements in the SLFP were unhappy about these developments. Attention was focused in this regard on Mangala Samaraweera, who lost the Foreign Ministry in the reshuffle, though maintaining the Ports and Aviation portfolios which it was claimed he had in fact preferred. Unfortunately, though Rajapakse and Samaraweera may well have been able to work together satisfactorily, given indeed the sterling support the latter had provided during the Presidential election, those associated with either were not likely to promote consensus.

In particular Samaraweera suffered from the fact that Kumaratunga, with whom he had continued to maintain good relations, seemed inclined to prefer Wickremesinghe to Rajapakse, and business associates of his had also shown similar predilections. When a newspaper with which Samaraweera had been linked began to attack the President, it provided ample ammunition for those who wished to provoke conflict. Simultaneously it was alleged that Samaraweera maintained close links with the JVP, which was ironic given the hostility of the latter to Kumaratunga and indeed to the UNP.

The vagaries of Sri Lankan politics however preclude no combination of forces. Meanwhile Rajapakse also had to be careful that the recent successes in the East, and his inclusion of so many diverse interests in his cabinet, did not blind him to the need for bold measures of reform. His Prime Minister, Ratnasiri Wickramanayake, was quoted as having claimed in Delhi, at the Mahatma Gandhi Commemoration a couple of days after the new Sri Lankan Cabinet was sworn in, that Sri Lanka faced a terrorist problem, rathern than an ethnic one.

This may have been true, but it is essential that the Sri Lankan government notes and responds to not only the terrorism of the Tigers, but also the state terrorism of the Jayewardene government that precipitated such a forceful reaction. Recent developments in the East may suggest that most Sri Lankans, of whatever ethnic background, do not want Tiger authoritarianism, but equally they would not want a return to the centralized patronage cum neglect of the past. Constitutional and administrative reforms based on principles that put people first, rather than the temporary repositories of government power, are essential if all Sri Lankans are to enjoy opportunities for development, free of the assaults as well as the attractions of terrorism.

Select Bibliography

Section I – The background to separatism and violence

Balasuriya, Stanislaus Tissa, (ed), *Race Relations in Sri Lanka*, Colombo 1978.

Bush, Kenneth D, *The Intra-Group Dimensions of Ethnic Conflict in Sri Lanka – Learning to Read between the Lines*, Palgrave, Macmillan 2003.

Committee for Rational Development (ed.) *Sri Lanka: The Ethnic Conflict, Myths, Realities, Perspectives*, New Delhi 1984.

David, Kumar and Santasilan Kadirgamar, *Ethnicity: Identity, Conflict and Crisis,* Hong Kong 1989.

De Silva, K M (ed), *Managing Ethnic tensions in multiethnic societies: Sri Lanka 1880–1985,* London 1986.

Little, David, *Sri Lanka: The Invention of Enmity*, United States Institute of Peace Press, 1994.

Nayak, Subash Chandra, *Ethnicity and Nation Building in Sri Lanka*, New Delhi 2001.

Rajanayagam, Ishwari and Siridasa Banda, *Hope beyond the Terror: Ethnic Supremacism and Class Conflict in Sri Lanka*, Bangalore 1996.

Russel, Jane, *Communal Politics under the Donoughmore Constitution 1931–1947*, Colombo 1982.

Vittachi, Tarzie, *Emergency '58: The Story of the Ceylon Race Riots,* London 1958.

Wijesinha, Rajiva, *Richard de Zoysa: his life, some work...and a death*, Colombo, 2000.

Wilson, A J, *Politics in Sri Lanka 1947–1979* (2nd Edition), London 1979.

Section 2 - The Jayewardene Years

Alles, A G, *The JVP 1969-1989*, Colombo 1990.

de Silva, K M & Howard Wriggins, *JR Jayawardene of Sri Lanka: A Political Biography*, London 1988.

Gunaratne, Rohan, *Sri Lanka: A Lost Revolution*, Kandy 1990.

—— *War and Peace in Sri Lanka*, Colombo 1989.

Hoole, Rajan Daya Somasunderam, K. Sritharan and Rajani Thiranagama, *The Broken Palmyrah: The Tamil Crisis in Sri Lanka, An Inside Account*, Claremont (USA) 1989.

Hyndman, Patricia, *Sri Lanka: Serendipity under Siege*, Nottingham 1988.

Manogaran, C, *Ethnic Conflict and Reconciliation in Sri Lanka*, Honolulu 1987.

Manor, James (ed.), *Sri Lanka in Change and Crisis*, London 1984.

—— *The Expedient Utopian: Bandaranaike and Ceylon*, Cambridge 1989.

O' Balance, Edgar, *The Cyanide War: Tamil Insurrection in Sri Lanka, 1973-88*, London 1989.

Ponnambalam, Satchi, *Sri Lanka: The National Question and the Tamil Liberation Struggle*, London 1983.

Nissan, E. and R. L. Stirrat, *State, Nation and the Representation of Evil: the Case of Sri Lanka*, Brighton 1987.

Parliamentary General Election of Sri Lanka 15th February 1988, Report of International Observer Group, Colombo 1989.

Piyadasa, L, *The Holocaust and After*, London 1984.

Ratnatunge, Sinha, *Politics of Terrorism: The Sri Lanka Experience*, Melbourne 1988.

Sivanayagam, S, *Sri Lanka: 10 years of Jayawardene's Rule*, Madras 1987.

'Sri Lanka: Racism and the Anthoritarian State', *Race and Class*, Vol. 26, No. 1, London (Summer) 1984.

Thambyah, S J, *Sri Lanka Ethnic Fratricide and the dismantling of Democracy*, London 1986.

The Tamil National Question and the Indo-Sri Lankan Accord (papers presented at first International Tamil Conference, London 1988) Konark Publishers 1989.

Select Bibliography

Vaidik, V P, *Ethnic Crisis in Sri Lanka: India's Options*, New Delhi 1986.

Wijesinha, Rajiva *The Current Crisis in Sri Lanka,* New Delhi, 1986, expanded as *Sri Lanka in Crisis, 1977-88: J R Jayewardene and the Erosion of Democracy*, Colombo 1991.

Wilson, A J, *The Gaullist System in Asia: The Constitution of Sri Lanka*, London 1980.

—— *The Break up of Sri Lanka: the Sinhalese Tamil Conflict*, London 1988.

Warnapala, W. A. Wiswa and L. Dias Hewagama, *Recent Politics in Sri Lanka: the Presidential election and the Referendum of 1982: A Study of Electoral Practice and Behaviour in an Asian Democracy*, New Delhi 1983.

Section 3 – Developments after 1988 and the peace process

de Silva, K M and G H Pieris (ed), *Pursuit of Peace in Sri Lanka: Past Failure and Future Prospects*, Colombo 2000

Hoole, Rajan, *Sri Lanka: The Arrogance of Power – Myths, Decadence and Murder*, Colombo 2001

LTTE in the Eyes of the World, Ministry of Foreign Affairs, Colombo 1997

Moonesinghe, Major General Sarath, *A Soldier's Version: An Account of the on-going Conflict and the Origin of Terrorism in Sri Lanka,* Colombo 2000

Mukherji, Apratir, *The War in Sri Lanka – Unending Conflict*, New Delhi 2000

—— *Sri Lanka: A Dangerous Interlude*, Colombo 2005

Narayan Swamy, M R, *Tigers of Sri Lanka: From Boys to Guerillas*, Konark Ltd., New Delhi, 1994.

Orjuela, Camilla, *Civil Society in Civil War: Peace Work and Identity Politics in Sri Lanka*, Gotebord 2004.

Pratap, Anita, *Island of Blood: Frontline Reports from Sri Lanka, Afghanistan and other South Asian Flashpoints*, New Delho 2001 (Colombo 2002).

Raman B, N Sathiya Moorthy and Kalpana Chittaranga (Edited), *Sri Lanka: Peace Without Process*, Colombo 2006 (The introductory Overview by Professor S D Muni provides a perceptive summation of events between 2001 and 2004).

Rupasinghe, Kumar (Ed), *Neogiating Peace in Sri Lanka: Efforts, Failures and Lessons*,Colombo 1998

Sivanayagam, S, *Sri Lanka: Witness to History (A Journalist's Memoirs 1930–2004)*, London 2005.

Wijesinha, Rajiva, *Civil Strife in Sri Lanka: the United National Party Government, 1989–1994*, Colombo 1995.

Index

Abeygunasekera, Ossie 215, 225
Amaratunga, Chanaka 215, 223
Amirthalingam, Appapillai 34, 58, 59, 166, 239, 286
Amparai (*see* Digamadulla) 54, 105
Anandasagaree 285, 286, 291
Ashraff, M H M 165, 201, 215, 244
Athukorale, Gamini 227, 228, 245, 246
Athulathmudali, Lalith 90, 91, 92, 106, 110, 119, 121, 140, 155, 162, 163, 176, 183, 184, 185, 187, 188, 191, 197, 202, 211, 216
Attanayake, Tissa 308
Balasingham, Anton 267, 268
Bandaranaike, Anura 34, 43, 63, 71, 89, 153, 246, 281
Bandaranaike, Chandrika (*see* Kumaratunga, Chandrika Bandaranaike) 62, 63, 64, 205, 206, 211, 212, 233, 234, 236, 237, 239, 240, 241, 242, 244, 250, 252, 260

Bandaranaike, S W R D 18, 19, 20, 21, 22, 28
Bandaranaike, Sirimavo 23, 24, 25, 27, 32, 33, 34, 49, 50, 51, 58, 62, 66, 68, 84, 89, 100, 101, 102, 113, 128, 129, 132, 141, 142, 146, 148, 149, 151, 152, 177, 179, 182, 188, 189, 216, 217, 221, 222, 228, 244, 258, 268, 294
Catholics 258
Ceasefire Agreement 279
Ceylon National Congress 11, 12
Ceylon Workers Congress (CWC) 25, 31, 34, 74, 101, 204, 215, 223, 248, 258, 282
Chandrasekaran, P 216
Chelvanayakam, S J V 20, 30, 44
Choksy, K N 199, 240, 258
Communist Party (CP) 26, 89
Cooray, Sirisena 191, 193, 197, 202, 203, 209, 210
Council for Liberal Democracy (CLD – *see* Liberal Party))

Counterpoint 199, 200, 216, 246
De Mel, Ronnie 70
Democratic People's Alliance (DPA) 141, 149, 150, 153, 222
Democratic United National Front (DUNF) 187, 190, 197, 198, 202, 205, 208, 217, 225, 278
Democratic Workers Congress (DWC) 141, 153
Deshapremi Jathika Vyaparaya (DJV) 121, 131, 133, 134, 137
Devananda, Douglas 236, 239, 245
De Zoysa, Richard 160, 163, 176, 177, 182, 190, 199
Digamadulla 106, 144, 150
Dimbulagala 55
Dissanayake, Gamini 37, 46, 54, 89, 107, 138, 140, 155, 163, 176, 177, 187, 188, 197, 198, 206, 210, 213, 214, 218, 219, 220, 221, 222, 223, 224, 225, 226, 227, 228, 229, 236, 239, 245, 256
Dissanayake, S B 215
District Development Councils 26, 45, 51, 52, 53, 240
Dixit, J N 107, 124, 137, 138
Eastern Province 120, 138
Eelam People's Democratic Party (EPDP) 216, 236, 245, 248, 265, 285

Eelam People's Revolutionary Liberation Front (EPRLF) 103, 109, 137, 143, 154, 165, 167, 170
Eelam Revolutionary Organisation of Students (EROS) 104, 154
Eksath Lanka Jathika Pakshaya (ELJP) 120, 141, 147
Federal Party (FP) 13, 19, 20, 24, 26
Fernando, Neville 58, 59, 70
Gandhi, Indira 52, 86, 95
Gandhi, Rajiv 95, 97, 99, 100, 104, 108, 113, 115, 160, 225
Gandhiyam Movement 55, 83
Goonewardene, Dinesh 141
Gunasinghe, Ronnie 163, 191, 192
Hakeem, Rauff 245
Hameed, A C S 81, 168, 169, 172, 177, 245
Indian Peace-Keeping Force (IPKF) 120, 125, 126, 143, 160, 167
Indian Tamils 9, 10, 12, 14, 42, 83, 142
Indo-Lankan Accord 114, 119, 121, 123, 133, 169, 174, 223
Interim Self-Governing Authority (ISGA) 271, 290
Jaffna 9, 12, 13, 28, 30, 45, 46, 52, 55, 56, 58, 77, 80, 82, 92,

Index

93, 106, 107, 108, 109, 112, 125, 127, 128, 152, 166, 168, 170, 236, 238, 242

Jaffna Public Library 46, 240, 270

Janasaviya Programme 222

Janata Vimukthi Peramuna (JVP) 27, 33, 51, 64, 69, 72, 80, 85, 88, 102, 121, 129, 130, 131, 132, 135, 138, 139, 141, 144, 145, 146, 147, 148, 152, 154, 160, 161, 162, 167, 176, 190, 216, 247, 278, 279, 281, 282, 287, 288, 290, 291, 307, 310

Jathika Hela Urumaya (JHU) 280, 281, 282, 293, 294, 295, 310

Jayasuriya, Karu 245, 246, 249, 282

Jayewardene, Harry W 129

Jayewardene, Junius Richard 19, 21, 22, 32, 33, 37, 38, 39, 43, 44, 48, 49, 59, 60, 61, 62, 63, 64, 65, 66, 69, 70, 74, 79, 81, 84, 85, 86, 87, 89, 90, 97, 101, 102, 105, 106, 107, 111, 112, 113, 114, 115, 120, 123, 124, 125, 128, 135, 136, 137, 139, 140, 144, 145, 146, 155, 166, 177, 178, 181, 182, 190, 194, 199, 202, 225, 229, 235, 239, 242, 243, 257, 260, 262, 263, 278

Kadirgamar, Lakshman 217, 234, 235, 281, 282, 288, 293, 295

Karuna (Vinyagamoorthi Muralitharan) 284, 285

Kobbekaduwa, Hector 63, 64, 152, 173, 174, 175, 190

Kotelawala, Sir John 19, 20, 21, 22

Kumara(na)tunga, Chandrika Bandaranaike 62, 63, 102, 131, 146, 189, 203, 204, 209, 211, 213, 214, 216, 217, 220, 221, 222, 223, 225, 227, 228, 229, 233, 234, 235, 236, 237, 239, 241, 242, 243, 246, 247, 249, 258, 262, 267, 271, 272, 273, 277, 278, 279, 281, 282, 287, 288, 290, 291, 292

Kumara(na)tunga, Vijaya 71, 131

Kuttimani 83

Lanka Sama Samaja Pakshaya (LSSP) 26, 31, 83

Liberal Party (LP) 132, 133

Liberation Tigers of Tamil Eelam (LTTE) *see* Tigers

Lokubandara, V J M 282

Mahajana Eksath Peramuna (MEP) 26, 129, 152

Maharaja Organisation 191, 212

Marapana, Tilak 273

Mathew, Cyril 46, 52, 53, **58**, 60, 87, 90, 97, 106, 129, **152**, 207

Moragoda, Milinda 272
North-East Merger 169
Norway 246, 264, 291, 301
Panditharatne, N G P 55, 89, 130, 257
Parthasarathy, G 86, 95
Paskaralingam, T 191
People's Alliance (PA) 189, 198, 203, 208, 215, 221, 246
People's Liberation Organization of Tamil Eelam (PLOTE) 265
Pieris, G L 212, 221, 234, 243, 248, 263, 271, 272
Ponnambalam, G G (Snr) 11
Post-Tsunami Operational Management Structure (P-TOMS) 290, 291, 293, 294
Prabhakaran, Velupillai 31, 105, 113, 124, 168, 225, 241, 252, 269
Premadasa, Ranasinghe 38, 39, 48, 89, 90, 113, 121, 129, 136, 139, 140, 146, 147, 148, 149, 150, 151, 155, 160, 163, 164, 165, 167, 168, 170, 173, 175, 176, 178, 179, 180, 181, 182, 184, 185, 187, 188, 192, 193, 197, 199, 202, 208, 209, 211, 213, 225, 233, 238, 242, 285
Provincial Councils 26, 99, 104, 111, 112, 123, 128, 129, 131, 132, 135, 138, 142, 145, 148, 149, 151, 152, 199, 204, 208

Rajapakse, Mahinda 281, 288, 291, 295
Rajasunderam, S. 83
Ratwatte, Charitha 179, 256
Research and Analysis Wing – India (RAW) 92, 127
Samaraweera, Mangala 293, 300, 301, 311
Senanayake, D S 18, 21
Senanayake, Dudley 18, 21, 22, 26, 32, 38, 43, 45
Senanayake, Maithripala 62
Senanayake, Rukman 120, 141, 210
Senaratne, Rajitha 189, 278
Sihala Urumaya (*see* Jathika Hela Urumaya)
Sri Lanka Freedom Party (SLFP) 18, 23, 26, 30, 31, 33, 34, 40, 50, 55, 56, 60, 62, 63, 64, 67, 70, 71, 84, 85, 86, 88, 102, 105, 114, 120, 129, 131, 133, 139, 141, 142, 146, 148, 149, 150, 151, 172, 185, 201, 203, 211, 212, 213, 219, 220, 229, 233, 244, 245, 246, 281, 287, 293, 310
Sri Lanka Mahajana Pakshaya (SLMP) 89, 120, 131, 205, 206
Sri Lanka Muslim Congress (SLMC) 106, 132, 133, 141, 143, 147, 150, 151, 153, 165,

Index 321

169, 215, 216, 222, 245, 246, 247, 248, 282
Tamil Congress (TC) 11, 12, 13, 19-20, 31, 63, 141, 152
Tamil Eelam Liberation Organisation (TELO) 103, 105
Tamil National Alliance (TNA) 251, 282, 285, 286
Tamil National Army (TNA) 167, 168
Tamil United Liberation Front (TULF) 31, 33, 34, 42, 43, 44, 45, 46, 51, 57, 58, 60, 63, 68, 69, 73, 80, 81, 82, 84, 85, 86, 87, 99, 104, 108, 112, 137, 143, 152, 154, 183, 217, 239, 243, 245, 248, 249, 262, 270, 284, 286
Thamilchelvam, S 45
Thondaman, Sauviamurthy 25, 31, 34, 42, 43, 59, 74, 78, 80, 89, 94, 102, 149, 204, 205, 215, 223, 224, 282
Tigers 31, 79, 103, 105, 106, 107, 108, 109, 112, 121, 122, 123, 124, 125, 126, 127, 136, 137, 143, 148, 154, 164, 165, 166, 167, 168, 170, 171, 172, 174, 185, 188, 189, 190, 192, 201, 220, 223, 224, 225, 227, 233, 234, 236, 237, 238, 239, 240, 241, 242, 244, 247, 248, 249, 250, 251, 252, 255, 263, 264, 265, 266, 267, 268, 269, 270, 271, 272, 273, 278, 279, 280, 282, 283, 284, 285, 286, 287, 288, 289, 290, 295, 296, 298, 301, 302, 305, 306, 307, 309, 311, 315
Tiruchelvam, Neelam 44, 60, 82, 166, 236, 239, 240, 286
Trincomalee 54, 56, 109, 115, 122, 143, 150, 170, 237, 307
United National Party (UNP) 17, 18, 19, 22, 23, 26, 32, 33, 34, 38, 39, 40, 42, 46, 52, 53, 54, 59, 60, 64, 65, 66, 70, 71, 74, 86, 88, 89, 105, 106, 113, 114, 115, 120, 121, 129, 130, 133, 134, 135, 136, 139, 140, 141, 143, 144, 148, 149, 153, 154, 162, 176, 181, 182, 176, 181, 182, 183, 185, 192, 198, 202, 203, 207, 211, 213, 216, 217, 218, 219, 220, 221, 222, 224, 225, 226, 227, 228, 234, 236, 242, 246, 247, 248, 257, 259, 268, 273, 278, 279, 280, 281, 290, 294, 307
United People's Freedom Alliance (UPFA) 280, 281, 282, 287
United Socialist Alliance (USA) 131, 133, 134, 135, 145
United States (US) 54, 250
University Teachers for Human Rights – Jaffna (UTHE) 284
Vavuniya 54, 60, 93, 238, 241

Voice of America (VOA) 96
Weerasooriya, Wickrama 256
Weeratunge, Lalith 258, 259
Weerawansa, Wimal 287
Wickramanayake, Ratnasiri 281
Wickremesinghe, Esmond 83, 97, 98, 135
Wickremesinghe, Ranil 48, 66, 113, 155, 179, 187, 193, 197, 202, 203, 205, 214, 215, 226, 227, 236, 243, 246, 247, 249, 252, 256, 257, 261, 262, 263, 264, 265, 267, 270, 271, 277, 278, 279, 280, 282, 285, 288, 292, 293, 294, 295
Wijeratne, Ranjan 136, 140, 148, 155, 160, 162, 163, 174, 190, 191, 216, 217, 309
Wijetunge, D.B. 155, 179, 193, 197, 200, 201, 204, 209, 210, 213, 214, 221, 225, 226, 235, 249, 259, 278, 281, 288, 289
Wijeweera, Rohana 27, 33, 161
Wilson, A J 44, 45, 60, 82, 240
Yoheswaran, Sarojini 286
Yoheswaran, T 166, 286